P9-CAM-619

THE CRITICS HAIL
COCKPIT

"HIS BEST AND MOST ACCESSIBLE NOVEL
SINCE *THE PAINTED BIRD* . . . Its rich
prose, vivid incidents and solid themes make it
fully rewarding."

—Jonathan Yardley, *Miami Herald*

"MERELY BRILLIANT. Kosinski is an articulate social critic who will not sentimentalize his
parable; a ruthless writer who formulates the
Age of Corruption and transmits it into the realm
of art."

—Larry Swindell, *Philadelphia Inquirer*

"A PROFOUND, CHILLING VISION OF
CONTEMPORARY LIFE—glittering, cruelly
sharp-edged and as bleak as a cinder from which
all warmth and life have fled."

—Richard R. Lingeman, *The New York Times*

"IF YOU CAN IMAGINE ROBIN HOOD CREATED BY GOGOL AND NARRATED BY KAFKA, you will have an idea of the power of this story. So we enter this world, are drawn into it, because in the people he tells us about . . . we recognize portions of ourselves, deeply buried fantasies, visions of power and flight, of entrapments."

—Robert Kirsch, *Los Angeles Times*

"THIS NOVEL READS LIKE FICTION BUT COULD BE MOSTLY FACT. And that is the terrifying beauty of it. Kosinski has made some kind of quantum jump in the art of story-telling. His plot takes on the colorations of all our lives. *Cockpit* achieves a state of pure psychological truth, and it may be more than that."

—Asa Barber, *Chicago Daily News*

"A MASTERLY PICTURE of figures in a landscape—a landscape that is glacial and merciless . . . As a commentary on contemporary Western life, the book is devastating."

—*John Barkham Reviews*

"ALMOST ALL BEHAVIOR IN KOSINSKI'S WORLD IS THEATER, a cover, a role to protect some anonymous deeply buried self. Like Melville's confidence man, Tarden is a different person in each of his disguises."
—*The New York Times Book Review*

"JERZY KOSINSKI'S WORK GLISTENS with social observation and psychological apprehension. Not since Conrad has an Eastern European found so profound a voice in the English tongue."
—*Time*

"PERTURBING AND EXCITING . . . The clarity of Kosinski's prose leaves one no chance of escaping from its dense, demanding moral perplexities. It reads as easily as a thriller, but will not be easy to forget."
—*Times Literary Supplement*

"KOSINSKI IS A FICTIONIST OF THE FIRST ORDER whose stunning verbal snapshots of violence and terror, bespeak restraint, modesty even."
—*Commonweal*

Bantam Books by Jerzy Kosinski
Ask your bookseller for the books you have missed

BEING THERE
COCKPIT
THE DEVIL TREE
THE PAINTED BIRD
STEPS

Cockpit

Jerzy Kosinski

BANTAM BOOKS · TORONTO · NEW YORK · LONDON

*This low-priced Bantam Book
has been completely reset in a type face
designed for easy reading, and was printed
from new plates. It contains the complete
text of the original hard-cover edition.*
NOT ONE WORD HAS BEEN OMITTED.

COCKPIT
A Bantam Book

PRINTING HISTORY

Houghton Mifflin edition published August 1975
2nd printing .... August 1975
3rd printing .... August 1975
4th printing .... September 1975
Book-of-the-Month Club edition published October 1975
Bantam edition/October 1976

2nd printing
3rd printing

All rights reserved.
Copyright © 1975 by Jerzy Kosinski.
*This book may not be reproduced in whole or in part, by
mimeograph or any other means, without permission.
For information address: Bantam Books, Inc.*

ISBN 0-553-02613-5

Published simultaneously in the United States and Canada

---

*Bantam Books are published by Bantam Books, Inc. Its trade-
mark, consisting of the words "Bantam Books" and the por-
trayal of a bantam, is registered in the United States Patent
Office and in other countries. Marca Registrada. Bantam
Books, Inc., 666 Fifth Avenue, New York, New York 10019.*

PRINTED IN THE UNITED STATES OF AMERICA

To Marc Jaffe, who helped to sustain my conviction in writing *Cockpit*, this edition is dedicated.

For Katherina,
the sound and touch of my life

Author's note. This book is wholly fiction. Any resemblance to the present or past is gratuitous and similarity to any actual event or character is accidental and not intended.

But I dwell now well in the making of the future. Little by little, time is kneading me into shape. A child is not frightened at the thought of being patiently turned into an old man. He is a child and he plays like a child. I too play my games. I count the dials, the levers, the buttons, the knobs of my kingdom.

ANTOINE DE SAINT-EXUPÉRY, *Flight to Arras*

Although we have known each other for a long time and have spoken often, we have never spoken intimately. I was intrigued by you the first time we met at your party. Since then, I have wanted to see you alone but could never bring myself to ask.

You probably do not recall that, during the party, I headed toward one of the bathrooms, locking your bedroom door behind me. If anyone had tried to enter the room during my inspection of it, I would have explained I had locked that door because I had not been able to lock the one to the bathroom. I opened your closets and checked the proportion of evening dresses to sports clothes, noting their quality and condition. I examined your underwear and the heels and soles of your shoes. Then I flipped through some of the letters I found on your desk, read a few, and glanced over your checkbook, telephone and hotel bills and airline ticket receipts.

In the bathroom, I surveyed your cosmetics and studied the vials of pills in your medicine cabinet. I wrote down the name of each doctor on the label, the prescription date and indicated dosage, then took a sample from every bottle.

That evening, I talked to a couple in their thirties who said they had known you for years. The woman, a bit drunk, said, "Look at me, Mr. Tarden. Once, a long time ago, I was soft and moist and supple. It was a time, if you can imagine, when staying thin wasn't a losing battle, when I didn't suffer from lower back pain, when I wasn't on my way to a drying-out tank like so many other women. Now my only unique features are my fingerprints, which developed even before I was born. When I was in high school, any idiot could foresee the kind of man I would marry, what our children would be like and the sort of home we would live in. Anyone could have predicted then that my life would become as dried out and bleached by alcohol and boredom as my hair and skin are by the sun and wind." She raised her Scotch in a mocking salute. Her husband joined her in the toast and they both laughed, displaying their capped teeth, white against their dark tans.

When I returned home from the party, I took out the pills I had stolen from your bathroom and looked through the most recent edition of the *Physicians' Desk Reference*, which includes full-sized, color reproductions of all currently marketed medications. I identified the proper chemical name of each of your drugs and read about its composition, use and side effects. For some reason, learning these details increased my desire to know you. The afternoon we met by accident and I drove you home, I wanted to invite you to the apartment I rent as Tarden, the only name you know me by. But I was afraid that, if I did see you alone, you might be upset by what I had to say, by my desire to share my life with you. I did not want to just tell you about my past. I wanted you to relive it.

Instead of taking you to my apartment, I dropped you off at your home and drove toward the theater district. I pulled alongside the curb, where prostitutes lounged against the buildings waiting to be picked up, made my choice and motioned her to come over. I told her what I wanted and we agreed on a price.

Later, at my apartment, while she was taking a shower, I felt terribly dizzy. I sank into a chair, exhausted and sweating.

I had difficulty breathing and suddenly my heartbeat seemed irregular. I heard the girl singing in my bathroom, and wondered what would happen if I should die right then. It wasn't the thought of dying that disturbed me, but that I might die without leaving a trace.

I saw it all: the girl would come out of the bathroom and find me sprawled on the floor. Having made sure I was dead, she would look through my pockets, take whatever money she found, pick up anything that seemed valuable and start to leave. But to open the door from the inside, she would have to know the three-digit combinations of the locks. She would panic, take a drink to build her courage and struggle unsuccessfully with the locks once more. Then she would give up and put back the money and the stolen articles before calling the police.

I could see the detectives force open the door, discover the body, then ask her sarcastically what she had done to break my heart. They would search the apartment for papers that might identify me and would then try to determine the cause of death. The locked drawers would contain hundreds of negatives and photographs of women taken in the apartment, nothing more. The police would joke about the man whose passion for women had killed him, and leave without finding any identification.

I have stored my important documents in vaults I rent under assumed names in residential hotels, banks and post office boxes, all prepaid on a long-term basis. I can retrieve the most essential papers at any time, and if I need to leave the country suddenly I can do so without having to return to any place that might be identified as my home.

Ever since I left the Service, I have simultaneously maintained similar apartments in major cities, every apartment located on one of the top floors of a large high-rise, each rented from a different landlord under a different assumed name. All the buildings can be entered through separate lobbies on different streets, as well as by underground garages and service entrances.

I keep master keys for all my apartments in each location, in order to be able to enter any apartment without carrying many sets of keys with me all the time; a duplicate set to each apartment is hidden somewhere in every building. I put the keys inside a small, magnetic box, which I then attach to a basement steam pipe, an incinerator shaft or some such inconspicuous place.

To be completely satisfactory, each building must have more than one staircase and elevator. I have always alternated among the apartments and never stay in any of them more than four weeks at a time. I don't know the other tenants and I doubt if they would recognize me. Each of my apartments consists of a furnished central room with floodlamps set up for portrait and figure photography, a small kitchen, a bathroom and some space that I have converted into a photographic darkroom. I have covered the walls with a layer of cork and hung heavy curtains between the main rooms and foyers to make each apartment soundproof. I have installed locks on every door. Under each darkroom's large work counter, I have cushioned a space large enough to sit up or stretch out in, and covered the front of it with a false wall. I can remain there for hours, unseen, hearing every sound in the apartment. With an ear-plug listening device that feeds from the main phone wiring, I can monitor incoming and outgoing telephone calls.

From my niche, I can also trigger various explosions all over the apartment. Those in the kitchen and bathroom would stun anyone who happened to be in either room and give me ample time to escape unseen. I have also set a charge in the main room that would create enough diversion to let me dash from the darkroom, through the foyer and out the door. It would also shatter the window, and, should I suffer a sudden seizure when alone and be unable to telephone for help, I could set off an explosion that would bring the police and the emergency rescue squad.

I always pay three years' rent in advance. I also give the management a substantial cash deposit to pay bills including utilities, telephone and cable television. The landlords welcome the front money and probably assume I am a bachelor or a widower who travels a lot, and is anxious not to let the rental agreement lapse during his stay abroad. No landlord has ever bothered me about my absences.

I recently read about a man who lived alone in a small house in the suburbs. He, too, had no family and went out so seldom that few of his neighbors ever saw him. They had forgotten he even existed, until the postman noticed his mail piling up and notified the police. They found the old man at his kitchen table in front of a portable television set, his shirt unbuttoned, his tie loosened, his body already decomposing. The coroner confirmed what the police assumed from the date of the newspaper under his hand: he had been dead for two months. The set had burned out. I realized that with only a prostitute in attendance at my death I would be no better off than this man.

As soon as the girl finished her shower and left, I called Valerie, whom I had been dating for over a year. She was a resident in orthopedics whose field was joint injuries, especially those incurred by athletes. Among her patients at a suburban medical institute were men who had been perfect physical specimens, whose limbs were now useless conglomerations of torn cartilage and shattered bones.

Because of her heavy schedule, Valerie had to live at the hospital in the suburbs and could spend the night with me in the city only twice a week. I would drive out to the hospital and when she was on call, we would sit in the cafeteria for hours talking and drinking cup after cup of coffee. She told me that, at first, the other residents and the athletes from the outpatient clinic openly ridiculed her for seeing me, a man so much older than herself. Some of them thought I was keeping her. Yet once they found out I was wealthy, they all suggested she give up medicine for the good life I could provide. She knew that, although a lot of my funds were frozen, there was plenty for both of us to live on and I promised to set up an unconditional trust fund for her, in case she ever decided to leave me. I assured her that I did not expect her to love me. She would live with me, but she would be as free as I to see other people.

Valerie said that, by appointing myself her liberator, I was actually prohibiting her from shaping her own existence; I was concerned only with my own future and had created an illusion of what I wanted her to be.

She admitted that she was too detached to love anyone but was intrigued by this system of mutual independence. She wanted to continue with me in order to see if she could become emotionally or physically involved and still retain her independence.

Valerie promised she was not seeing anyone else: my need stimulated her desire to be possessed. She wanted me to memorize every inch of her body, every gram of her flesh and hair and bone and muscle.

One evening, as I sat with her in the hospital cafeteria, I saw a man passing by who glanced at Valerie as if he knew her. She did not look back at him, but I sensed she had noticed him.

A few days later, I told her I had to go to the Coast immediately. Since Valerie had planned to spend the weekend in the city with me, I suggested she come along, but she declined, saying an old girlfriend had just come to town. I gave her the keys to the apartment she knew, and phoned her on Friday that I wouldn't be back before Monday.

I spent all Friday afternoon preparing for her visit. I wrote her one note listing my San Francisco number and another in which I explained that the sound system controlling the TV, radio and record player was out of order. I put the first note on a table and taped the second to the phonograph, which I disconnected. Next, I loaded a camera, attached an electronic flash to it, screwed in a zoom lens and put the camera in my darkroom hiding place.

At dusk I heard the first key turn. I knew I had a good minute before all three locks were opened, and, after turning off the light switch and drawing the soundproof curtain behind me, I went into the darkroom. Before the last lock turned, I had pulled aside the false wall and climbed into the niche behind it.

The front door opened and I heard Valerie and a man's voice. As she turned on the lights, she joked about the three locks and the soundproof curtain, and he remarked he didn't understand why she was intimate with someone as peculiar as Tarden. Valerie found my first note and read it aloud, then turned on the radio. When it remained silent for several minutes, she began checking the controls and discovered the second note.

I listened to Valerie showing her guest around the kitchen and the darkroom. When the man examined the enlarger, he was standing inches away from me.

They discussed going out, but, before they left, they made love on the carpet only two feet from my hideaway. Sitting in the darkness, I felt like a blind man with an acute sense of hearing. Valerie was much more vocal in her lovemaking with this man than she was with me. Later, as they took a leisurely bath together, I learned that he was married but was getting a divorce and that, once he was free, he planned to marry Valerie.

They dressed and left the apartment. I fixed myself a sandwich, read for a while, then climbed back into my niche and fell asleep. Valerie and the man returned late, chattering drunkenly about the bar where they'd been dancing. I was amused that Valerie, drunk as she was, remembered to secure all three locks and pull the curtain to slow me down if I came back unexpectedly. The man went off to the shower, singing happily, while she opened the convertible couch and pulled blankets and pillows out of the closet. When he came back from the bathroom, he fixed drinks while she took a shower.

After they made love, he kept asking questions about me, especially about the trust fund. Valerie suspected that I had made the proposal only to see how an American would react to such a bizarre concept and that I had never believed she would accept it.

8

The man suggested that since my deepest desire was to liberate her, she should use the money to be free of me.

Later he asked, "What is it about you Tarden likes so much?"

"Maybe it's the same thing you like about me," she replied.

"No, seriously. What do you do for him that no other woman can?"

"What do I do for you that no other woman can?"

"I love you," he said. "I want to marry you and have a child with you. I don't care what you can or can't do. But Tarden isn't in love with you; you said so yourself. He'll drain you emotionally, sexually, any way he can. He'll even let other men use you if it amuses him. Tell me: what does he want from you?"

"He says he wants me to be part of everything he does. He's tired of not being able to share his life, of picking up girls he has no intention of seeing again, girls he uses to excite himself. He tells me how he makes love to them. Then, lying on his back with a hard-on, he raises his legs over his head and sucks himself off."

"Jesus, he must be limber!" The man laughed. "Then why does he need the girl? As an audience?"

"The girl makes him excited by his own flesh. She is there even while he is tasting himself. He says it is as if the two of them are making love to a third person."

"And what about you and him?"

"Those other women make him feel inferior: he chooses them and they come willingly. But he's never sure of me. Maybe it's because I spend so much time among other men. When he's with me he feels superior because I'm choosing him over all of you."

"Over me," said the man.

"Over you," she agreed.

A moment passed before he spoke again. "I just can't imagine you thrashing around with a bony old bird like him. What a picture! That pervert poking his beak into you. No, I bet he watches you, right? While you lick yourself. That's it. Show me what he makes you do."

The man must have tried to maneuver her because she started to giggle, then yelled in pain. "Stop it! You're hurting me!" she cried, and they both gave up.

"What if he finds out about me?" asked the man.

"He won't care."

"But if he sets up the fund and then you marry me . . . ?"

She paused. "So what?"

The talking stopped abruptly. When I heard the man begin to snore, I left my niche, moving stealthily into the main room. I stood behind the sofa bed, looking at the naked bodies. I could see only the vague shapes of their forms in the dark. I aimed the camera at them and took a test picture. The quick flash did not wake them but I could see Valerie's lover. He was the man from the hospital cafeteria. I took several photographs in rapid succession, zooming the lens progressively closer. I captured Valerie's breast resting near her lover's shoulder, her leg brushing his, his elbow touching her belly.

They slept undisturbed. For a moment, I wanted to wake them and ask Valerie why she had lied about her reasons for staying in the city, a choice that disturbed me, considering the freedom of the agreement I had offered her. But I did not wake them. Instead, I silently returned to my niche and fell asleep. I didn't come out until the next afternoon when they had gone.

Two days later, I called Valerie to say I was back

in town and eager to see her. She told me that staying in my apartment without me had made her miss me. She would get someone to take her place at the hospital and spend the night with me.

She was subdued when she arrived but tender and affectionate. "While you were gone," she said, "I decided to leave the hospital and live with you."

I paced the room as I spoke. "I wanted to free you from all obligations. Do you still think that's possible?"

"I do," she answered. "More than ever."

I sat down opposite her and placed my hands on her shoulders. "There isn't anyone else in your life?"

She smiled radiantly. "No one. Why would there be?"

Casually, I said, "One of the building attendants told me that he saw you during the weekend with a young man he thought was my son."

When she answered, her voice was calm. "Oh, yes. I ran into an old friend from medical school. We hadn't seen each other for years, so I brought him up for a drink. We talked for a while and then he left. That's all."

"Does he resemble me in any way?"

"Not at all," she laughed. "He's fat and already bald."

Laughing with her, I suggested, "He could still be the son of a bony old bird like me."

She sipped her coffee. " 'Bony old bird.' Where did you get that expression?"

"A lot of people call me a bony old bird because I'm thin and have a nose like a beak."

"You look more like a camel to me."

"Are you sure you want to live with a camel?"

"When should I leave the hospital?" she asked.

I got up and walked over to the desk. "The sooner

the better." I sat down and removed several black and white photographs from a large envelope.

She walked over to the desk. "What are those?"

"Just some photos I took a while back. Look." I handed her the first one, which she held up to the light.

"Not too clear. Someone's elbow?"

"How many great elbow photos are there? What about this one?"

"Is it a shoulder? Are they all this dark?"

"You're too critical. Their sole intent is to show people engaged in an act. Here." I handed her the rest of the photos.

As she looked at one after another, she grew tense and slightly pale, but continued until she had replaced the last photograph on the table with a hand that trembled only slightly.

"Congratulations," she said, moistening her lips with her tongue. "Pity you had to trust a hidden camera." She scanned the walls and ceiling, looking for it. "Do you have tapes, too?"

"No. Just the photos."

"Too bad. If you'd taped our conversation, you'd know that he was just a one-night stand. I can tell you don't believe me, but I guess even that doesn't matter now."

"What matters is that you didn't tell me the truth."

"I would have told you."

"When?" I took her hands in mine. "Valerie, I was here while you were talking about me."

She looked at me with disbelief. "You couldn't have been."

"But I was, Valerie."

"Come on, Tarden! It's bad enough that your camera was spying for you."

"Remember 'bony old bird.' I have a very good idea what you said."

"You mean that he and you . . . ?" Her voice had taken on a new edge. "Oh, really, Tarden. You're actually trying to make me believe . . ."

I said, simply, "There are some things all men share."

She walked to the couch and picked up her bag. As she passed me, she didn't even try to mask her resentment.

Looking at the pictures of Valerie and her lover now, I realize how badly they record my experiences with Valerie, how much more accurate and explicit my memories are. My past emotions are etched into my mind like a display in a store window ready to be called up at any moment.

I often walk through the city streets, and stop at windows filled with radios, tape recorders, stereos, watches, pens and dozens of other gadgets. As I scan the display, I memorize each object's position in relation to every other object. Then I enter the store and walk over to the counter. The owner approaches me.

"You must have the largest window display in the city," I tell him.

"Thanks. Can I show you something?"

I lay a twenty-dollar bill on the counter. "I think I have a pretty good memory," I tell him, "and I enjoy betting on it from time to time. In fact, I'll bet you twenty dollars I can remember the price of every item in your window. How about it?"

The owner looks puzzled. I take out a piece of paper. "Why don't you make a list of the merchandise in the window? When you're through, I'll write down the correct price next to the item. Or you write down the prices and I'll match the items to them. If I make a single mistake, you win twenty dollars. If I get them all right, you lose twenty. I'll even impose a ten-minute time limit on myself."

The owner goes over to the window, takes stock of the merchandise and returns to the counter. "You're on," he says. He lists about fifty-five items on the back of a sales slip and pushes the paper across the counter. Then he glances at his watch.

I close my eyes and recreate the window display, carefully separating from the group each item on the list, and writing down its price. I am finished long before the ten minutes are up.

The owner takes the list from me, calls over a salesman and tells him to keep an eye on the twenty-dollar bill while he returns to the window. He eagerly begins matching my notations against the merchandise, but slows down as he realizes I am scoring one hundred percent. Finally, he walks back to the counter, shaking his head. "I can't believe it," he says, returning my money. He stares glumly at the floor for a moment, then looks up at me and opens the cash register. Reluctantly, he hands over the worn bills.

If I evoke a single memory picture, others will spring up automatically to join it and soon the montage of a past self will emerge. It's an autonomous process, and the fact that I have no control over it excites me.

As a child, a similar lack of control terrified me. I once cut my foot on a piece of glass and its healing process fascinated but bothered me. After that, several times I intentionally wounded my leg. I observed how the cut bled, how the blood ebbed and eventually stopped flowing and how the wound began to mend. Every day, I would check the scab forming to protect the healing wound. When it was fully developed, I carefully peeled off the scab and opened up the wound again. Then I examined it through a magnifying glass, trying to see what it was that made my body heal independent of my will. Although I often tried to keep a wound open and bleeding, it always sealed itself overnight, challenging my power over myself. I hated the sense of an autonomous force in my body, determining what would happen to me.

Years later, when I was an associate professor at the State Central Academy of Science, a young dental surgeon told me that one of my teeth had to be extracted at once.

He assured me that one shot of a local anesthetic would guarantee painlessness. While he loaded the hypodermic syringe, I sat back in the chair, hypnotized by the powerful light before my eyes. A student nurse from the dental school was standing next to me and I felt I had to conceal my fear from her. I barely felt the needle when the dentist injected my gum, but almost instantly became aware that my heartbeat was accelerating rapidly. I wanted to tell him about it, but my throat was too constricted for me to get out the words. I grew weak and my limbs began to shake uncontrollably. My feet and hands felt as if they were being pricked by internal needles. A great fear of dying flooded my mind and body. To counteract the terror, I forced my mind backward to the moments before I had arrived at the office. I watched myself wandering through the arcades in the bright daylight, looking at my reflection in shop windows. I struggled to warn myself to cancel the appointment. I saw myself reach the university square, wait for a green light on the corner, then enter the huge lobby of the dental clinic and disappear into darkness. I shouted after myself not to go to the office but I would not listen. I witnessed myself shaking hands with the dentist and smiling at the student nurse, saw myself pressed back against the chair in fear, my eyes following the gleaming tip of the needle until it disappeared under my lip. I struggled one last time to urge myself to escape while I still could, but it was too late. I felt a stab of pain as the needle pierced the gum. Suddenly, my chest began to fill up with a fluid so heavy it made my lungs give way. I felt my heart weaken under the burden of the ever-thickening blood it was trying to pump. I was becoming too faint to breathe. My lungs wheezed one last time and surrendered; my heart lay still.

I woke to find a blurred face hovering over me. Slowly it began to come into focus. I pulled off the oxygen and as I was inhaling warm air I became aware that my lungs had resumed their natural rhythm. A disembodied voice explained that I had suffered an uncommon reaction to the anesthetic and that I had survived after my heart stopped only because the incident had happened in a clinic. Thanks to the State's sophisticated medical equipment, my vital functions had been restored.

I was kept in the clinic for a few days, then dismissed, feeling shaky and humiliated. Like the elusive substance that had once healed my wound, now the State had saved me without my consent.

Most people surrendered their lives to the State's omnipresence. I could not deny its existence, but I could abstract myself from its power.

As a prize-winning photographer, I had free access to the Academy's darkroom. Among the chemicals stored there were cyanide pellets used for retouching photographs. I selected a single pellet and wrapped it in the foil from a chocolate bar to keep it safe.

I walked the streets of the Capital with the pellet in my pocket, as if I were a tourist, staring at grandiose government buildings, at the monuments erected to past and present heroes, at State banks, museums, department stores. Even though I was still at the State's mercy, I mentally projected myself to a time when I would be free of it.

I had been fortunate enough to qualify for scientific training, an invaluable protective device which I planned to eventually turn to my own advantage. In the State's eyes, I was its property. The State had even decided on the service I would perform to repay the cost of my education. According to the identity card I always carried, I was a researcher at one of the most important political and scientific institutes within the State Central Academy of Science.

The card not only created immediate respect, but granted me privileges not available to ordinary citizens. When I was stopped by the police for a routine document check, I would casually offer my card. They would salute and immediately wave me on, for, as minor servants of the State, they had been taught to respect their betters. My card enabled me to buy food and clothing at discount prices in special shops reserved for top-level bureaucrats, to vacation in resorts closed to the general public, to eat in restricted clubs where State leaders gathered under the protection of security men. Yet for all this liberty, I sensed freedom only when my fingers stroked the foil-wrapped pellet in my pocket.

The State was a vicious enemy. Whether I escaped abroad or committed suicide, it would punish those who had known of my plans. What had begun as my personal challenge to the State would end with the destruction of innocent people, and I had no more right to destroy them than the State did.

I traveled to an ocean resort on the pretext of visiting a friend in a fishing cooperative. I walked along the water under the border guards' surveillance. I studied the empty beaches, searching for a spot where I could hide long enough to launch a boat, but found none. Finally, I gave up, realizing that, even if there were such places, no craft could evade the police speed patrol or the State fishing fleet.

I considered learning to fly in order to escape by air. I enrolled at the gliding school but did not get clearance for a pilot's license; instead, because of my slight frame and low weight, I was used as living ballast on the gliders. Each time a powerful gust swung our glider high into the clouds, an air force monitoring plane circled and followed us, ready to abort any attempt to glide toward the border. I also learned that even the most trusted pilots were permitted to fly planes only when paired off with a surveillance craft. As an escape route, the sky, like the sea, was closed to me.

The Academy of Science, my employer, was a mammoth institution responsible for all aspects of the State's educational and scientific life. It was located in the Capital's tallest skyscraper, referred to as the "Palace" of Science and Culture. Each one of the thousands of people who worked day and night in the Academy's offices had been selected through national competitive examinations, for their political or academic achievements.

The Academy was comprised of various different institutes in specialized studies, editorial offices of scientific publications, publishing houses and, above all, hundreds of offices that belonged to full Academy members or candidates, and to other scholars and their staffs, including research assistants like me. The Palace of Science and Culture was a Vatican governing the church of State.

Using the official stationery of my Institute, I wrote a letter to the Academy, stating that, since my research

18

required me to photograph certain classified materials from the archives, a private room was essential to the completion of my project. For the same reason, I requisitioned a direct-dial telephone for outgoing calls, an item usually given only to senior personnel. No space was available at my Institute, so I was assigned a smaller room in another section of the Palace. Only the Academy's Personnel Bureau kept records of room allocations; as I had applied directly to it, my own Institute was unaware that I had received the separate space.

Again using Institute stationery, I suggested that, owing to the political sensitivity of my work, new locks must be installed on the door. Because I was solely responsible for the room's security, I requested that no duplicate keys be issued to the maintenance staff.

As soon as my routine was established, I asked for an after-hours pass. Usually, such passes were issued only to senior staff members on high-priority projects that necessitated unlimited work hours. However, since my Institute was often involved in highly classified research commissioned by the Party's Central Committee, my requests were processed immediately. The room became my private vault. I brought in a folding cot so that I could spend the night there if I chose.

The Palace was located in the center of a barren square nicknamed the "Tundra." Every morning, whipped by northern winds that penetrated their inadequate coats, thousands of people rushed across the Tundra to work. From my room on one of the Palace's highest floors, they resembled faceless extras in silent-movie crowd scenes. Yet, important as these people might look, their identity papers had to be checked at the doors of the Palace by the most experienced security men. Once in from the Tundra, the crowd separated into individuals. Some took express elevators reserved for members of the Academy whose offices were on the top floors; others were consigned to locals that stopped at every fifth level. Many visitors were not allowed to enter the Academy's inner recesses at all. Others were brusquely directed to conference rooms and amphitheaters, while still others lined up in silence at the Postal Center, bearing written authorizations to collect mail for themselves or their superiors.

Every day on my way home, I passed the main ticket office of the State Airlines. Peering through the window, I could spot officials with their passports in hand, waiting to collect tickets to foreign cities. They had the drab, anxious look of minor Party and government officials. I speculated that the State found them good security risks, not only because they were leaving families behind, but also because they were considered too old to begin new lives. Once, one of them caught my eye and stared at me like an animal that had just picked up the scent of an enemy.

To leave the country legally I needed a passport. I knew it would be impossible to get an official Academy one, so I decided to apply for a short-term tourist passport. Before the Internal Security Police would issue me one, I had to present them with an authorized application specifying the State's reason for sending me abroad, my itinerary and my foreign sources of maintenance. But once I had the passport, I hoped to trick the State National Bank into believing I had an Academy passport, for which they would automatically provide the foreign currency required for a round-trip ticket.

One morning, I was looking out over the Tundra as the fog lifted, unveiling a mass of swarming bodies.

The scene reminded me of something my father had often said: that the whole country was an endless, bureaucratic jungle in which the brush and undergrowth grew dense and intertwined. I decided to turn that confusion back on itself, to make it work for me.

Afraid to trust my memory under the stress, I placed a large sheet of accounting paper on the floor and spent the next twenty hours listing in code everything I had to do if I was to leave the country without seeming to break the law.

I would need the services of four prominent Academicians in different research fields that frequently required foreign study. Scholars of this rank would have influence in the State agencies that issued passports and authorized tickets for foreign trips. They would also be familiar with the necessary documents and procedures.

The four should be able to judge my good qualities and be ready to justify my bad ones. Ideally men with Internal Security Police connections, they all would receive denunciations against me from my friends, enemies and State and Party officials. The four should send and receive mail at the Academy's Postal Center.

Obviously, I could never find actual Academicians with such qualifications who would help me. I would simply have to invent four such people. I started by giving each of them a name, a title, and a unique, yet plausible, bureaucratic assignment.

At that time, no communication was valid without written substantiation. Because of government secrecy, few people knew what any Academician was actually doing, under whose auspices he worked, whether he was in disfavor or even if he was still employed by the State. In the Palace of Science and Culture, individuals were merely sum totals of titles, documents and dossiers. The power to impress the Academy's seal on official documents was real and perpetual, but the person who wielded that power was often anonymous. Because my plan capitalized on that anonymity, there was a good chance it could work.

I finished my chart, folded it up neatly and taped it to my rib cage. My plan was intricate and I knew I would often have to consult my map to ascertain where the five of us were at a given moment.

I had each of my Academicians officially apply to the State Printing Office for stationery with his new letterhead. Since they all gave prestigious promotions as the reason for their requests and filed the requisitions following proper procedures, the Printing Office filled the orders immediately.

The letterheads listed the four men's full Academy credentials along with their titles and affiliations. I manufactured one member of the National Council of Humanities. Another was the editor of the *Quarterly Review of Current Trends*. The third was a Senior Fellow at the Institute for Coordination of State Planning. And the fourth was a vice chairman of the High Commission for Technological Development and Progress, a man who was also the editor of the police journal, *Problems of Internal Security*. I doubted that anyone would question the existence of my men or their jobs.

I also requested rubber stamps and seals for these make-believe authorities, and had them shipped to the Academy's Postal Center. I made a separate visit to collect each Academician's order, presenting the appropriate authorization, which I wrote on my Institute's stationery, to a different staffer each time. By the end of the week, the stationery, stamps and seals of the Academy's four newest members were in my room, safely packed away in boxes of photographic paper whose labels warned that the contents would be damaged if exposed to light.

In order to divert any future State inquiries, I knew my Academicians should have complete information about me. I spent several days listing every person and establishment I had ever dealt with. Using the list, my Academicians sent letters of inquiry to all schools and institutions with which I had been connected, to fellow students, teachers, professors, ski instructors, neighbors, casual and intimate friends, as well as to my parents' acquaintances. I had the letters marked "Official and Confidential" and sent by registered mail.

Two of the Academicians occupied positions in the humanities and the other two in the sciences. Academy personnel involved in the humanities received formal letters from my two scientists, while those in science heard from my humanists. Not only did this make the inquiry seem more objective, but it greatly decreased the chances of anyone's discovering that my Academicians did not exist.

The letters stated that the Academy department listed on the letterhead was considering me for a foreign research scholarship. They asked for thorough evaluations of my academic performance, character and political allegiance, and guaranteed that all replies would be kept strictly confidential. I had my Academicians request that their original correspondence be returned with the replies. They also requested that any past or future inquiry made about me by other State agencies be forwarded to the Academy for reply. Since the Academy was the highest authority regarding politically sensitive material, any information gathered in a real State investigation of my life would be sent directly to my four nonexistent Academy members. To expedite the responses, with each letter I enclosed a prepaid self-addressed envelope stamped "Official and Confidential" and bearing the name and official address of the signing Academician.

During the weeks that followed, I collected dozens of replies. A former girl friend spoke of my sexual obsessions, which seemed alien to the Party spirit; a current one listed unpredictability as my dominant character trait. A professor with whom I had studied warned I could be a camouflaged enemy of the State and if allowed to leave the country might never return. My parents' neighbors wrote scathing denunciations, calling my father a reactionary who was openly contemptuous of the State, and my mother a cosmopolite, a remnant of the old regime. Some of the friends with whom I had studied, skied and spent summer vacations evaded the issue by claiming that I was too inaccessible to be evaluated.

A few professors praised highly my academic achievements but hesitated to give me political recommendations. Letters from the offices of the Rector, the Dean and the University Military Reserve training unit were accompanied by my academic transcript, with confidential reports by the university's Party cell. There were several references to a police investigation of my family and me shortly after the Party take-over.

Having assembled the most complete dossier possible on myself, I now possessed written proof that, when questioned by the State, even my most trusted friends would inform against me. My fear that the State could at any point build a case against me was not an imaginary one.

Meanwhile, friends called to congratulate me on my good fortune in being considered for a trip abroad, but I always dismissed my chances of foreign travel as slight, and tried to divert further curiosity. My parents wrote that their neighbors and business associates had received requests for information from high academic authorities. My father speculated that this was actually a hostile police investigation but I persuaded him not to worry. Everyone in the country, I said, had been under investigation at one time or another. It was the Party's only method for establishing the innocence of the majority of the population.

To those professors who inquired about my proposed research abroad, I replied that I had just learned the project was about to be abandoned, thus ruling out the chance for overseas study.

With all potentially damaging material locked away in my darkroom, I was reasonably certain that I would have time to avert any Party or police inquiry before it could reach me. Meanwhile, I advanced to the second stage of my plan. Rather than apply for a passport at the overefficient and always suspicious central office in the Capital, I utilized a little-known regulation that permitted requests to be made at the place of voter registration.

I was banking on the ignorance and lethargy of my home town's Provincial Passport Bureau. It issued few passports and always to the most deserving applicants. The Academy letterhead would impress them and make the Bureau especially susceptible to official pressure from the Capital. Since the passport application had to be filed by the Academy member in charge of my research, one of my creations duly submitted the forms along with instructions to address all inquiries directly to him.

I had every original document notarized at the offices of the Central Committee of the Party. The Central Committee was the highest authority in the land, and I presented the documents to its notary with the explanation that they would eventually be submitted by the Academy to one of the Central Committee's departments. I knew that the Party's official seal on my papers would have an additional impact on a Provincial Passport Bureau. That seal meant absolute power, especially to a petty official.

After several weeks, my Academician had still not received the passport. I decided to speed things up. I made a special trip to my home town and went directly to the Provincial Bureau. Identifying myself as an employee of the Academy, I asked for a brief appointment with the major who was the Bureau Chief. The secretary asked to see my identity card and was obviously impressed, because she went immediately to the major's office with it.

When she came back, she announced he would see me in fifteen minutes. At the appointed time, I entered a large room decorated with portraits of State and Party leaders. The major was a tall man in the uniform of the elite Internal Security Police. He rose from behind the desk. We shook hands; then both of us sat down.

Out of the corner of my eye, I saw a manila file open on his desk. Among its contents I recognized the Academy stationery.

"So you're the young genius the Academy wrote us about," he said jovially. "But it is the Academy that acts for you," he added reflectively, "and your presence here is out of order." He was still smiling broadly.

"I am aware of it, Comrade Major," I said contritely, "but what brings me here is a matter of the utmost importance. I would be betraying the State if I kept it from you."

"You sound concerned. Still and all . . ." he rose from his chair, uncertain whether or not to stop me. He walked around the desk, then sat down on the edge, his polished jackboots dangling in front of me.

"Well, let's not be so formal," he said, breaking the silence. "Go ahead. Speak up."

"I came to ask you, Comrade Major . . ." I hesitated. Then, as if I were mustering my courage, I looked straight at him. "I came to see you, Comrade Major," I repeated emphatically, "because quite suddenly, you see, I have found a woman." I faltered again, and again mobilized myself. "A woman I love. I have never been in love before."

The major stood up, barely restraining his laughter. "You're in love, then. Unfortunately, we issue passports here, not marriage certificates."

I forced a weak smile. "Yes, of course. But, Comrade Major, I wondered whether . . ." I paused, and pretended to be having difficulty swallowing, ". . . whether the issuance of my passport could possibly be delayed for at least a month so that I can get to know her better?"

He drew his brows together in exaggerated disapproval. "You came here to request I delay what the highest authorities require you to do? Now, young man, there are limits to what I can listen to, even from someone as accomplished as you. Yours is a highly immature request. If I were to go by the book, I'd have to report you to your Institute."

I was flushed and breathing shallowly. "I know," I said, "but I had to risk that and tell you the truth, Comrade Major. The truth is I want to marry her and give her a child. And if I go abroad as soon as they want . . ." I stopped, then corrected myself. ". . . as soon . . ." I faltered several times, pretending to be overwhelmed by emotion. ". . . I might not come back alive from the mission which the Central Commit . . ." I stopped abruptly, as if I were on the verge of giving away top secrets.

The major frowned and gestured for me to stop

talking. He returned to his chair and leafed quickly through my file, stopping at a document I could not see. I hoped he had noticed the seal of the Central Committee. He raised his eyes and glowered at me.

"I never again wish to hear you speak as you have just done," he scolded. "You're a grown man, and I gather a very bright one." Casually indicating his decorations, he said, "I have been in every historic battle of the war, so I can tell you from experience that every man, no matter how brave, fears losing his life." He now spoke like a commander addressing his troops. "But the Academy, the State . . ." He paused, then stressed, "and the Central Committee of our Party, they all have faith in you." He paused again, trying to show me he understood the real significance of my mission, then added, "That's why you are being sent abroad on this . . . mission. Go back home," he said, winking knowingly as he ushered me to the door and opened it. When his secretary handed me back my identification card, I realized she must have been verifying it while I talked to the major.

If my stratagem had worked, the major now believed I was a Party operative ready for his first important assignment abroad.

I returned to the Capital, where I began spending every day in the Academy library, to make it seem that I was still involved in my studies. I used to sit in the hushed reading room, watching other men and women studying.

From a raised desk separated from the room by soundproof glass, a middle-aged librarian in thick glasses maintained constant watch over the readers. One day, after glancing repeatedly in my direction, she picked up a telephone. My heart pounded: if the major had reported me to the Party and security personnel should attempt to visit any of my Academicians, I was finished.

Even as I sat reading, Internal Security men might be gathering outside to arrest me. I reached into my pocket to feel for the cyanide pellet. After waiting an anxiety-ridden hour, I got up and left the library. No one stopped me and, as far as I could tell, no one followed me home. I was safe for the moment.

Toward the end of the week, a clerk at the Academy's Postal Center casually handed me a small packet covered with "Official—Confidential" stamps and addressed to one of my Academicians. I opened it in the privacy of my darkroom and found inside a brand-new passport issued by the Provincial Bureau. As I leafed through it with reverence, my eyes met the eyes of my photograph. In a covering letter, the major apologized for the delay in processing the passport.

I immediately applied to the State National Bank for a round-trip airline ticket. At the bottom of the application I listed all the documents required by the State Bank, but in place of every unobtainable document I attached letters from my Academicians concerning my Academy position or the importance of my research.

As an employee of the Academy, I could request a personal interview with the Deputy Chief of the Foreign Travel Division of the State Bank. Shortly after I requested one, I was told to come to his office, bringing with me my official application, my passport and all the required documents.

I entered an enormous hall partitioned into large open areas, each filled with desks, file cabinets and bustling office workers. I asked one of the clerks to point out the Deputy Chief's desk, and he told me to join the long line of State officials already waiting to see him. When my turn finally came, I approached him, presented my Academy identification card and introduced myself. He was a middle-aged man with a round face and bull-like neck, who asked for my papers with undisguised indifference. I placed the application, the documents and the passport on his desk. Ignoring the rest of my papers, he picked up my passport with two fingers and sneered, "With this tourist passport, my dear Comrade, all you need is a rich relative to pay your way. But I see from this application that you consider the State your rich relative. Where is your official Academy passport?" I pretended to grow suddenly tense, as if I were being accused of a serious crime against the State. When he saw I was worried, he shrugged his shoulders and continued in a sarcastic tone, "All you low-flying butterflies from that flower bed in the sky . . ." He screwed his face up into a mirthless smile and continued, ". . . are so absent-minded . . ."

I took a deep breath. "I have given you everything that I understood was required. I resent your attitude, Comrade, and find your vocabulary most offensive," I announced loudly. "I'm not a 'butterfly' but a scholar employed and paid by the Academy. That 'flower bed' is the scientific avant-garde of the working class and of the heroic Party that guides it."

The Deputy turned pale, started to rise, then dropped back into his chair. He glanced around the room as if he were inviting others to rally to his defense.

Everyone in the office froze. Several officials waiting in line ceased talking when they heard what was said. "But I did not . . . I did not mean it that way," he mumbled. "All I said was . . ."

I interrupted him, speaking even more loudly than before. "Your statement, Comrade, degrades the Academy and all its devoted staff, among whom I am proud to number myself. May I remind you, Comrade, that both you and I represent institutions. They are significant; we are not." I withdrew my passport but pushed my application closer to him. "This document as well as all its enclosures were prepared by the Academy for the State Bank. As the Academy employee who delivered it to you, I am at least entitled to proof that you have received it. May I have a receipt?" I demanded, hoping to distract him.

Eager to terminate the incident, the Deputy Chief reached for the document with trembling hands and, without reading it, signed the bottom of the carbon copy. He was as anxious to be rid of me as I was to leave him, and he hastily handed me the copy. After checking it for a moment, I said, "This is not sufficient; the regulations governing circulation of confidential State materials require you to list legibly on this receipt your name, position and the date and hour of this delivery. Then you must affix your department's stamp to validate the information. These procedures are for security's sake, Comrade, and I admit I am astonished that you appear to be unfamiliar with them."

The man could barely restrain himself. His face and neck were becoming discolored by swelling blood vessels. He snorted to clear his nose, stamped the receipt and, with a shaking hand, dated it. He pushed the duplicate application, passport and identification card across the desk without looking at me.

I calmly took the papers from him and began to walk toward the door, past nervous clerks and apprehensive officials who pretended not to see me. When I turned back, I saw the Deputy Chief angrily tossing the documents I'd given him into a desk-tray marked "File."

On my way down, I asked the elevator operator, "What's the name of the red-haired woman in the Foreign Travel Division? I've just finished talking to her but I've already forgotten her name."

The man leered at me. "You liked her?"

"Maybe that's why I looked at her instead of listening to her."

He shrugged his shoulders. "I can't tell you her name. It's against the law, Comrade." I gave him a tip, which he quickly pocketed. Then he told me the woman's name.

I called the Foreign Travel Division from a public telephone booth and asked for her. When she answered, I introduced myself, citing my official position at the Academy as well as the exhibition of my photographs at the State Experimental Arts Gallery not far from the Bank. I told her that I had noticed her in the Bank and asked her to meet me in a café after work. She hesitated; I promptly assured her I wanted only to discuss a business matter of mutual interest.

She was nervous when she arrived, but slowly relaxed as I showed her some of my recent photographs.

"The Academy is sending me abroad for research," I said, gazing pensively at the first snow falling outside. "I don't mind the trip but I do mind leaving before I can do some skiing. I always spend Christmas in the mountains."

"What do you want me to do?" she asked suspiciously.

"The Academy sent your division a routine application for my ticket. You could delay it simply by misfiling the folder. Mistakes happen. My file is in the December requisitions, but it could accidentally end up among the March or June requisitions."

I pulled out an envelope. "This contains a reward for two seconds of absent-mindedness. I am giving you a voucher for two prepaid weeks of Christmas vacation at an excellent hotel in a beautiful ski resort."

She took the envelope, opened it, checked the voucher and leafed through the colorful booklet promoting the resort.

"I've never been to the mountains," she said.

"Now's your chance," I suggested.

We both stared through the window for a moment. Outside, the bitter winter wind forced spiraling clouds of snow down upon the city. The woman turned to me. "I'd better take this with me right now before I misplace it. I'm so absent-minded these days." She laughed, put the voucher in her purse and reached for her coat. After I escorted her to the door, I returned to my table and looked out the window. Propelled by the wind, she walked faster and faster, coming perilously close to stumbling with every step. It occurred to me that I had forgotten to advise her to try skiing at the resort.

The following day, she telephoned me at the Academy to tell me how excited she was about her vacation. She remarked again that she was growing more absent-minded every day. Only minutes before, she said, she had mislaid an application she was working on and still couldn't locate it.

Immediately after she called, I applied for an appointment with the Director of the Academy, whose office administered all research jobs and approved all changes in the status of the employees.

He had been selected for his post by the Party because he was an experienced bureaucrat, and many of the Academy's research personnel, all of whose salaries and appointments depended on him, did not hide their contempt for his lack of formal education and often mocked his manners and speech.

The receptionist ushered me into a waiting room,

whose huge windows showed a panoramic view of the city. Soon the Director's personal secretary, a young woman in a military-style blouse and skirt, appeared and led me to his office. The Director, whom I had met two years earlier when he admitted me to the Academy, greeted me warmly. "Welcome, Comrade. Sit down." He gestured toward a chair. "I don't often have the pleasure of talking face to face with our young scientific talent!"

He was a short, slender man who looked rather puny behind an enormous desk cluttered with four telephones and replicas of missiles, Earth satellites and rockets. He opened a drawer.

"How about a Havana? Or an American cigarette?"

"No, thank you. I don't smoke," I answered.

"Good for you. Neither do I. How about a cognac? Napoleon's choice?"

"Thank you, Comrade Director, but I don't drink."

"Wise. I don't either. Coffee, perhaps? Brazilian. Very strong and aromatic."

"Too strong for me, thank you," I apologized.

"Never touch it myself," he reassured me. "How about tea? Chinese. Very fragrant."

"With pleasure, thank you."

He pressed one of the buttons below his desk and gave his secretary the order. The tea was brought in almost immediately.

He must have assumed that I had come to denounce an associate, for, as we sipped our tea, he encouraged me to gossip about the Academy and asked who in my Institute was sponsoring my doctoral project. I mentioned two of my professors, both abroad at the time.

"My secretary tells me," he said, "that when you called her to ask for this meeting you spoke of an emergency."

"I did, Comrade Director. An emergency that concerns not just me but the Academy."

"What is it then?"

"As you probably know, Comrade Director," I enunciated carefully, "I am about to be sent abroad to complete my research project in the West. In fact, I have already received my official Academy passport."

"Good, good! Enough of ass-licking our political allies across the border!" he exclaimed. "It's high time for you and all the other young bucks to know our true enemy and prepare for the battles of the future. When are you supposed to leave?" He leaned across the desk to pour me another cup of tea.

"I can't answer that, Comrade Director. Yesterday, I went to the State Bank to see the Deputy Chief of the Foreign Travel Division. I expected simply to pick up my round-trip airline ticket . . ." I opened my attaché case. "This is a copy of the Academy's application on my behalf, which I personally delivered yesterday to the Deputy Chief at the Bank." I placed the sheet in front of him, politely indicating the list of enclosures at the bottom of the page. "As you know, Comrade Director, for an application to be approved by the Academy, all documents must be presented and all originals must be inspected."

He noted each item on the list carefully. "You certainly submitted all the necessary data to the Bank. What's the problem?"

Pretending to feel uneasy, I gulped and jerked my neck and shoulders as if I were wearing a collar that was too tight. "When I handed the application and enclosures to the Deputy Chief, he said that I was— here I must quote him, Comrade—'a low-flying butterfly from that flower bed in the sky.' Those were his exact words, Comrade Director."

The Director clenched his teeth. "Flower bed in the sky? Are you certain he said that, Comrade?" he asked, looking at me intently.

"I am positive, Comrade. I reprimanded him loudly enough for everyone in the room to hear what I was saying."

"Good. How did he reply to your reprimand?"

I pretended to restrain my rage as I replied, "He did not apologize. He did not do anything, Comrade, except throw my documents into his wastebasket."

The Director picked up my application and scanned the list of enclosures. "He threw original documents into the wastebasket?" he asked incredulously.

"That's correct, Comrade Director." I paused to emphasize the seriousness of my reply. "However, upon my emphatic request, the Comrade Deputy Chief confirmed in writing his receipt of the application and enclosures," I continued.

The Director studied the signature and stamp at the bottom of the page. "Indeed he did," he said angrily, pounding the desk with his fist. "We'll settle this matter right away," he roared, reaching for one of his phones. I rose as if ready to leave his office.

"You stay here," he commanded. "I want you to witness this." He pressed a button and an older woman with gray hair entered the room. "Get me the Deputy Chief of the State Bank's Foreign Travel Division and don't say who's calling," he ordered her. She nodded and left hurriedly.

Almost at once, the telephone rang. The Director picked up the receiver. "Is this Comrade Deputy Chief?" He looked at me, smiling vindictively. "You don't know who I am, do you, Comrade? Well, I'll tell you who I am. I am the high-flying butterfly in charge of the highest flower bed in our land, Comrade; that's who I am. If you look out your window,

36

you'll be able to see my office way up in the sky. A butterfly. Yes, that's what I said; a butterfly. Hello? Hello?" He pulled the receiver from his ear, looked at it as if he wanted to smash it, then slammed it down and buzzed for his secretary. "He hung up!" he screamed at her through the intercom. "Get him back right away and this time inform him who is calling."

When the phone rang again, he grabbed it. "Comrade Deputy Chief? If I were you, I would wet my pants before I hung up again. I have here a copy of an Academy application and the list of required documents that you received yesterday." He grinned at me, delighted with himself, and continued, "How do I know? Because you confirmed their receipt in writing. In fact, I am looking at the copy as I speak to you and I can clearly read your signature, the date, even the hour when the documents reached your desk. Here is the name of our Academy applicant." He spelled out my name and asked the Deputy Chief to repeat it to him. "Yes, I'll hold on," he said impatiently.

He kept the receiver pressed to his ear but covered the mouthpiece with his hand and turned to me. "When does the Academy want you to go abroad?"

"In a day or two, Comrade. Of course, this unfortunate delay . . ." I sounded dispirited.

"There will be no delay," he interrupted. "Anytime I want, I can have him turned into a butterfly cavorting in a six-by-eight flower-bed cell." We chuckled together over his joke.

Minutes passed. He pressed the intercom button. "Call him on another line," he yelled at his secretary, "and tell him I am waiting."

The phone rang a third time. Again the Director picked up the receiver. "Ah, you're still here. I thought you had already defected to the enemy. Do you have the file?" He listened to the reply. "What do you mean you 'can't find it'?" he screamed. "This 'it' is a bright young scientist who is sitting here right now staring at your signature, Comrade." He paused. "You what? You can't locate the file?" he roared. "No, I won't wait. We know you received the material because you signed a formal receipt for it. Is it possible, Comrade Chief Deputy," he shouted, intentionally reversing the Deputy Chief's title, ". . . is it possible that you threw it into the wastebasket? Not possible? Then it is all right for me to send a messenger from my flower bed to your kennel right now with a copy of the receipt you signed. Within the hour, you will deliver the authorization to the State Airlines, where it will be picked up by the applicant. You will follow regulations but this time you will also demonstrate your competence, your willingness and your promptness in fulfilling official requests . . . Let me remind you, Comrade Chief Deputy . . ." as he once again reversed the Deputy Chief's title, he winked at me pointedly, ". . . before you fail again, that there are wasps as well as butterflies among the flower beds." He hung up and rang for his secretary, who rushed into the room. He handed her the application, instructing her where to take it. After she left, he calmed down and stretched out in his chair.

"This was a good lesson for you, Comrade," he said, picking up a small replica of the Earth and its first artificial satellite, then replacing it on his desk. "A good lesson in authority. Down there," he said, looking out the window on the Tundra, "that's all that matters." We both rose; then, thanking him profusely, I left his office.

An hour later, I joined the line of State officials in the Airlines office. My ticket was waiting for me at the desk. As others watched, I casually placed it in my attaché case.

The first available plane was leaving late that night, and I decided to take it. I called my parents to say I was leaving for my vacation. My father asked me to call him from the ski resort, but I explained that my friends and I were planning a long drive through the mountains and wouldn't reach the resort before the weekend. He told me to be careful.

As I crossed the Tundra in the darkness, the Palace looked like a Byzantine basilica, incarnating the State. I locked myself inside the darkroom for the last time and packed all the Academicians' correspondence in two suitcases. Even though I realized that the documents could destroy me at airport control, I decided to take them with me: they had been my dueling weapons. If I won the duel, they should be preserved. If I lost, the police would destroy them anyway.

Fifteen years later, in Washington, D.C., immigration officials informed me of the arrival of an older man who claimed to have been my professor. He was trying to find me to obtain the professional recommendation needed to remain in the United States.

I went to see the man and we recognized each other instantly. "You haven't changed. Still that angry parrot glint in your eyes," he said.

"You haven't changed either, Professor. Still the same powerful voice."

"You won't believe it," he said sadly, "but I, who served the State for so long, was thrown out of my country. At my age; so close to retirement. You were wise, quite wise, to leave when you were still young. Now it's too late for me to start a new life."

"Why were you thrown out?"

"Do you remember my monograph on the plight of the nineteenth-century revolutionaries?" he asked.

"To me they were visionaries," I said.

"Visionaries, if you will."

"Now, twenty years after the Party journal commissioned and published it, the same Party charged me with writing it to highlight the role of the Jews as martyrs. Also, because my first wife was Jewish, the Party expelled me from the country as a Zionist agent! I a Zionist! Imagine that!" He looked at me for sympathy.

"It's hard to imagine," I agreed. "Because, when you mentioned Jews in your monograph, you claimed that the pogroms were legitimate revolts of the proletariat against its Jewish exploiters."

He grabbed my arm. "You know very well that what I claimed was based on specific instructions from above. In any case," he continued, "it's not important who was beaten by whom so long ago. What matters now is that, because you were my student once, I took enormous personal risks to help you."

"Did you?"

"Yes. And you didn't even know it. A year before you left the country on that research scholarship, you were seriously investigated by the Academy's highest echelons." He lowered his voice almost to a whisper. "The investigation was extremely confidential and had obviously been instigated by the Ministry of Internal Affairs. When I was approached, I wrote to the Academy that among my students you were the most intellectually stable and highly qualified candidate for travel abroad." He looked to me for an acknowledgment of appreciation and, when I did not respond, he grabbed my arm again. "Of course, I can't claim that I decided your fate. But you should be aware of what your old professor risked for you."

I looked at my watch as if I were in a hurry. "Have you ever seen the safe-deposit vaults in an American bank?" I asked.

"No. Should I?" He seemed relieved by the change of subject.

"I have to retrieve something I stored in a vault. It won't take long. Why don't you come with me?"

Soon an escalator was carrying us down to the bank vaults, where a clerk opened the gates and admitted us. I signed a card so that he could compare my signature to the one in his files. Then he led us into the vault, took my keys and opened the compartment.

"It's a steel bunker," said the professor. He looked around, impressed.

I reached inside the safe-deposit box and pulled out a thick folder. "A bunker of stock certificates, wills, manuscripts, jewelry, money." I removed two letters from the folder and put them aside. "By the way, are you sure, professor, you accurately recall that investigation you spoke about?"

"Indeed I do. I received several inquiries from a scientist who was a high-ranking member of the Academy."

I picked up one of the two letters and handed it to him. "Do you recognize this?" I asked.

He put on his glasses and looked at the letterhead, then at the signature. "This is that very letter!" he exclaimed. "It is marked 'Official and Confidential.' How did you obtain it? Was the Academician who wrote it to me also exiled from our country as a Zionist agent?" he asked, astonished.

Without replying, I handed him the other letter. It was his response to the Academy inquiry. He read it transfixed, as if for the first time.

"I wrote this out of fear," he said dully, after his shock had diminished. "Out of the same fear you yourself experienced when you were there. Out of fear. Forgive me," he begged, with tears in his eyes. Suddenly, he halted and asked, "But how did you get hold of that letter?"

"The Academician to whom you replied never existed. I invented him," I said.

"That can't be true. He was a well-known man. He personally signed the letter I received and when I sent my reply both he and the Academy officially confirmed its receipt."

"I invented him," I repeated. "I wrote to you in his name and when you answered, it was I who confirmed receipt of your reply."

Uncertain what to do next, the professor stood up, stubbornly searching his memory. "I recall that many of my associates at the university also responded to such confidential inquiries from the Academy about you."

"Indeed they did," I answered.

"But who wrote these inquiries?" he asked.

"Dead Souls. They are all here," I said, pointing at my vault.

Under the bright fluorescent light, his skin was pinched and gray, stretched taut over his bald skull. He started to say something. Instead, he blinked his eyes as if the light were suddenly too bright for him, and walked out. As soon as he was gone, I regretted having told him the truth.

Soon after arriving in America, I moved into the university dormitory and advertised in a student paper for someone who would like to learn Ruthenian in exchange for helping me learn English during the forthcoming summer session. The most promising reply I received was from an assistant professor in the Economics Department.

I contacted him and we arranged to meet. Robert was about my age and height, but substantially heavier and more powerfully built. His crew-cut hair was blond, his eyes were blue and he had the kind of pale skin that burns easily. He was dressed casually and explained that since his discharge from the army he favored clothing that did not restrict movement. Although he was not handsome, his gentle and attentive manner was appealing. He spoke elementary Ruthenian with a heavy accent, often confusing regular and irregular verbs.

When he inspected my dormitory cubicle, he warned me that as the room was not air-conditioned it would be unbearable during the summer. He suggested that for the sake of my comfort and our mutual language lessons I should move into the apartment he shared with his girl friend.

Robert lived in a two-bedroom apartment with a river view, on the eighth floor of a university-owned building. From the living-room windows, I used to watch transatlantic ships making their way from the river's mouth up to their slips in the docks. On smogless days, I could see the skyscrapers of the financial district and the blurred silhouette of the Statue of Liberty.

My bedroom was small but air-conditioned and comfortable. Robert and Martine, his girl friend, occupied the large master bedroom, which had its own bathroom. There was another bathroom, which I used, a big living room, a good-sized dining room and a kitchen.

By the time I moved in, Martine had left for Europe to spend the summer with her family. From her photographs she appeared to be a chubby brunette, with large, expressive eyes. Robert told me he had met her in Germany, where he had been stationed with the army. He and Martine had become engaged, and a year before I met him, he had convinced her to come to the United States. They planned to marry in the winter.

Robert seldom spoke of his own family. All I knew was that both his parents were alive and that he had three married sisters who lived near Seattle. The family got together at most once a year, but they kept in frequent touch by telephone.

Over the next weeks, Robert became one of the closest, most thoughtful friends I had ever had. He insisted on my speaking to him in English, although he himself could have used practice conversing in Ruthenian. He continually corrected my speech, checked my term papers for grammatical mistakes and often helped me rewrite them. He relentlessly dragged me to movies and plays, especially those that would acquaint me with regional American dialects and slang; often, he went to see them first to decide whether they were worth my while.

It was a particularly hot summer and I found that taking several hours of classes every day was exhausting. I had begun to lose weight and looked drawn and tired. Robert worried about my health, and to be sure I ate properly he insisted on keeping me company at meals. He also took me swimming in the university pool to make certain I got exercise. For every hour of Ruthenian I spoke with him, he paid me back with many more hours of English.

When the heat had become stifling, Robert urged me to buy a summer suit to replace the heavier European ones I always wore. He went with me to a well-known men's shop and saw to it that I was fitted with a light-weight suit. It was a very expensive model but, fortunately, on sale at half the original price.

I was so pleased to be unburdened of my heavy clothing that I decided to buy another summer suit before the sale ended. This time, a different salesman asked if he could help me and I told him I wanted to see the suit I was wearing in another color. The second one fitted me as well as the first, but when I asked if it was still on sale the man replied that these suits were the finest models in the store and were never reduced. I contradicted him, quoting the price of the first suit, but he continued to insist I was mistaken. I called over the manager, who reluctantly revealed that Robert had paid half the cost of the suit. At home, I confronted Robert, who apologized for his deception but felt I wouldn't have been able to manage without a summer suit. He said he had every right to buy me a present he could easily afford, and suggested I pay him back gradually after I had repaid my university loan.

Late in July, my father wrote to say he had received several long letters from my American roommate. Robert's letters had moved him and my mother greatly. They were letters about me written by a man who understood my character and my roots intimately. He saw in me what my father thought only he himself had detected. My father said he had translated all of Robert's letters for my mother, and each time he read them to her she wept. But if my mother cried over Robert's account of my new life, it was not merely that she was reminded how much she missed her only child, but because she was happy that, on a new continent, among strangers, I had found a friend so wise and so devoted. My father, who had usually disapproved of my friends and seldom found them worthy of his praise, considered my relationship with Robert a good omen. If I was capable of eliciting such a friendship, he wrote me, I could look forward to a bright future in a new country.

Robert's own life was very predictable. He got up

early every morning, took a cold shower, then dressed in a fresh shirt and neatly pressed pants. Next, he prepared our breakfast. He never appeared to mind waiting on me.

During our lunch breaks Robert and I would often meet in the cafeteria or have a sandwich by the river. Sprawled on the grass, cooled by the breeze coming off the water, we listened to the distant foghorns and watched the boats moving in front of us. I experienced a tranquillity I had never known before.

Toward evening, Robert and I often met in libraries to review the most recent American, English and Ruthenian journals and magazines.

We attended many lectures, concerts and parties given by various departments in the university, and I began dating a girl I met at one of them. Robert would occasionally join us for dinner, but toward the end of the evening, under the pretext of having to work, he would leave us alone.

He often invited us along to visit his friends, who seemed to be as impressed by him as I was. I was struck by his ease among them, how he never raised his voice and remained calm during even the most heated discussions.

There were nights when he did not come home, but he would always call in the morning to say he'd slept at a friend's and was going straight to work. I began to suspect that while Martine was away he was seeing another woman; but he would never discuss his love life with me.

One afternoon, a man telephoned Robert at home. When I said he wasn't in, the man asked where he could be located. Although Robert had stayed out the night before, he had not called me, so I could honestly say I didn't know where he was. The caller asked who I was and I told him I had been Robert's roommate for the last few months. When I suggested he leave his name and number, he reluctantly admitted he was Robert's doctor and was calling to inquire why Robert had missed two appointments. He said he had already called the Economics Department and been told that Robert hadn't shown up for work for the last three days. The doctor asked me to remind my roommate he had an appointment on the following day.

Robert came back late the next afternoon, unshaven, filthy and exhausted. He cheerfully told me that he had been in a rough neighborhood assisting social workers. After he had bathed, shaved and changed, I gave him the doctor's message, which he shrugged off. He mumbled something about not needing an annual check-up yet.

In the middle of that night, I was awakened by a flashlight glaring in my face. Without thinking, I leaped off the bed and flung myself straight at the figure inside the doorway. The impact of my body against his threw us both down. He must have fallen against the light switch as he sank to the floor because light suddenly filled the room. As I started to get up, I got my first chance to look at the intruder. It was Robert.

He was wearing a clean white shirt and immaculate white pants and still clutched the flashlight in his hand. By now, we were both on our feet and when he saw how upset I was he tried to calm me. He told me he thought he had heard me cry out and had come in to see what was wrong. He sounded as though he were telling the truth. When he smiled, his face was as gentle and friendly as ever. There was no question of my going straight back to sleep, and I asked him to watch the late TV movie with me. He hardly spoke during the program. Half an hour later, he said he was going to sleep and went to his bedroom, but on my way back to bed I noticed the light under his door. When I peered through the keyhole, I saw Robert lying on top of the bed, still dressed, his hands folded behind his head and his ankles crossed, apparently staring at the ceiling. I was struck by the fixedness of his expression. I wanted to ask if something bothered him, but I decided not to disturb him.

When I got up in the morning, he had already left but there was a note reminding me it was my turn to do the laundry and food shopping. He added that he might be away for a day or two.

That afternoon, I answered a long-distance, person-to-person call from Robert's father. As soon as he heard me informing the operator that Robert was away for a couple of days, he said he would speak to me. He told me he was surprised to learn that Robert had a roommate, because Robert had never mentioned me. Then he asked me off-handedly if I knew why Robert was not seeing his doctor. I said Robert felt he didn't need an annual check-up yet. His father paused, and weighing his words, suggested that I urge Robert to see his doctor. He ignored me when I asked whether Robert was ill, and insisted I take the doctor's home phone number in case Robert needed it.

Robert did not return that night, and as I left for school in the morning I wrote him a note saying that his father had called him about contacting his doctor.

When I got back from classes that day, I found the front door wide open. My first thought was that we had been robbed, so I entered quietly in case the robbers were still there. I walked slowly down the long corridor to the dining room, carefully checking each room I passed but everything seemed in order. As I walked through the kitchen, I saw that my note to Robert was still on the table.

I found Robert in the dining room, hunched in a

chair facing the wall, his hands folded in his lap. His shirt and pants were torn and filthy. His feet were gray with dust and grease, as if he had been walking the streets barefoot. When I got closer, I smelled his stench. He was breathing almost imperceptibly. I went back, closed the front door and returned to attend to him.

I put my hand on his shoulder, but he did not respond. I dragged the chair away from the wall, got down on my knees and stared at him. His eyes were open and blinking sporadically but his expression was vacant. He could neither see nor hear me. I had never encountered that blankness in anyone before, and I could not imagine what had ever possessed him.

"Robert, please answer me." I was practically shouting but he did not respond. Placing my fingers on his temples and my thumbs on either side of his jaw, I gently pushed back his head; he froze where I had moved him, his eyes glassy, his face colorless.

I hurried to the kitchen to get water, then ran back and splashed it on his face. Shivering and confused, he began to come out of the trance. "Robert," I urged him, "please tell me what happened. Shall I call the doctor? Please answer me!"

Suddenly, his eyes cleared and he sat back in the chair, mumbling a phrase I gradually began to comprehend. "I'm going to kill you," he muttered over and over in a voice drained of all inflection. "I'm going to kill you. I have to. I have no other choice. Do you understand? I am going to kill you. I have no choice."

I backed away very slightly. "You are sick, Robert, and you don't mean what you're saying," I said. "Please tell me what you feel." He jumped abruptly from his chair, pushed me aside and dashed into the kitchen. I stood for a few seconds, trying to decide whether to go to him. When I finally moved toward the kitchen, he appeared in the doorway. One hand held a long carving knife and the other was extended for balance. "Robert," I pleaded, "why do you want to kill me?"

"I have no other choice," he apologized in a toneless voice. "I am going to cut your head off. Now. Please don't try to run away." As he moved toward me, I withdrew behind the heavy mahogany dining table in the center of the room. I was paralyzed by the unreality of it all and could not make myself believe he wanted to kill me.

"Please put the knife down, Robert. Let's talk," I reasoned. He stared at me, then lunged, barely missing my head with the knife.

It was real. I had no time to take off my jacket to ward off the blows with it. Robert stalked me around the table while I maneuvered desperately to stay on the opposite side. When he leaped onto the table, I grabbed a heavy vase and hurled it at him. It hit with enough force to knock him to the floor. As he was struggling to his feet, I grabbed a chair and swung it at him, trying to knock the knife out of his grip, but he wrested the chair from me with his free hand and threw it against the wall, where it splintered.

Suddenly, he was above me, wrestling me to the floor with the knife at my chest. As he raised the blade, I rolled over on my stomach, crawled backward, grabbed a broken chair leg and struck his shoulder. He did not drop the knife, but the blow slowed him down. Before he could recover his strength, I grabbed another chair and hurled it at the window to get attention. The glass shattered and I could hear the chair smash as it hit the ground. I counted on someone noticing the commotion and calling the police.

Just then, Robert attacked again. He had me cornered and he thrust like a duelist ready to deliver the coup de grâce. I yelled, ducked and grasped his leg with my hands, trying to pull him off balance. He slipped but got back on his feet. Before I could run out of the room, he blocked my path to the corridor, standing with both arms extended, his knife slicing the air. I was breathless but he showed no sign of fatigue.

For an instant, we faced each other without moving. Then, with his free hand, he cleared a path between us by throwing the three remaining chairs out the window one after another. "I have to cut off your head. Now," he repeated. "I have no other choice."

"We're friends, Robert," I shouted at him. "Why do you want to kill me?"

"You know why," he said, jumping onto the table to bridge the distance between us. He waited for me to move, then threw himself at me, but I leaped sideways and he missed. We began running around the table like two boys playing tag. I was tempted to make a dash for the corridor but knew he was too fast for me.

Suddenly, he halted at the old-fashioned bookcase that stood against the wall, and pulled it over. It hit the floor like thunder, strewing books over the floor. Now there was another obstacle, and Robert had resumed the chase. Because he was a trained jumper, his chances of catching me increased each time I hurdled the bookcase. Twice I fell over it and bruised myself, getting up only seconds before his knife reached me. I was saved not by my speed but by his choosing to aim only at my throat.

An hour had passed since I entered the apartment. My strength was ebbing, but the deadly game of tag continued. Suddenly, we heard hammering and shouts of, "Open up. Police," at the front door. Robert paused, distracted by the sounds, and I took advantage of the interruption to pick up a thick dictionary from the floor and throw it into the corridor to further distract him.

The hammering and shouting increased. Determined to finish me off, Robert attacked again. I tried to run away but tripped over the bookcase, and the distance between us shortened. The police still pounded on the door. I took a desperate chance and bent down to pick up another book; just then Robert lunged again. He missed my neck but nicked my jacket collar. Again, I managed to break away and hurled the book into the corridor over his head.

At that moment, the police shot open the lock and entered with guns drawn. I shouted to them not to fire because Robert was sick. They raced down the corridor. Reaching the dining room, their guns still cocked, they ordered him to drop the knife and raise his arms above his head.

Robert's face suddenly regained its alertness and he turned from me, charging at the two men with a speed and ferocity far beyond what he had shown in chasing me. It was then I realized he could have caught and killed me at almost any point, but that he had intentionally slowed himself down.

Against the policemen, he became a natural killer. Within seconds, he had cut one officer's uniform twice. The policeman was about to shoot but I pleaded with him not to. For the first time since the police entered, Robert became aware of my presence. He turned his head in my direction and, as he did, the other policeman slugged him. Robert's body went limp and he fell at our feet.

He was taken to the hospital and I to the police station. The officer in charge referred to Robert as my "schizo friend" and told me that Robert had a record of violent attacks and was supposed to have been under psychiatric care. I made a deposition and went to visit Robert, but the attending doctor told me Robert was under heavy sedation and was not allowed any visitors. The doctor's only comment was that I was lucky to be alive.

I called Robert's parents. When his father answered, I told him what had happened, and he said he would fly in immediately to see Robert and me. He stopped by the apartment the following afternoon, having spent the morning at the hospital. He was in excellent shape for a man his age, with a handsome, impassive face. He surveyed the wreckage in the dining room and looked at my bruised head. "Robert has been under medical supervision ever since he returned from the army," he said. "He has been hospitalized many times before."

"Why didn't you warn me when I talked to you the first time?" I asked. He didn't answer. "Why did he stop seeing his doctor?" I demanded.

He looked at me blandly. "You should know. You lived with him." We both stopped talking, strangers with only one hideous interest in common.

"When did Robert become ill?" I finally asked.

"When he was in the army," he said. "When they realized how sick he was, they discharged him."

"Was there any indication of disturbance before he enlisted?" I asked.

Robert's father rose and picked up his hat from the table. "When Robert was a small boy, I gave him a dog," he said. "A big, strong animal. The kid loved it more than anything else in the world. Two years later he cut off the dog's head."

Shortly after Robert was committed I went back to Europe. Even now, whenever I become involved with others enough to expect certain patterns of behavior or to rely on them, the memory of my experience with Robert returns to alert me. In a sense, Robert continues to be a close friend, reminding me from time to time of the estrangement that may lie beneath apparent mutual understanding.

I settled in Switzerland and began working in a small chemical laboratory. To earn money for ski weekends, I worked overtime in the lab and did freelance translations. I boarded with a family in their small house to make my money last. The couple worked on weekends during the tourist season- and asked me if I would mind taking their ten-year-old daughter to the ski slopes with me. The little girl loved to ski, but her parents wouldn't let her try the higher slopes by herself and were pleased that I accompanied her.

Shy and withdrawn, she became friendly only after I offered to teach her some stunts performed by the better skiers. Soon, she wouldn't leave me alone. When we ate lunch, she angrily told any waiter who addressed her as my daughter that I was not her father but her best friend.

We agreed that I despised my work as much as she hated school and that one day the two of us would visit places where together we would do only what we liked. We would wear beautiful clothes and ski the highest mountains. We would fly south to swim in warm, turquoise oceans. She hung on every word as I described the strange animals we would see in the jungles and the parties we would attend on the rooftop terraces of skyscrapers. As we talked, she would pull at my parka, demanding that we escape right away. When her parents complained about her grades or reprimanded her for sleeping too late on school days, she gave me a conspiratorial glance.

We went skiing on the last Saturday of the season,

though the slopes were already bare in many spots. When I hit places where the snow or ice was too thin, I removed my skis and walked the trails, but the girl insisted on skiing even the baldest patches, laughing and making fun of me.

At dinner that night, I mentioned that I would be leaving early on Monday. The girl's mother proposed a toast to my return the following year, but I told her that I might not even be in the country then. The girl said nothing.

During Sunday supper, the girl ate little and sat quietly at the table. She surprised her parents by volunteering to go to bed early and, as she went upstairs, I embraced her and she kissed my cheek.

The next morning, I awoke while it was still dark, dressed and finished packing. I was attempting to leave the house without waking anyone when I saw the girl standing in the hall. She was wearing her best coat and clutching a small suitcase in her hand. She whispered that she was ready to go. I tried to explain that our trip had been make-believe and that she was too young to be allowed to travel alone with me. She replied that she was planning to escape secretly.

Once I realized that she was determined to go, I went upstairs to wake her parents. When we returned to the hall, we found that she had disappeared. We assumed she was upset about my leaving, that she had decided not to see me off. As her parents walked me to my car we spotted her poised on the roof of the chalet. Her mother pleaded with her to come down, but the girl insisted that if I left without her she would kill herself. She swore she would jump if I abandoned her. Her father urged me to leave at once so that his child could see I had no intention of taking her with me. I fastened my skis onto the car, stowed my luggage in the trunk and started the engine. When the girl saw me going, she stood up, swaying very near the roof's edge. I wanted to get out and talk to her, but her father slammed the car door and ordered me to go. I backed the car out of the driveway, but, just as I began to move forward, I heard her mother scream. The girl had fallen off the roof, and was rolling down the slope.

She was unconscious by the time we reached her and we were afraid to move her. While her mother and I sat with her, her father called an ambulance. At the hospital, waiting for the doctor's report, her father kept trying to explain to me how much he had loved his daughter, as though I had blamed him for her accident. The doctor appeared with the x-rays and told us that the girl had broken her spine and fractured several ribs; she might never walk again. I have never seen her or her parents since.

When the French scientist whose works I had been translating came to see me, I asked him to help me find a better job. He took me to a cocktail party given for him by a prominent Swiss industrialist and his wife who, he felt, might provide good job connections.

Our hostess was tall, olive-skinned and very glamorous. I learned from the scientist that she was of Lebanese descent and had been an actress in second-rate French and German films.

Since she was constantly surrounded by admirers, I had no chance to talk to her alone. She was too busy to bother with me until she overheard me speaking English with one of the guests. In the middle of a conversation, she abruptly turned to me and complimented me on my fluency and then returned to her conversation. A few days later, she called to say she would like to refresh the English she had learned as a child. I agreed to give her lessons, which began the following day.

The lessons were held in her study while her husband was at his office. I saw him infrequently, only when she invited me to one of their parties. During our lessons she read English prose and poetry aloud, and I criticized her pronunciation. She always remained cool and distant.

One morning, I was awakened by a phone call. She said she had to see me and would be over at once to pick me up. As we drove, she insisted that what made her call was not boredom and restlessness. She told me that her need to see me was too desperate to wait the twenty-four hours until our lesson, that what she wanted to say was too important for the time we had alone. Rather than reveal only part of what she felt, she had said nothing, but now she had to speak. That afternoon we became lovers.

Our physical intimacy only increased the ambiguity of our relationship. She said that she wanted to be more than an afterthought tacked onto the main part of my existence. She wanted to be the center of my life and would not settle for less. Since she knew this need made unreasonable demands upon me, to spare me, she suggested we consider our relationship unsalvageable and part.

After several days, we began to meet again. Still she blamed me for holding back. She claimed that each time she had tried to get a response from me, I had moved away; she was always the one to suggest we make love.

She also told me she assumed our every meeting would be the last, and that she would do anything to keep me. She grew more anxious every time we were together, our encounters became more and more tense, and she again demanded that we part. We did, for about three weeks, then she wrote that she could no longer suppress the tenderness she felt for me. We began to meet again.

Since she claimed to want to build her life around me, I was puzzled by her frequent trips abroad. She always went alone and her husband did not seem to mind, but I suspected she was meeting a lover and she finally admitted it.

A year later, her husband was about to move his base of operations to Washington, D.C. During the last few weeks in Switzerland she insisted on seeing me more often. The evening before they were to leave, she came to ask if I would consider returning to the United States. I said I could not afford to go back.

Then she took an envelope from her purse and handed it to me. The package, she said, contained coded documents of considerable value. She gave me the names of foreign intelligence agents who would all be eager to buy these secrets at a high price. The originals, she assured me, were abroad, in the private safe of her lover, who was a prominent member of a powerful government. She had photographed the documents and developed and printed the copies herself; no one but she and I knew she had done it. I could become wealthy by selling the documents, she said, and if I wanted to could even begin a new career. But she warned me not to betray her.

Soon after she had left the country, I sold the contents of the envelope to the highest bidders, the Americans, who also made me an offer to join the Service. I accepted.

I recall vividly how, upon arriving at the training center, I was asked to wait in a small room packed with over a hundred men roughly my own age. The room had a large exit that was locked from the outside. An official stepped onto the podium at the far end of the room, announced that we would soon be called for a medical examination and left through a small door behind the podium.

We waited an hour. Most of the men began to grow impatient. Then the door opened again, another official entered, closed the door and mounted the podium. He apologized for the delay and told us to undress completely and to leave our belongings where we were standing.

We undressed in the cramped space and hot, smelly air. Many of the men grumbled as they were elbowed, inadvertently, by others. Some left their clothes in a heap, some tucked one garment into another, but they all clung to their wallets and watches.

When we had stripped, the first official returned and conferred with the second, who said with some embarrassment that the order had been intended for another group. He asked us to dress again and await further instructions. After both officials left, the men sullenly started to gather their belongings together. The sealed windows could not be opened and cigarette smoke was further polluting the already stale air.

Fifteen minutes later, when we were dressed, one of the officials came back looking agitated and asked for our attention. As soon as we had quieted down, he said he was sorry and that we actually were the group that had been ordered to undress. His apologies were labored and profuse, mixed with bad jokes about bureaucracies, which served only to irritate the men around me. Some of them angrily threw their clothes onto the floor, while others refused to undress at all. The official pleaded with us and, in the end, everyone stood naked.

Thirty more minutes passed. By the time another man entered the room, the crowd was at the boiling point. This official did not ask for silence but simply glared at us. He finally announced that complications had delayed the other group's examinations and that we might not be taken that day at all. His tone managed to suggest that we were somehow to blame for the inconvenience and disruption of the schedule. He ordered us to dress again and left without another word.

Men trampled upon their clothes and smashed their shoes against the wall. A fight broke out, but the combatants were restrained. A man next to me popped the buttons off his shirt sleeves. When another man's zipper stuck, he angrily yanked at it until it broke. Few men bothered to lace their shoes; almost no one redid his tie.

The next official who entered the room was greeted with boos and curses. He was the one who had pleaded with us earlier, and now, his voice heavy with contempt, he confirmed what we had been told. Our examination would not be held that day and we were free to go as soon as he finished speaking.

Some men went on swearing and gesturing. Others, exhausted and listless, merely followed instructions and continued dressing. Still others began to nod with delayed comprehension. Those who had behaved most theatrically were now the most calm. At last, there was general quiet and the man continued.

He explained that during our repeated dressing and undressing we had actually undergone the examination. Our physical would come later. Today, we had been filmed by teams of psychologists, who would study our behavior. The sullen candidates looked suspiciously around the room, checking for cameras.

Days later, during one of many interviews with people from the Service, I was told I had achieved one of the highest scores in the examination. I had undressed and dressed each time with approximately the same speed, removing, piling and picking my clothes up again in the same order. I expressed no visible emotion during the test and accepted the changes in orders as if I had expected them all along. They noted that I circulated, joined no group but conversed easily with whomever stood near me.

After months of training, I began my intelligence work in the United States. I made a formal Service inquiry about the Lebanese woman and was told that she had been an intelligence agent for years, but when she failed to acquire some strategic European documents she had been dropped.

Apparently, her marriage to the Swiss industrialist had been arranged for intelligence purposes, and for those reasons had also been ended. The divorce had left her penniless and she was forced to work for a living. She was now settled in New York City, where she was known as Theodora.

When I arrived at her apartment, she said she had known I would turn up sooner or later. I was shocked at the change in her. She had aged badly and become obese. Her face was heavily powdered a pasty white, and she wore thick false eyelashes, bright lipstick and garish rouge. She was dressed in a skin-tight black leather pants suit and an ill-fitting wig. Later, she told me she had lost so much of her own hair that she had to wear the wig all the time. Her living room was filled with books inscribed to her, autographed movie stills and photographs of her and her ex-husband.

She told me that after her dismissal, within a year of their arrival in America, she had found her first job with a real estate firm. One day she was asked to show a luxurious, furnished duplex apartment to the new United Nations' representative of a recently founded republic. It was one of the most expensive apartments the agency had ever handled, and she would receive a substantial bonus if the diplomat bought it.

The diplomat was a distinguished-looking older man dressed in a long, elaborately draped robe, his country's national costume. Reserved and polite in the best British colonial tradition, he accepted a cup of tea and told Theodora how anxious he was to find a good home for his family. While he drank his tea and nibbled at the canapés, he chatted about his children. As he and Theodora toured the apartment, he inquired about its air conditioning, the closets, the kitchen facilities and the house telephone system.

They had reached the upper floor. Just as she was about to show him the master bedroom, he grabbed her by the neck and tripped her with his leg. When she fell, he ripped off her underpants, and, with a single, rapid movement, shed his robe and covered her mouth with it to muffle her cries. He dropped onto her and spread her legs with his kness. He moaned and gasped as he raped her. When he was finished, he rolled off her, got up, wiped himself with her panties and neatly rearranged the robe around himself. In the most exaggeratedly polite manner, he apologized for his behavior, insisting that nothing like that had ever come over him before. He had simply been overwhelmed by her beauty, he explained, and would never forgive himself. Then he left.

Since she needed the commission and was afraid to make trouble, Theodora reported to her agency that the diplomat required a few days to make a decision. On the following afternoon, she received a giant bouquet of roses from him accompanied by a note of thanks. Her employer was delighted and congratulated her for having made such a good impression.

About a week later, she received an invitation at the office to a reception celebrating the opening of the diplomat's mission to the UN. Her first reaction was to refuse but her employer was anxious for her to go. To check whether there really was a party, she telephoned the mission and was told the reception would be attended by the diplomatic corps, by the city's most distinguished citizens and by reporters. Under those circumstances, she felt she could attend.

As soon as she arrived at the party, the rapist came over to her. This time he was wearing a robe embroidered with gold and semiprecious stones. He introduced her to his wife, an elegantly dressed woman much younger than himself. The diplomat looked into Theodora's eyes, then gallantly kissed her hand. He complimented her on her dress and asked in a whisper if she had forgiven him for the most irresponsible moment of his life. She didn't reply.

During the reception, she mingled with the other guests to avoid the diplomat. In one of her attempts to stay with a large group, she joined a tour of the mission's art collection. The rapist, who was escorting his wife, discreetly followed in the long line of visitors.

On the third floor, as the guests were being guided to a group of sculptures, Theodora felt secure enough to head for a bathroom around the corner. As she was opening the door, she was suddenly shoved inside from behind. Before she could cry out, a large hand covered her mouth and another unzipped her dress. She recognized the diplomat's cologne even before he turned her around. He was not drunk and seemed perfectly in control. With his hand still on her mouth, he pinned her to the wall, ripped off her brassiere and pressed her cheeks between his fingers until she opened her mouth; he then stuffed a guest towel into it.

His robe dropped to the floor as though he had pulled a ripcord. Naked and excited he stood before

her, squeezing her breasts as his knees parted her
thighs. When she attempted to twist free, he deftly
turned her over, ripping her pants as though he had
rehearsed it, and thrust into her. He climaxed rapidly,
then pulled out and let her go. He carefully wrapped
his robe about himself; he looked into her eyes and
whispered how sorry he was that once again he could
not restrain his passion for her. Then he glanced into
the mirror to smooth his hair, opened the door and
swiftly left the bathroom.

The diplomat failed to buy the apartment, and
Theodora lost her job. Afterward, she worked as a
nightclub hostess, a cosmetics saleswoman, a transla-
tor. When I met her, she was supporting herself by
gathering data for a small sex research institute. Assisted by professionals, she conducted interviews with
men and women who had responded to personal ads
in pornographic tabloids. It was not a bad job, she
said, although many of the men she talked to pursued
her constantly. She was looking forward to ending the
project and planned to restructure her whole life.

She was getting old, and even though she realized
it might be too late, she had decided to try to have a
baby. She planned to increase her chances of concep-
tion by taking hormone shots and finding a lover for
intercourse with her at least twice a day. I mockingly
remarked she had a better chance of becoming pregnant than of finding a lover, but she said I was wrong:
I would be her lover. Before I could protest, she offered to provide me with a different woman every day
on the condition that Theodora could join us in bed
and collect my sperm. When I objected, she insisted
I should first test the sexual skill of her protégées.

She fixed lunch and, while I ate, made several
phone calls. Soon a teen-aged girl arrived. Theodora
asked whether I wanted her, and when I said I did the

girl took off her clothes. I undressed and got in bed beside her. Theodora, still dressed, reclined on the edge of the bed next to the girl.

I told Theodora to leave the room and she obeyed. I played with the girl and she began working on me, determined to accomplish what she had been brought in to do. Soon we both knew she would not succeed.

Finally, I called to Theodora, who appeared immediately, as if she had been expecting my call. She moved toward the bed in high-heeled slippers and a black robe, descending like a monstrous bat upon the girl's body. Almost at once, the girl had loosened Theodora's robe and their heads were locked between each other's thighs. They swayed rhythmically until Theodora moved away and told me the girl was mine.

The bed was warm and the sheets were fresh. In the soft glow of the bedside lamp, I felt sheltered from the outside world. Theodora perched against the headboard, her face hidden in the shadows, watching every move I made. The girl was still excited from being with Theodora. As I took her, she screamed and cried. Anger suddenly swelled in me; I pushed her across the bed, straddled her head and sat on her face until she went limp. As I climaxed, Theodora arose from her corner to collect my semen in the palm of her hand, then glided off to the bathroom.

I occasionally hinted at my sexual needs to guide Theodora in selecting the women. Whenever a girl could not arouse me, Theodora would help; watching her make love to another woman invariably excited me. Eventually, regardless of how much the girls attracted me, I would prefer to have Theodora prepare them. I never penetrated Theodora with my flesh and never kissed her mouth.

Once in a while, I brought a girl I had picked up myself. Theodora would fix lunch or dinner for the three of us and by the end of the meal she would have captivated our guest. While the girl was changing into the nightgown Theodora offered her, Theodora would put on one of her black lace or leather outfits. She always managed to seduce the girl before I did.

When one of her girls did not show up, I threatened to find my own partners and make her find another sperm bank. Theodora laughed. She told me she was sure I could trap plenty of women on my own because the passive, repressed types I preferred were always the easiest to find. But in the end, she said, it was I who would be trapped: these women were just the opposite of what I really wanted.

One day, Theodora phoned me to announce she was pregnant. Although I did not believe it, she continued to insist exuberantly that she was going to have my baby, and the next time I saw her she immediately showed me the result of the hospital test. In the following weeks, she told everyone the news. Even though she refused to reveal who the father was, many people assumed the child was mine.

A few months later, I arrived at one of Theodora's parties to find her wearing a gown that accentuated her prominent belly. During the evening, she reproached a guest, a playwright, for using experiences from her life in his latest play. The man, who was quite drunk, accused her of faking the pregnancy by wearing padding under her dress. He lunged at her, trying to tear off her gown, and Theodora fled the room in tears. From that night on, no one believed she was pregnant.

When she bought a crib and began knitting baby clothes, people thought she was losing her mind, and even her closest friends soon abandoned her. She continued to work with the sex research institute and stopped discussing her pregnancy.

I was curious to know whom she was seeing. I began following her and found out she was being tailed by two detectives from the vice squad. I thought they might have discovered drug addicts among Theodora's research subjects, and since an investigation could also involve me, I decided to steer clear of her.

For the next few months, I moved from one to another of my apartments. I made no attempt to see Theodora or any of the people she had introduced me to. Late one night, I returned to the apartment where she had once visited me. An envelope written in her familiar scrawl had been pushed under the door. She wrote that she had given birth to my son and was enclosing a picture of him. It was a large glossy photograph of a newborn baby lying in an incubator with its face partly obscured. I could tell from the sharpness and angle of the photo that it had been taken by a camera used for scientific documentation.

Suspecting that the child in the photo was not Theodora's, I took the picture to the largest photo laboratory in the city and asked to have it traced. Two days later, I was notified that the picture had been taken by a photographer specializing in textbook illustrations. When I went to his studio, he identified the photograph as one he had taken about ten years earlier and sold many times for use in medical books. He recognized my copy as one of two hundred recently delivered to an uptown address and gave me the catalogue number of the original stock photo.

I called Theodora to tell her I had received the photograph. She said the baby was well, although the delivery had been difficult. Postnatal difficulties had led to some disturbing test results, including the possibility that she might have bone cancer. Afraid of what might happen to her son if she died, she told me she had found foster parents for him in a small suburban town. She still visited the child, but as her health failed, her trips became more and more exhausting and infrequent.

I asked when the child's photograph had been taken and she told me a day or two after the delivery, adding that she had sent the picture to all her friends. I promised to see her when I was next in town.

It occurred to me that Theodora might have told her friends that I was the father of her child. To put an end to her story, I typed short, anonymous notes to all the people whose addresses I had once copied from her address book. I stated that Theodora's child did not exist, that the photograph she had sent was of another child and had been taken ten years before. To substantiate this accusation, I gave the photo's catalogue number and the name of the studio where the original could be found. I mailed the notes on the day I left the country.

Returning from Europe almost a year later, I was walking down Broadway when I recognized a black girl to whom Theodora had once introduced me. The girl asked if I knew Theodora was dying of cancer in a charity ward. Although it was very late, I went directly to the hospital. The night nurse was hesitant to let me into the terminal ward, but when I told her I had arrived in New York that very night and was the woman's only living relative, she allowed me to see her.

I walked down the darkened center aisle of the room, looking at each patient until I found her. Next to her bed stood an oxygen tank from which two extending tubes had been inserted into her nostrils. Her yellow skin sagged on the bones of her face, and the wig had slipped back, exposing her bald scalp. She had no eyebrows or eyelashes left. The thin sheet that covered her emphasized her sharp, fleshless bones. On

the night table, among the make-up creams, magazines and books, I noticed a Polaroid photograph of
a baby in a playpen. I left the room without waking
her.

The following day, I returned and spoke to the doctor in charge. He told me Theodora had been hospitalized when her pelvis collapsed. Initially, she had
been given injections to slow the cancer, but since she
had entered the terminal phase she was being given
only strong pain killers. He said it was now a matter
of days.

I found her propped up against a low headrest, staring at the wall. As I approached the bed, she shifted
her gaze and looked at me. Slowly lifting her hand,
she centered the wig on her skull. While I spoke, she
attempted a smile. The corners of her lips stretched
sideways under the oxygen tubes as she strained to
speak, but could not. Her eyes returned to the wall,
and she refused to look at me again. As I left, I asked
the nurse to call me if there was a change. By the end
of the next week, she called to say that Theodora was
dead.

Weeks later, I received a message from a law firm,
informing me that Theodora had left me all her
books. The lawyer said he had obtained my phone
number from the nurse at the hospital and asked if I
was related to Theodora. I remarked I was not and
that as far as I knew she did not have any living relatives, but the lawyer answered that she had a one-year-
old child. I told him that her pregnancy had been a
hoax, but he insisted that Theodora had given birth
to a boy. I explained how she had sent out to friends
a professional photograph of another baby; he replied
that she had done so because her own child had been
born cross-eyed, but that an operation had since corrected the defect.

I asked about the boy's father. The lawyer paused, then said Theodora had not named him. Furthermore, it had been agreed that the child's foster parents would never tell the boy he had been adopted. After I asked where the child was, the lawyer said he was not free to tell me.

Soon after Theodora's death, I took out one of the nurses from the hospital. She said the doctors had told Theodora that she was dying five months before she actually died. Since then she had been aware that the injections would do nothing but extend her agony. When the nurse had asked Theodora whether there were any relatives or friends she would like to have visit her, she answered there was only one man, the father of her child. She refused to contact him, but she was sure he would come. Even when Theodora was being fed intravenously and had to be given oxygen, she would still prepare for the man's visit. She wore her make-up and wig all the time, and when, as a result of hormone injections, she began to grow a dark mustache and a slight beard, she diligently shaved every morning.

Months went by, but the man did not come. Theodora stopped caring about her appearance. When the young nurse brought her a television set, she refused to watch it. Theodora told the nurse that, although her body was dying, her brain was still alive and she didn't have time to waste. She was too busy looking at her memories, each memory as fresh as a young green sprout.

I had Theodora to thank for leading me to the Service. She had helped me find a shield for the self I wanted to hide.

I was one of many Service operatives assigned to track down an agent of ours who had disappeared five years earlier. I had met him socially many times during his Service days, and, since he had never known I was an agent, it was thought that I would have an excellent chance of making contact and eliminating him. We had no information on his present whereabouts, name or occupation, and not even any assurance that he was alive.

After months of pursuing one futile lead after another, I was ready to admit defeat and suggested that the search be abandoned. My report was accepted, and I was reassigned.

A year later, in early spring, I was passing through the Val d'Anniviers. As I was driving toward a small mountain resort, an unusual sports car sped by. I recalled that the agent used to drive an earlier model of that same car, in the very same color. I also noticed that the spare tire was attached to the roof in exactly the same manner as it had been on the agent's previous car. I thought it would be strange for the agent to stick to old habits if he were trying to erase all contact with his past. Still, I felt he might be behind the wheel. My own car was not fast enough to catch up, though. I reached the village and searched every parking lot and public garage but failed to locate the car. I was about to give up when I saw the agent crossing the street, but by the time I parked my own car he had disappeared. I decided to remain there and make contact.

I rented a room in a small hotel and strolled around the town. Outside a large camera shop, I paused to study pictures taken by local photographers in the town's restaurants, nightclubs and hotels. I was glancing idly at the display when I spotted a picture of him. He looked years younger in the photo than he had during his final Service days. His face was completely unlined; his once thinning hair was thick and full. I assumed he was wearing a toupee and make-up. I went into the shop so that I could check the back of the print and find the name of the hotel where it had been taken.

I purchased the photograph, took it to the hotel and asked the concierge to identify the man in the picture, saying he resembled an American friend I hadn't seen for some time. The concierge gave me the name under which the agent was registered and I pretended to recognize it. I telephoned the room, and when the agent answered I called him by the name he had been using when we last met. He was surprised, but he had no reason to suspect my motives. We arranged to have lunch together in the hotel restaurant.

When we met later, I told him the strange story of how I had come to find him. I mentioned I had seen him in his car. He laughed and explained he had not owned a car for years and was now driving a rented sedan. Furthermore, he told me, at the time I thought I had seen him on the street he had been lounging by the hotel pool. But the photograph was unmistakably of him. We joked about the strange coincidences, but I believed nothing he told me.

I asked him why he had left America. He said he had run into some problems five years earlier, and decided to settle in Europe, where life was easier. He had changed his name to simplify his existence and, when he was able to afford it, had undergone radical cosmetic surgery. The changes of country, name and appearance, he said, had altogether altered his view of himself. Looking in a mirror no longer made him self-conscious, and he could now enjoy dating girls half his age.

Throughout lunch, he continued to reminisce; then he asked what was I doing in the mountains. I said I had just completed an exhausting business trip and, since I was already in Europe, I'd decided to spend a couple of weeks relaxing in the Alps. After lunch, I suggested sightseeing. I knew that his sedan was equipped with a standard antitheft device. If the ignition was off, the steering mechanism automatically locked in position, immobilizing the car's front wheels. I asked if he would drive, since he knew the area.

We drove up a steep road for almost forty minutes, chatting and occasionally stopping to admire the view. As we passed a school where small girls were playing in the yard, he remarked how sad it was that both of us might die before these girls became women.

The road ended where the glacier began. We drove back along a narrow road with no safety railings and almost no shoulder. I watched him snap his seat belt on but made no move to fasten mine. As we drove on, he told me about an old mountaineer he had once known in Vercorin who had trained an eagle to hover high above him as he climbed. Whenever the mountaineer was in trouble, the bird flew off to alert guides who came immediately to the man's rescue.

I half-listened to his story. The car made two hairpin turns and was about to enter a third when I quickly leaned forward, placed one hand on the door handle and, with the other hand, switched off the ignition. The agent did not seem to grasp what had happened. Just as the engine died and the steering wheel locked, I opened my door and rolled out onto the ground. The car shot across the road, and dived over the shoulder. I heard a crash from the chasm below, followed by a small rockslide. When I got up, painfully aware that I had bruised my thigh and knee, I peered over the edge. On the lower slopes everything was quiet. There was no trace of the car.

I walked down the road for about an hour without

encountering anyone. I reached the highway, pretending to be an afternoon stroller, and hitched a ride back to the village.

The evening news reported that a man had died when his car veered off a mountain pass and crashed several hundred feet below in a ravine. The following day, another announcement stated that the driver's partly burned body was being held at the local morgue pending identification. Promptly, I called my contact to inform him I had eliminated the agent, and he complimented me on my success.

As I walked through the village, I saw the sports car that had originally alerted me that my quarry was nearby. The car was driven by a young man who bore no resemblance whatsoever to the dead agent. As I turned into my hotel, pondering that coincidence, I nearly bumped into a man with the agent's exact build. At that close range his face and hair only roughly resembled the dead man's, but as he walked away, I realized that this was the man I initially took for the agent: from a distance they were identical.

A day later, on the terrace of an old hotel, I was approached by a stranger who told me in code that he was from the Service. He sat down, ordered a beer and tersely congratulated me on achieving success where so many others had failed. Then he asked me how I had been put onto the man's trail. I told him about the weird string of coincidences that had led me to him.

The operative looked at me unconvinced, then reminded me that the agent had been underground for years. He suggested that I must have had help in finding him and insisted that the Service be told who the informants were.

I repeated what I had already told him. He remained skeptical, but instead of persisting with questions, he proceeded to fill me in on my next assignment, for which I was to be sent to Indonesia.

After arriving in Djakarta, I attempted to contact our resident agent in order to begin my assignment. Under my cover identity, to prepare for which I was given a suitcase full of books and papers, I was a member of an international group of psychiatrists and anthropologists who had come to compare primitive concepts of madness with psychiatric theories of emotional disturbance. If the tribal term "illness of the spirit" described the same behavioral states as the Western concept of "insanity," we would be able to define mental imbalance as a culturally independent phenomenon.

The local governmental authorities in charge of all scientific research were most anxious to have us flown immediately to a remote part of Borneo for our field work. In the rest of the country, the civil strife that had followed an army-led rebellion was still going on. There was a rumor that the mass slaughter of suspected opponents to the new regime was being performed by bands of army-appointed civilians, mostly university students, and by members of religious sects, who struck by night. In many hamlets, prisoners and even whole families were stabbed and hurled into pits, rivers, wells and ponds, where they were left to rot. In the larger villages, towns and cities, people were dragged through the streets, their heads shattered by stones hurled by the crowds. No one knew how many men, women and children had actually been slain. The official figure was in excess of a million. Miles of mutilated bodies lined the highways.

In Djakarta, we were told that no international body would dare intervene to stop the mass killing. Western diplomats stationed in Indonesia did not want to be accused of interfering in another country's

internal affairs and had confined themselves to be-
wailing in public forums the extent of human
brutality.

When my contact did not show up during the first
two days, I assumed that the mission had been can-
celed, but on the third day, the local radio announced
the capture of an American spy who had confessed
there was a second American operating in Indonesia.

The captured man had never seen me and had been
arrested before being told of my cover. Although the
Indonesians knew there was another operative in the
country, they would not be able to apprehend me unless I revealed myself. Since now I could not leave the
country without the risk of alerting the police, I decided to play out my cover role and join the conference.

The group had turned out to be far larger than anticipated. Many of the psychiatrists had brought wives
or husbands, and we had only three small planes at
our disposal. It took several trips to transport our
group from Djakarta to the institute in Borneo, and,
once there, we discovered that there were not enough
accommodations. Eventually, we were separated by
sex and assigned to two large classrooms, each crowded
with beds about two feet apart. A single door connected the dormitories, and each room had its own
entrance to the outside.

Among the psychiatrists was a young couple who
appeared to be newlyweds. During the lectures and
discussions that preceded the actual field work, they
were constantly holding hands or caressing and were
very protective of each other. Once, when I casually
made a joke at her husband's expense, the wife began
cross-examining me angrily, questioning my theories
and my scientific credentials. I answered her with the

expert data prepared for me by the Service, but she remained hostile and suspicious.

Strolling in the institute garden one morning, I saw her walking alone. I went over to join her, and she reluctantly allowed me to accompany her. As we were walking, a stray cat brushed against her leg. The cat's arrival prompted me to test out a new defense device that I might have to use if I were discovered. I bent down and began to stroke its fur. The woman's skirt brushed my forehead, and I looked up at her legs. Realizing I was staring at her, she turned away in embarrassment, and it was at that moment that I pressed the ring on my third finger into the cat's neck. With my thumb, I moved the ring's concealed activator to the release position and shot two pressurized doses of poison into the animal's flesh.

I had been ordered to take one shot to kill myself if I were ever captured. With two times that dosage in its system, the cat instantly shivered, grew rigid and fell dead at the woman's feet. She screamed and jumped back, averting her eyes when I picked up the corpse and threw it under a bush. Walking back toward the institute buildings, I speculated that the animal must have died of a heart attack. She seemed to accept the explanation.

During our afternoon break, I looked through a window into the woman's dormitory and saw her sitting on her bed, fifteen cots away from the connecting door.

About an hour after the lights were turned off that night, I slid from my bed and lay down on the floor. The only sounds in the room were the hum of the ceiling fans and an occasional snore. I began to crawl down the aisle between the rows of narrow beds, wearing only my short bathrobe; I could not tell whether the men I passed were fast asleep or only lying still.

By the time I reached the connecting door, my chest and thighs were dusty and scratched from the rough wood. I opened the door just wide enough to be able to slide through.

The women's room was lit only by a dim red bulb over the main door, and I had to inch along, counting the beds. Someone coughed. A woman stretched and turned over. The psychiatrist's wife was sleeping on her back, with the sheet pulled up to her chin. I made my way to the edge of her bed and tugged at the sheet. She shifted but did not wake up. I pulled the sheet again, and this time she began to open her eyes. I covered her mouth with my hand, pinning her head to the pillow. Still kneeling on the floor, I whispered that if she made a sound her husband would die as silently and quickly as the cat.

I climbed onto the narrow bed, pressing hard against her, my hand covering her mouth while the other moved under her nightgown. She tried to push me away, but I reminded her to think of her husband, and she stopped resisting. I caressed and kissed her, but I did not enter her. After an hour, I lowered myself to the floor, whispered that I would come to her every night and slowly crawled back through the door, inching carefully along the floor until I reached my own bed.

At breakfast, I sat across from her and her husband, pretending to listen to his pretentious theorizing. The woman said nothing and didn't even glance in my direction.

That night, I waited until well after midnight to slide off my bed and crawl through the door. I sat motionless on the other side for a few moments, waiting to see if I had been followed. If she had told her husband what I had done, he and others might be waiting for me to make my move. After I made sure no one had followed me, I began to crawl along toward her bed. She was awake. I motioned to her to undress, and she obediently slipped off her nightgown. I slid into bed alongside her. As my hand moved over her belly, she stifled a gasp and covered her mouth with the sheet.

I turned her over and eased into her from behind. She stifled a moan, and I deliberately forced myself deeper into her. She was sweating, but she did not scream. I whispered that if she could reach a climax by exciting herself I would stop hurting her. At first she refused. I slid onto the floor, my head between her thighs. I bit into her flesh and held fast to it until her hand moved to push me away. She began to caress herself and I pressed my mouth against her hand. Wet from my tongue and warmed by my breath, her fingers moved back and forth frenetically. Before each climax, she bent forward, pressing her hand against the back of my head.

The next day, the psychiatrist and his wife did not attend the afternoon session. I inquired about them and was told they had left that morning for another part of the country.

Several days after the field work ended and I returned to Djakarta, I decided to leave Indonesia on the scientists' charter flight. My passport was checked, and I was told I could go directly to the plane. I knew that if I was going to be arrested it would have to happen before I boarded.

Walking to the plane, I spotted the psychiatrist and his wife ahead of me, both suntanned and wearing safari jackets. I caught up with the couple, who were burdened down by their heavy luggage, and, as I carried only a light attaché case, I offered to help them. The psychiatrist handed me a bag containing his movie cameras, but his wife barely acknowledged me.

The three of us joined the large crowd waiting to board. Suddenly, I saw a military police car racing toward us. My legs felt weak. I had trouble catching my breath. I put down the camera bag and the attaché case. The police car screeched to a stop and two officers got out and approached us. My thumb located the activator on the inside of the ring. I raised my hand toward my face, but, before I could trigger the shot, the psychiatrist's wife bumped into me and I staggered backward and fell. She was smiling as I got up. She had tripped over her bag, she said, and apologized for her clumsiness. One of the policemen announced that all passengers were to board through the rear door in the tail of the plane. Then they saluted, got into their car and drove away.

The psychiatrist's wife said she hoped I hadn't smashed my ring when I fell, and I assured her that it didn't matter because it wasn't worth much. Taking my hand, she remarked that she never trusted a man who wore jewelry and hated animals. She and her husband sat nine rows behind me on the plane. Just after takeoff, she curled up in his arms and, whenever I looked at her, she seemed to be sleeping.

During my later years in the Service, I was frequently sent to western Europe as an industrial representative. I addressed large gatherings, gave press interviews and appeared frequently on television in many foreign capitals.

Once, in the course of a live TV news program, I found myself disagreeing with local reporters, who rebutted me angrily and at length.

Later that evening, I was supposed to attend a dinner given by the head of the opposition party, but by the time the TV program ended I was angry and tired and hardly up to a formal social occasion. Irritated that I had to go, I rushed back to the hotel, forced myself to sleep for an hour, then took a shower, shaved and changed into my dinner clothes.

By the time I arrived at the state rotunda, the courtyard was filled with limousines. I hurriedly presented my invitation to one of the guards and was escorted through long, mirrored corridors teeming with reporters and security men.

I entered a drawing room where guests were gathered, and was relieved to see that cocktails were still being served. Bored and tired, I wandered through the crowd looking for my host, whom I knew only from his press photographs. I noticed several guests whispering to each other as I passed, and it occurred to me that they had seen the TV program and were probably as shocked by my opinions as the reporters had been.

At the far end of the room, I noticed a tall, exquisite woman. As I stared at her, she suddenly came toward me. Her presence made me uncomfortable.

"I am your hostess," she introduced herself. "How good of you to come. I saw you on the news tonight." She extended her hand, which I kissed, feeling how cool her smooth, long fingers were. "My husband and I watched you defend yourself against the members of our press." She attempted to put me at ease. "Here you were, a guest of our government, and they treated you as an enemy," she continued, guiding me gracefully through the crowd. Her tall, distinguished husband had spotted us and was making his way through the crowd to greet me. After we had exchanged pleasantries, he turned away to speak to other guests, leaving his wife and me alone.

"You must forgive my staring at you," I said to her, "but I was wondering why nature gave you so much and others so little."

She smiled. "Perhaps nature was not as generous as

you think. After all, you don't know me." She paused as two reporters photographed us.

"No, I don't," I replied, when they moved off. "It must be difficult for any man to know you." I pointed to another photographer who was aiming his camera at her and said, "As a beautiful woman and as the wife of a man destined to govern his country, you're always watched."

She abruptly changed the subject by asking how long I would be staying in the city.

"I'm leaving for Paris early in the morning," I told her.

"I envy you. Paris is magnificent at this time of year."

"Do you often visit Paris?" I asked.

"I do, but always with my husband on official business. There's never enough time for me to just stroll or sit in a café."

Her relaxed attitude made me feel easy, even a bit brash. "I'll be in Paris for a week, staying at the Bradley," I said. "It's a new hotel where no one knows me. Why don't you join me there?"

She returned my gaze and, in a cool voice, asked, "Is this what Americans would call instant seduction?"

Her husband was heading toward us with two couples in tow. "Not seduction," I said quickly. "Merely an attempt to discover if nature is as generous as it sometimes seems."

In a second, her husband was at her side, playfully chastising her for abandoning the other guests, then he whisked her away. During dinner, I often looked in her direction but she never returned my glances. While coffee and liqueurs were served, I slipped away, returned to my hotel and prepared for Paris.

My first two days there were hectic. I attended long conferences, tedious seminars and executive dinners with industrial representatives from the provinces. The talk was taxing and the food heavy. After dinner, too exhausted to accompany my colleagues to a night-club, I usually went straight back to my hotel room.

The third morning the telephone woke me. Half asleep, I groped for the receiver and heard a woman's voice whispering my name in a heavy foreign accent. The accent was familiar, but the voice was not. "You left our reception without saying goodbye," she said.

It was then that I recognized her. Suddenly, I felt elated and fully awake. "Are you in Paris?" I asked.

"Of course not. I am in my country, in my bedroom and in my bed. Where else would I be at this hour in the morning?"

"But where is your husband?" I asked.

"In the bathroom, taking a shower."

I caught my breath. "Suppose he hears you?"

"He can't as long as the shower's going." She paused. "I'm coming to Paris."

"When?"

"Tomorrow. On the noon flight."

"For how long?"

"One day."

"With your . . . ?" I began.

"Alone," she answered. "Are you still curious how 'generous' nature is?"

"More than ever."

"Please reserve a room for me at the Hôtel de La Mole. I used to stay there when I was married to my last husband, so use my former name, Leuwen." She spelled it for me.

"Shall I meet you at the airport?" I asked.

"Please don't. Someone might see us. I'll call you from the hotel."

"I'll wait for your call. Until tomorrow, then."

"Until tomorrow," she whispered and hung up.

I couldn't sleep. Feeling a need to fill the time, I dressed and went at once to La Mole. It was an elegant old hotel, which could be entered either from the main lobby or through a bar on the side street, as well as through the garage.

I presented myself to the reception manager as a travel agent who had come to select a room for Madame Leuwen, a client of mine. The manager checked his reservations and asked if Madame would like a single room. I suggested a suite, instead, and after visiting three or four of them I settled on a large corner one whose door did not open off the main corridor and could not be seen by anyone looking out from the elevator. I ordered flowers to be delivered for Madame Leuwen's arrival and asked the manager to give the lady's reservation his personal attention.

I spent the rest of the day concluding as many of my business affairs as possible. By midafternoon I felt nauseated and my body ached. I realized I was feeling the strain of the trip and decided to see a doctor. Several physicians recommended by my associates could not see me soon enough. I checked the phone book and found a physician whose name suggested my own national origin. I called him, introduced myself and told him I needed immediate medical assistance. I asked him in Ruthenian whether he still spoke his parents' language, and he answered fluently in it that, even though his schedule was full, he would see me at once.

His office, which was also his home, was in an old section of Paris. He was in his sixties, gray-haired, with a beautifully chiseled face. His suit was cut in the fashion of the late twenties, and he wore a monocle. He led me through a dark apartment filled with massive old furniture.

His white examination room contained old-fashioned, enamel medical equipment and evoked the atmosphere of another century. He apologized for the disorder in his office by saying that his wife had died a few months earlier and the paid help he now had to rely on was very poor. He asked me to undress while he put on a white lab coat and washed his hands; then he checked my weight and gave me a cursory examination.

"Barring some invisible malady, you're not ill but simply underweight, run down and overworked," he pronounced. "Your heart seems to be slightly arrhythmic, but you are a sportsman, which might explain it. Your present exhaustion combined with increased metabolic rate and radically low blood pressure produces occasional dizziness. What you need now is rest, exercise and a sound diet."

"Nevertheless, doctor, I came to you for help with a specific complaint," I said as I dressed.

"What is the problem?"

"I have an important engagement tomorrow and I need a drug, injections if necessary, to get through it."

"But you're not ill, only over-tired," he reiterated.

"A lady friend of mine is arriving tomorrow for a one-day visit. I may never see her again and I want to be strong enough to have a memorable time with her."

The doctor got up from his desk and looked at me. "Is she your fiancée?" he asked.

"No, but I want to know her as intimately as if she were."

He moved closer, winking at me with an eye surrealistically enlarged by the monocle. "Is she, by chance, married?"

"I can't see what her marital status has to do with my request," I said, barely hiding my annoyance.

"If you want my help, you must be honest with me."

"She is married."

"Is her husband alive?"

"Yes. But he is not coming with her."

"Do they have children?"

"I believe so."

"What are their ages?"

"I should think they would be in their teens," I said.

He rubbed his chin. "Then this woman is older than you?"

"Possibly."

The doctor paced the room and returned to where I sat. "How well do you know her?" he asked.

"I met her only once, a few days ago. I need to know her and I don't intend to fail. Do you understand me, doctor?"

"Don't excite yourself," he said. "By the way, does she love you?"

"She hardly knows me, but perhaps one day she might love me, and I don't want to postpone that day for a minute."

The doctor sat down across from me. He removed his monocle and put on a pair of glasses. "I could be your father," he said sternly. "If I were, would I condone what my son is about to do? Are you an only child?"

"I am."

"I knew it. Would your father want his only son turned into an instrument to satisfy an aging, adulterous wife?"

"I am nobody's instrument. Besides, my father never dealt in such matters. My mother was his only woman."

He tapped his pen against the wood of the desk. "You are living an existence contaminated by vice," he said. "Why don't you settle down with a woman who loves you? You could irrigate the dry land, help bring peace to the region."

"I haven't come to ask if I should join a kibbutz," I interrupted.

"What have you come for?"

"A remedy. You know what for."

"If I possessed such a remedy, I would be listed in the *Kamasutra*, not in the Paris telephone directory."

"There must be a drug that would . . ." I pleaded, but he interrupted me.

"There isn't. There are certain combinations of drugs and injections and long-term therapy."

"I'm not impotent, doctor. Merely cautious."

"When is she arriving."

"Noon tomorrow."

He frowned as he scribbled a prescription, which he then handed to me. "You can have this filled in any good pharmacy. Take the pills every two hours, the tablets every three and one capsule every six." I paid him in cash and he cautioned me, "Don't expect miracles."

"I never do," I said.

I stopped at the first pharmacy I came to, had the prescription filled and swallowed the medication before I left the store. I had a busy day ahead of me. Pleading illness, I had postponed several less crucial appointments, but there were two important meetings and a large press conference that I had to attend. Between meetings and mail and telephone calls, I had no time to rest or eat, but I took the medications without fail. I returned to my room after midnight, tired and short of breath, with my heart palpitating, feeling no pick-up from the medicines. I thought about the woman who in twelve hours would arrive to see me. I recreated her image as I had last seen her at the

dinner party, reviewing her features, her gestures, her
expressions. I tossed restlessly until at last the sleeping pill I had taken diluted her image. At dawn, I
fell asleep.

I woke up a few hours later, walked to the window
and looked out. The city sparkled in the sunlight and
the sky was cloudless. Having completed my remaining business commitments before noon, I returned to
my hotel, shaved once more and waited restlessly for
her call. In order to have my medicines on hand
throughout her visit, I loaded my pockets with a good
supply of all three drugs.

I was apprehensive. I lay down but could not sleep.
Just as I decided her call would not come, the phone
rang. I let it ring three times before I picked up the
receiver with an unsteady hand.

She sounded relaxed and composed as she told me
she had just arrived at the Hôtel de La Mole. She
thanked me for the flowers and for choosing such a
beautiful suite. When I invited her to lunch, she
asked me to come to the hotel to pick her up.

The convertible I had rented was waiting in the
hotel driveway. I put its top down and drove slowly
through the sunlit city, familiarizing myself with the
car and with the Paris traffic. Each time I glanced at
the empty seat next to me, I could almost see her sitting there, her legs stretched toward me, her arm resting on the seat behind my back, her fingers inches
from my neck.

At La Mole I told the garage attendant to keep my
car ready, then took an elevator to the floor above
hers, inspected the staircases and the corridors and
went down the stairs. Listening outside her door, I
could faintly hear her footsteps.

I paused for a moment to calm myself and knocked;
she opened the door immediately. She was wearing a

tweed suit with a skirt that ended below her knees and accented her slender calves. Her hair fell abundantly onto her shoulders, and I noted that in daylight it looked lighter than it had the night I met her.

She ushered me into the room. "It's hard for me to believe you're here," I said. "At your party, I was sure I would never see you again."

"But when I tried to find you after dinner, you had gone."

"I was restless and you were so inaccessible. Now, the more I look at you, the more awe-struck I am."

She laughed and told me, "Proust says, 'Leave pretty women to men without imagination.' Do you disagree with him?"

"Not at all, but I also know your beauty can be fully appreciated and defined only by a man with imagination. In any case," I continued, "I am taking you out to lunch. My car is waiting downstairs."

At the restaurant, she explained that her husband had left that morning on a campaign trip. She had told him she was going to visit her sister and brother-in-law at their farm fifty miles from the capital and would be staying overnight. She had confided in the couple about her Paris escapade, and they had agreed to cover for her.

She left the table to go to the ladies' room; I removed two pills from my pocket and swallowed them before she returned.

After lunch, we drove out to Combray. I parked the car and we walked through the woods. I had brought my camera with me, and I asked if I could photograph her. I examined her through the lens as she posed. I approached her for a close-up and pushed her hair back gently. She did not move. I put the camera aside.

We stood facing each other without speaking. Suddenly, she reached for my shoulders and drew me against her while her hands explored the contours of my hips. Kissing her lips and thrusting my body against her, my flesh remained flaccid in spite of my excitement. I realized that if I continued to press against her, she would know I was not aroused. I disengaged myself and stepped away.

"Let's go back to La Mole," I said, as if suddenly overcome by desire.

She stepped in front of me, her fingers stroking my face, and asked in a husky voice, "Which way do we go? By Méséglise? It's shorter, isn't it?"

"Let's take Verrières. It's prettier," I said. By the time we reached Paris, it was dark. I let her out on the street around the corner from the hotel, so that if she were being watched, she would be seen entering La Mole alone. I left the car in the garage, then rang her room. She said to come up.

She had changed into a soft white caftan that seemed to float around her as she moved. Her hair was pulled back loosely with a white ribbon. I wrapped my arms around her waist. We kissed, her pelvis grinding against mine, but I realized that, again, my excitement was not apparent. I moved away. "Let's order champagne," I said, pressing the service button. I sensed she was growing irritated and confused, but she said nothing to indicate her mood.

Before the waiter arrived, a maid appeared. She introduced herself and asked whether the suite was in order. She noticed my companion's robe and, while we waited for the champagne, she prepared the bed. Finally, the bed was ready, the champagne was open and we were alone in the room. I sipped the wine slowly, afraid that my drugs might not mix with the alcohol.

We moved onto the bed and kissed again. Her hands were aggressive and I could feel myself growing excited, but my body still failed to respond. I continued to kiss and stroke her and when, at the height of arousal she whispered that she wanted me, I felt as if my sight, touch, and hearing had abandoned me. I stood up; without a word, I dashed into the bathroom.

I looked at myself in the mirror. There was no perceptible change in my expression. I looked at my body; there was no perceptible change in it, either. I downed a double dose of medication even though I had last taken a prescribed amount only an hour before.

She looked at me anxiously but said nothing when I returned. I suggested that because it was late we should order dinner before the kitchen closed.

The waiter who previously had brought us champagne now arrived with our dinner. He assumed we were married, and as he wished us good luck and many children I caught her look of embarrassment.

Toward the end of the meal, I suggested we go to a show. She did not seem to mind and changed into an evening gown that she said she'd bought just for me, and put on a diamond necklace, a gift from her father-in-law. We went to a nightclub famous for its blatant sex shows. I tipped the head waiter in advance, and he seated us close to the stage, on which naked performers acted out seduction scenes. I could see she was enjoying the show as well as the attention she attracted from the performers and the rest of the audience.

Against the background of the stage light, her hair fanned out around her face like a copper flame. I became acutely aware of how beautiful she was and reached for her, cupping her breast in my palm. She moved closer to me and I felt her hand on my thigh. With many women from my past, this would have been enough to excite me; now that I was with one who really mattered, I remained sexually dormant.

We returned to the hotel. While she was undressing in the bathroom, I swallowed the remaining pills. She was giddy from the drinks at the nightclub and already aroused. A single need dominated my thoughts. I wanted to appropriate her, to imprint myself upon her. We went to bed. I caressed and kissed her and she murmured that she wanted to be taken. She placed her hand on my groin and tried to make me swell. She begged me to enter and saturate her, but soon realized that, even with her help, I could not do it.

She pushed me off her, climbed out of bed and went to the bathroom to take a shower. When I heard the water running, I immediately called the doctor. His phone rang several times before he answered.

I gave him my name, but he sounded too groggy to recognize me. I repeated the name and said, accentuating every word, "Yesterday you advised me to irrigate the dry land."

"Oh, it's you," he murmured.

"You prescribed pills and tablets and capsules for me. I took them all."

"Did they make you ill?"

"Not even that. They have done absolutely nothing."

"You wake up an old man to tell him that? I warned you not to expect a miracle."

I lowered my voice. "The miracle I expected is here, but the drugs that were supposed to help me worship it do not work."

"There are other ways of worshiping a miracle."

"They come later. Now I need the one enjoyed by the village peasants you and I left behind."

"If that's what you need, call these peasants instead of me. I can do nothing more to help you." He hung up.

As she returned from the bathroom, she overheard

the final words of conversation. I apologized for making a business call. "What language were you speaking?" she asked.

"Ruthenian. It's the language of the peasants I lived among as a boy."

She threw her clothes over a chair, put her necklace on the night table and turned off the light. I lay with my eyes open, listening to her breathe.

We got up early. She seemed at ease but slightly withdrawn. Her eyes were distant, but she still attempted to make conversation.

"Where did you get those boots?" she asked.

"I made them myself."

"Really?"

"As a boy, I worked with a shoemaker. Every few months, I select leathers and pay a shoe repair shop for the use of the equipment after hours. I now have three or four pairs of shoes and boots that fit perfectly."

"Why don't you get them custom-made?"

"I prefer making them myself."

"Do you always have a reason for everything you do?"

"Always," I replied. "Custom-made by me."

She hardly touched her breakfast and asked me to call a taxi to take her to the airport earlier than I knew was necessary. When I started to object, she placed her fingers over my lips. We embraced. She walked to the door, and, just before closing it, turned back to me and said, "God spare beautiful women from men with imagination." Then she was gone.

Soon after her departure, the floor maid, alerted by the concierge, came to collect her tip. She asked me why my wife had left before me, and I replied she had been notified of a death in her family and had to return to our home that morning.

During the afternoon, I was too preoccupied with business to brood about what had happened. Just as I returned to my hotel to change, the phone rang. I lifted the receiver, expecting a business associate; instead, the concierge said it was Madame Leuwen calling long-distance. Sounding desperate, she told me I must listen very carefully.

She had packed so hurriedly, she said, that she had forgotten her diamond necklace, which she must have left on the night table in her hotel room. She pleaded with me to retrieve it immediately and to arrange an absolutely safe way of delivering it to her.

"What if the necklace has already been stolen?" I asked.

"That would be the end of everything," she said.

"Why?"

"Once I report it missing, the insurance company will make a thorough investigation. The police and possibly even Interpol may become involved. They will drag you into it. The press will seize on the affair, and my husband's political future . . ." She faltered.

"What is the value of that necklace?" I asked.

"It's insured for over three-quarters of a million dollars."

"I'd better get moving," I said. "How do I get in touch with you?"

"Call me at home. My husband won't be back until tonight. But please . . ." Her voice broke. "Please find it."

I looked around my room, uncertain where to begin. From now on, if the jewels were not found I would be a prime suspect. I could see the headlines in the newspapers. My removal from Service. My trial. The end of her marriage.

As soon as I arrived at the Hôtel de La Mole, the reception manager recognized me as Madame Leuwen's travel agent.

"Was Madame pleased with the accommodations?" he asked.

"Delighted," I said. "She hopes to visit you again soon. Meanwhile, I want to pick up a necklace she left in her room."

"Let me check," he said, disappearing into his office. During his absence, it seemed that my life hung on that necklace, but he came back all smiles. "The floor maid found the necklace and locked it away in the second-floor vault. I told her that you will be right up to sign for it."

I thanked him, and handed him a large tip.

The maid recognized me as Monsieur Leuwen. "I just had a call from the reception desk that your travel agent is on the way here. What a coincidence!" she exclaimed.

I noticed her for the first time. She was in her late forties, a tall, powerfully built woman with uneven skin pigmentation and a high-pitched, resonant voice.

"I'm here to pick up the necklace," I said.

"Of course, Monsieur. But since your travel agent is apparently also on his way, let me check with the manager to make sure . . ."

When she reached for the phone, I removed her hand from the receiver. "There's no one else coming. To some, I am a travel agent. To others, a husband." I reached into my pocket and handed her a roll of bills. She took the money, counted it carefully, then, giving me a knowing look, handed me a rectangular package. "Please check it, Monsieur. And if everything is in order, please sign for it." She passed me a receipt.

I opened the package. Now that it was found, the

glittering necklace seemed so trifling. I wrapped it up again, signed the paper, and hired an insurance courier to deliver the necklace.

My business in Paris ended. I packed a small suitcase and drove aimlessly through the countryside. I ate in small local restaurants and stayed at out-of-the-way inns in solitary villages. I left by dawn every day and was well on my way by the time the sun had risen over the fields. I crossed the border into Italy and kept on driving. A gust of southern wind brought me the smell of manure mixed with the acrid odor of factories and mines. Soon it began to rain. After the downpour, the splotched fields were like stained glass windows, full of multicolored pools. Behind them, rotted by the poison of industrial waste, the woods looked gray and barren.

I drove on. In the rearview mirror, I saw a man in a small car coming up behind me. He was wearing a white shirt, a jacket and tie. He honked his horn ceaselessly and revved the engine to indicate he was in a hurry. I slowed down to let him overtake me. He took off, glaring at me as he passed.

An hour later, I saw a crowd gathered on the highway and stopped to see what had happened. The little car that passed me had hit a highway pole and been ripped in two, like an envelope torn apart by an impatient hand. Out of it fell scraps of flesh and crushed bones, jagged metal and broken glass.

I picked up my camera and began to take photographs. The crowd of bystanders said nothing to me but stared as I moved around the remains of the body taking pictures. I got back into my car and drove off.

As dusk fell, I stopped in a small town, checked into an inn, changed and went for a stroll. I walked idly through street after street, past broken-down houses surrounded by wooden fences, delapidated villas with iron gates, white-washed churches and cheap, pre-fabricated apartment complexes.

Slowly the streets emptied of pedestrians. Occa-sional cars roared down the road, and the drivers shouted to the streetwalkers, who pretended to ignore them.

One of the whores, who was dressed in a raincoat open to her waist, called me. I approached her.

"They call me Fiammetta. Don't you want Fiam-metta's love?" she asked.

I looked at her exaggerated make-up, at her full breasts pushed up by a tight corset, at the silver stock-ings and black patent leather shoes. "Maybe I do," I said. "How much does it cost?"

She looked me over, quoted the price and waited expectantly. "Is it too much for you?" she asked.

"It's reasonable. What do you do for the money?"

She smiled, exposing large white teeth. "I do every-thing. Everything." Then she reflected. "Except, not inside."

I wasn't certain what she meant. "Only outdoors?" I asked.

She laughed politely, as if I had made a joke. "Of course not, you stupid man. In a hotel. The room is included in the price. It has electric lights and even a basin to wash yourself."

"But you said 'not inside,'" I persisted.

"You can do everything with me," she emphasized, "but not inside." She glanced down at herself.

"Even if I wear a rubber?" I asked.

"Even if you wear a rubber," she replied.

"But what if I like to be inside?"

"What for?" She raised her voice. "I can undress very slowly for you. I walk naked for you. I touch you. You touch me." She began to unbutton the rest of her raincoat, revealing that she wore only a corset. "With

Fiammetta's body, you come like an explosion . . ."

"But not inside?"

"Not inside," she reaffirmed.

I paused. "What if, to go inside, I pay you three times as much as you asked?"

"I told you: no inside."

"If I pay you five times as much?"

"No inside."

"Ten times?"

"No inside, no matter what you pay." Then she threw up her hands in exasperation. "What kind of man are you? Why inside? Nothing special there."

"I'll look for another girl," I said.

She stood with her legs apart, inhaling deeply to expose her breasts even more. "In this town, no street girl goes inside," she insisted.

"I don't believe you."

"I'll show you. Fornarina! Fornarina!" she screamed at a woman who stood near us. "This one here," she pointed at me, "wants to pay ten times as much to go inside. How about inside, Fornarina?"

"No inside," Fornarina shouted back.

"Amorrorisca! Amorrorisca," she yelled to a woman across the street. "For ten times the price, he wants inside."

"No inside," yelled Amorrorisca.

"Ask any girl. Go ahead; ask Selvaggia, ask Gradisca, ask Alcina, anyone . . ." She gave me a withering look and left me for another man.

I walked on into the night and each time I passed a girl, I stopped.

"Ten times your price if I go inside?" I proposed.

They all gave me cold, haughty looks. "No inside," every one of them sputtered, looking at me with contempt. Soon others learned about my predilection and jeered, "No inside," even before I propositioned them.

I moved to another section of town, and approached a much older woman. "I want to go inside," I said. "I'll pay ten times your price."

"No inside," she said, wagging her finger at me.

"But you are on the street," I said.

"I am. That's why I do everything you ask for. Just like that!" She snapped her fingers. "You don't need inside."

"But I want inside," I said.

"Go north. There the women go inside, because they don't know how to excite men."

"But why won't you?" I persisted.

She came closer. "I am a virgin," she said. "One day I take the money I make here and go way down south, back to my family. I want to marry a nice man. His family will suspect me. They will check me with their fingers to see if I am still a virgin. Only when I marry a man I love, he goes inside. Not before."

I recall the whores and the incident at La Mole as vividly as if I had been in Paris two days ago, in Italy yesterday. Though I wish now I could forget the Paris incident, and wonder why I remember the whores so clearly, I can't free myself from either memory.

When I was ten, a psychologist visiting my secondary school gave me a routine memory test. She was astonished by its results and arranged for me to be tested by a group of psychologists. They showed me pages of technical jargon and statistics, complex drawings, film strips and dozens of photographs. Careful to question me on different days, they would ask me to describe what I had seen, to identify fragments of films and photographs, to extend a single curved line from a drawing or to recall the precise location of a particular face in a photograph of a crowd. After extensive testing, they concluded that I retained whatever I concentrated on, but they warned me to memorize only useful information. Otherwise, my mind would become an overcrowded attic, steadily but unselectively storing up everything I saw. One day, they added, the attic might collapse, wrecking the house beneath.

I began to experiment with my memory. I found that it automatically intensified while I slept. If I misplaced something, such as a set of keys, I took a nap. It was as if I were dreaming a film about losing the keys that was being run backward in slow motion. By the time I woke up, I recalled where I had left them. During exam periods, when my fellow students were staying up all night to study, I slept, to their disgust, twice as much as usual. In my sleep I reviewed all the texts which I had originally only skimmed, and by exam time had total recall of all the necessary material.

At the university, I enrolled in three separate degree programs, in the humanities and sciences, and took all available electives. Often, when asked questions in oral examinations, I took more time than I actually needed to answer. Carefully watched by those professors anxious to expose my ignorance, or my system of cheating, I produced correct answers only when I was sure they expected I did not know them.

Since my childhood, I have learned to guard my memory from becoming overloaded with unnecessary data. I have developed a set of mental exercises that prevent me from concentrating involuntarily on useless details. When I don't use the method and, for instance, allow myself to look at people on a subway, I instinctively memorize every detail of their features, coloring and expression, the clothes they wear and what they are carrying.

In searching out ways to make use of my memory, I occasionally help friends engaged in scholarly research. Many years ago, one of them was preparing an extensive critical study of a certain author, whose every work he had to read. I told my friend I had devised a program of speed-reading and memory-training that I wanted to test by skimming everything the writer had published. In order to evaluate my method effectively, I needed to know what to look for in various texts. My friend thought I was joking, but proceeded to give me a list of the writer's favorite topics and ideas.

Surrounded by the man's collected works, I began reading. Soon my mind took off, soaring above the jumble of words, expressions and notions, which slowly became abstracted into predictable patterns, just as rough farm fields seen from the air look like a neatly sown quilt of velvet smooth patches. As I read, I dictated brief bursts of thoughts into a tape recorder. Only when I finished scanning everything the writer had produced, did I become aware how flat and unchallenging the topography of his work was.

I gave the tape to my friend, who promptly had it transcribed. Later, he called to thank me for it and said that, if used indiscriminately, the map I supplied could not only discredit the author's work to date but might cripple his self-confidence and stifle his desire to write. He suggested that if I ever undertook another such survey I should extend my method to detect plagiarism.

When I was stationed in western Europe, I used to peruse the local literary journals and magazines in order to improve my linguistic skills. Every so often, I glanced at an influential weekly that carried a well-known critic's reviews of contemporary foreign literature in translation. On one occasion, he reviewed a recent translation of an early novel by the writer whose work I had investigated.

The critic cited examples of stylistic repetition that my friend had noted in a scholarly article he published years earlier, but my friend's article wasn't mentioned. It struck me how easy it must be for a critic to plagiarize foreign reviews: since a translation was usually published some time after the original-language edition, he could be reasonably certain that the source of his ideas about a book would never be discovered.

To see if my memory could operate simultaneously in two languages, I selected several of the critic's recent reviews, then looked up the original criticism of the same works. As I had expected, some of his opinions and turns of phrase were crudely disguised piratings of earlier foreign reviews.

I passed the information on to the chief of my Service section. At first, he was baffled by my devoting so much effort to matters as insignificant and dull as fiction, literary criticism and translation, but once he realized how damning my evidence really was, he complimented me. He was sure that, confronted with the choice of cooperating with the Service or of having his plagiarism made public, the critic would make a sensible decision. The chief suggested we could always use an internal source at the weekly.

About the same time, a fellow Service agent told me about an incident that had occurred in Washington, D.C. Within one month, a senator, a well-known journalist, two college students and five older people were all hospitalized with cases of acute hepatitis. The infected persons varied widely in age, medical history and lifestyle, and the doctors could not agree upon a single source of infection.

Two hundred more cases were reported over the next few days, and, since some of the stricken worked for a sensitive government agency, the Service was called in to investigate. Their check established that, weeks before falling ill, each person, complaining of a nose and throat infection or of a respiratory inflammation, had consulted one of eight well-known physicians who shared office space in the center of the city. The search then zeroed in on the doctors, their staffs, the medications they prescribed and the sanitary conditions of their offices and equipment, but nothing suspicious turned up. Strangely enough, the epidemic died as quickly as it had begun, and the various investigating teams never did uncover the origin of the disease.

A short time before his conversation with me, the agent had been talking to a middle-aged scientist in a bar. Accusing the medical profession of wholesale negligence, the scientist said that doctors made complex diagnoses based only on blood and urine tests, electrocardiograms and rapid check-ups, and felt free to take telephone calls about unrelated matters while examining a patient. Often, he complained, doctors prescribed drugs to alleviate particular complaints, but did not even attempt to review the patient's history to find out whether a drug was toxic to the individual's system or harmful under certain circumstances.

The scientist decided to prove how corrupt and immune to investigation the medical profession had become. Since he was then working in a private laboratory, it was easy for him to obtain minute samples of many hepatitis viruses. He began experimenting with them, and after a few weeks had successfully developed a vicious new strain.

Complaining of a severe pain in his chest, he made appointments with eight well-known Washington doctors. During the brief preliminary interview with each doctor's nurse, he would give a different false name, address and medical history. In the examining room, the nurse would always weigh him and then leave.

After an examination, the doctor would tell him to get dressed and come to his office. Alone in the examining room, the scientist would withdraw an aerosol vial of the compressed virus from his pocket, unseal it and quickly spray the hepatitis culture on disposable tongue depressors in an open jar and on metal nose and throat applicators. In addition, he sprayed stacked paper cups and the disposable rubber gloves used in rectal examinations.

The scientist had followed this procedure in the offices of all eight doctors. By the time the victims were hospitalized, the infected depressors, cups and gloves had long since been incinerated and the applicators disinfected, so no traceable source of the germs existed. The scientist was incensed at the helplessness of the hepatitis victims in the hands of their negligent doctors and at the failure of the top medical researchers to uncover the origin of the infection. He claimed his test made a mockery of the sanitary conditions of the entire medical profession.

The agent continued to listen intently to the scientist's rantings, and then excused himself to go to the men's room. Once out of sight of the bar, he went straight to the telephone and called his superior for orders on how to proceed. When he returned to the table, the scientist had disappeared.

Years later, inspired by the story, I decided to conduct an experiment of my own. I placed in my raincoat pocket a syringe with a short, fine needle and a half-pint bottle filled with a harmless solution that had no odor or taste but merely turned purple after contact with saliva. I would drive to a shopping mall and wander through the aisles of a supermarket, the small syringe concealed in my hand. By inserting the needle through food cartons, I expelled the substance into cottage cheese, milk, cream, butter, margarine, ice cream and yoghurt. Using one hand, I would refill the syringe in my pocket; no one ever noticed what I was doing. Before leaving a store, like a legitimate shopper I would purchase a few items.

In the first few days, I injected hundreds of containers in more than fifty shopping centers in the city's suburbs. Toward the end of the week, the newspaper and TV news programs reported a poisoned-food scare that threatened to escalate into an epidemic. Days passed, and the media devoted more time and space to the epidemic. After two weeks, the poison scare became the subject of a TV special on which a Nobel Prize-winning professor of immunology stated that, even though the substance apparently was not fatal, its long-range effects on an unsuspecting consumer had yet to be analyzed.

As the scare continued to build, other reports asserted that food products reached supermarkets already contaminated; countless people asserted that they had been poisoned by the substance fifteen to twenty minutes after swallowing the contaminated foods. They all agreed it caused shock, nausea and severe hallucinations.

At that point, I altered the composition of the solution so that it turned red after thirty to forty minutes' exposure to air.

I also started injecting other foods, which until now were considered to be clean. Consumers were horrified to find themselves poisoned by breads, ready-to-eat meats, cold salads, frozen puddings and pastries that turned the tongue and inside of the mouth scarlet half an hour after being opened; many claimed the red poison to be more lethal than the purple one.

The epidemic began to cause mass panic. Several

food and packaging manufacturers, as well as supermarket chains and consumer organizations, initiated
their own investigations, flooding the market with
conflicting reports, accusations and demands for
tamper-proof packaging. Meanwhile, several anonymous callers contacted newspapers and television and
radio stations, eagerly claiming responsibility for the
wave of terrorist acts, which included food poisoning
on a massive scale. One of them sent a tape recording
to the police in which he threatened to increase the
power of the red poison and hit food shops and supermarkets across the country unless the unfair immigration laws were immediately changed. Because of his
Middle European accent, the media labeled the substance "Polish poison."

While I was in the Service, I appropriated a number of eighteenth-century snuff and perfume
boxes. They were all made of gold, platinum or silver,
and were decorated with enamel and precious stones.
The methods by which I acquired them were unusual,
and I knew that if I was ever associated with the boxes
I would have to leave the Service immediately.

The boxes were very valuable when I first obtained
them, but by the time I disappeared from the Service
they had easily doubled in value and made me a very
rich man. I realized that my post-Service survival depended on being able to move quickly from one hiding place to the next and on having a source of ready
cash to buy my freedom if I were caught. The boxes
provided that source.

I began to think of suitable repositories for my
boxes. The caches had to be located in a country to
which I, with an American passport, would have free
passage without police surveillance, a country that did
not check too carefully into what objects or how much
cash were carried over its borders. That narrowed my

potential drop-sites to the few large democracies remaining in the West.

To guarantee the absolute security of the boxes, I planned to store each one separately in the safest hiding place I could devise. Such a place had to be unobtrusive, offering easy access at all times. Above all, it had to be an unlikely storage place for an object of great value.

It occurred to me that the water tanks above many old-fashioned public toilets contained simple, reliable mechanisms that almost never required cleaning or repairs. Toilets in large old hotels, restaurants, railroad stations and subways would become my safe-deposit vaults.

I made several trips abroad, each time carrying a few boxes concealed in my luggage. Where I came across a toilet with a water tank, I securely wrapped one of the boxes in chamois and moisture-proof plastic, then positioned it in the water at the bottom of the tank.

Eventually, I found all the toilets I needed and hid every box away. No map of these toilets has ever been drawn. I have committed every one to memory.

So far, I have never failed to get a box back when I wanted it, but each time I travel to reclaim one, I have to consider two contingencies: that the box has been discovered by a repairman, or that the toilet safe has been torn down.

Recently, I was driving across the Swiss-Italian border on my way to Livigno. As I approached Lago Nuovo, I took my place in the enormous line of cars waiting to enter the one-way, four-mile tunnel. Certain that the heavy traffic meant at least half an hour's wait, I left my car and walked to the public toilet. It was as clean as I remembered it, since people in line seldom risked losing their place or missing the green

entry light by going to the toilet. I closed the bathroom door, stepped on top of the seat, pulled the
chain and reached into the remaining cold water of
the tank. The package was still in the right rear corner where I had put it years before. I lifted it out,
threw away the wet plastic wrapper, put the box
wrapped in chamois in my raincoat pocket and returned to my car before the tunnel light turned green.

An hour and a half later, I checked into a hotel in
a mountain town and placed a call to an art dealer in
Milan. I told him I was putting a rare eighteenth-
century box up for sale and referred him to an art
catalogue that included a color plate of the object. I
also quoted him a non-negotiable price and requested
a decision within twenty-four hours. Three hours later
he called back to accept the offer, and the following
morning he and an expert appeared at my hotel. After
thoroughly examining the box, they handed me the
money I had asked for.

Just this year I decided to put one of my most valuable boxes on the market. Remembering the name of
a discreet London dealer, I sent him a letter describing the history of the box's owners and enclosing a
color photograph. I gave no return address and named
my final price. A week later I telephoned the dealer,
who told me he had been eagerly awaiting my call
because a rich American woman was willing to meet
the price.

Since I was about to fly to Latin America on a Swiss
passport and did not want to go through customs,
both the dealer and the client agreed to make the exchange at Kennedy airport. I suggested we all meet in
the international transit lounge to avoid attracting
attention. The dealer met my plane and escorted me
to the lounge, which to my surprise had been cor-
doned off from the public at his request. The woman

was waiting with an important museum curator, who was armed with various instruments, chemicals and magnifying glasses. The woman's lawyer and her current husband sat on either side of two suitcases.

After the box had been examined and authenticated, the lawyer locked it in his attaché case and the husband handed me the two suitcases. Even though I knew I was not being cheated, I opened both of them. Inside were small plastic bags containing prepared packets of fifty- and one-hundred-dollar bills. I quickly counted the bags, then closed both suitcases.

After the transaction was completed, the woman and her husband invited me to have a drink with them until my flight was ready. Over cocktails, the woman told me she owned a large collection of similar boxes and wanted to know how I had come upon the box she had just bought. I politely referred her to the dealer, claiming he could give her a more complete explanation of the box's history and said that, because of his political connections, the last owner preferred to remain anonymous. She inquired about other boxes, emphasizing how eager she was to see them all. I told her that, because of the high robbery risk and skyrocketing insurance rates, I kept each of my boxes in a different vault and would never dare show them all at once.

The husband commented that his wife's art collection was also stored in bank vaults. During the three years of their marriage, he had seen it only piecemeal, when he went with her to have the objects cleaned. I asked the woman if it had been difficult for her to get together so much cash on such short notice, and she assured me it was not; her bank was used to dealing with her whims. She obviously thought nothing of carrying around so much money, but her husband complained that it made him queasy.

Women who seek great risks don't bother me, perhaps because I've had so much experience with them. In my final Service years, I was one of a specially trained group of agents called "the hummingbirds." The men and women of this group are so valuable that to protect their covers no central file is kept on them and their identities are seldom divulged to fellow agents.

Most hummingbirds remain on assignment as long as they lead active cover lives, usually as high-ranking government, military or cultural officials based in foreign countries. Others serve as businessmen, scientists, editors, writers and artists. I recall a newscaster and a film director who, unknown to their millions of devoted fans, were among our most valuable operatives.

If a hummingbird runs into trouble, he counts on the Service to get him out, never knowing when, how or in what form the help will come. He also must expect to be called on by the Service at any time, but, again, he never knows when, how or by whom.

I have been called upon several times to eliminate agents who had defected years before. But I always used to wonder what would happen if a hummingbird vanished, leaving no proof whether he had defected, died or been captured. To date, I know of only one man who has never been tracked down: myself. I owe my survival solely to common sense. I seldom carry a gun. I consider guns crude, because their use involves an irreversible process. Instead, I rely on more recent inventions, ones that merely incapacitate temporarily: drug concentrates concealed in a tie-clip syringe or in a ring, button-sized gas pellets, aerosol cartridges and the like. Above all, I trust my intuition.

In a Los Angeles bar once, I struck up a conversation with a German industrialist who was visiting the States on business. We had an enjoyable dinner together that night and began to see each other often while he was on the Coast. About a month after he went back to Germany, he telephoned to invite me to join him and his family at their country home.

I accepted and a week later flew to Munich, where he met me at the airport. As we passed a newspaper kiosk on the way to his car, I decided to buy some postcards for a girl friend who collected them. I picked out a dozen or so, took them over to the counter and started to pay, but the salesman refused to change my hundred-mark note. My host impatiently withdrew a handful of coins from his pocket, stared at them for a moment, then paid for the cards.

As he drove, I looked at the scenery and thought back to the incident at the airport stand. My host had hesitated almost imperceptibly before paying, but his slight delay made me question whether or not the currency he held was native to him.

My suspicions were shortly confirmed. We turned onto a highway, which, he said, led straight to the village nearest his house. But at the first crossroads, he hesitated, and I saw his eyes shoot to a highway sign before he continued along the main road. Had he driven the road often, he would have known it better.

I decided it was not worth finding out if he was who he claimed to be. I asked him how long it would be before we arrived at his home. Approximately another hour, he said, and I told him I would appreciate it if he would stop at the next gas station so that I could use the toilet. In the large, American-style station, he said he would wait in the restaurant. As soon as I saw him sitting down at a table, I went to the men's room and stood near the door until I spotted four young men about to leave the restaurant together. I left with them, as if I were one of their group, crossed to the other side of the highway and hitchhiked back to

Munich. I have not encountered the industrialist again.

For emergencies away from home, I always carry money and chemical self-protective devices in secret pockets in my trousers, jackets and coats, but there are some times when I cannot rely on hidden money, weapons or intuition.

Late one night, walking down Fifth Avenue, I heard a cab driver quarreling with a passenger on the corner, and paused to see what was happening. Just as I was about to walk on, a slim, neatly dressed young man passed close by me, then turned back as if to comment on the argument. I felt the tip of a switchblade pricking my skin just above my belt, but could not reach any of my weapons. A few people strolled by us, but no one noticed.

The man pushed me against a wall. I watched the perspiration glistening on his forehead as he mumbled something about money and a hotel room. But when I told him that he was welcome to the three thousand dollars I had on me, he did not react.

I repeated that in the back pocket of my pants he would find a wallet containing thirty one-hundred-dollar bills. He mumbled incoherently. I mentioned the money a third time.

When he still failed to respond, I assumed he was insane or drugged. There I was, a former humming-bird, armed with the most advanced defense weapons yet unable to get away from an addict with a switch-blade. I continued to talk to him, aware that I might die in midsentence. The man tried to focus his eyes on me. Suddenly, retracting the blade, he stepped back and stumbled off.

I recalled this incident years later when I again found myself at the mercy of strangers. I had developed a serious throat infection, which lingered on in spite of all the drugs I took to cure it. I went to see a doctor whose credentials I first checked out in a medical directory.

The physician examined my throat and prescribed an antibiotic, which I was to take three times a day for several days. On my way home, I took the pills. Almost immediately, I felt an unbearable pressure in my chest. I checked my watch: it had been exactly five minutes since I took the medicine. The abrupt change in the mechanical functioning of my body took my breath away. An excruciating pain radiated down my left arm to my fingers and back up into my shoulder, neck and chin. My heart seemed to explode, stand still, and then explode again. As the pressure in my eardrums increased, the more desperate for air I became. My eyes began to blur, my legs began to tremble, and I knew that in seconds I would collapse. I knew no passersby would offer to help me to a taxi for fear that I was a drunk or an addict or that they would be sued later for unauthorized intervention. A traffic cop might eventually notice that I was ill and summon an ambulance, but it would barely be able to plow its way through the rush-hour traffic. By the time it reached me, I would probably be dead.

I staggered into the nearest store. The people inside drew away from me. I stumbled toward the counter and fell against it.

"Call the motorcycle police," I gasped, as I pulled some money out of my pocket and handed it to the clerk. "I have something important to tell them. Hurry."

The man nodded and went to the rear of the shop, while a woman helped me to a chair. When the owner returned, he said the police were on their way.

In less than five minutes, I heard motorcycles stop in front of the store. Two policemen entered and the manager brought them over to me. I pulled myself up until I was standing. I said, "I'm ill, I need medical assistance at once. I can't wait for an ambulance, so I want you to notify the hospital to have an emergency team ready to treat a toxic reaction to an antibiotic. Then take me there by motorcycle." I gave them both several large bills.

They looked at each other and then accepted the money. "You've got yourself a ride, mister," one of them said. They helped me out the door and onto the back seat of one of the motorcycles. To protect me in case I should faint during the ride, they strapped my thighs to the seat and instructed me to keep my arms around the chest of the driver. The other policeman radioed the hospital and took off, clearing a path through the cars and buses.

We speeded against the oncoming traffic on a one-way avenue, disregarding the lights, zigzagging between cars and trucks, cutting sharp corners and leaning hard on the curves. I clung to the driver, the wind drying my sweat.

Within seconds of our arrival at the hospital, three men in white overalls unstrapped me, lifted me gently off the motorcycle and helped me to an emergency receiving room, where a doctor and two nurses were waiting.

I took a folded sheet of paper from my inside pocket and gave it to the doctor. "This contains all the data and diagnostic summaries required for emergency admission as well as for your records," I said. The doctor took the paper and the nurses began to undress me. I checked my watch and realized that eighteen minutes had passed since I had first felt the pain and weakness.

Having been in uncertain health for many years, I have learned to turn my physical liabilities to my own advantage. Since I cannot survive unless I can order every aspect of my existence, my mind exploits my body. My choice of a life of adventure may well be a result of the fact that action raises my blood pressure, giving me enough energy to live.

A doctor of mine once stopped abruptly in the middle of a physical examination and called in his colleagues. He displayed me as proof that it is possible to function normally with radically low blood pressure, to structure an existence around the body's physiological demands.

Because of my blood pressure, I fall asleep easily. All I have to do is think about sleeping, rest my head on my shoulder and I am out in two to three minutes. I have been told that I do not shift in my sleep, barely breathe and maintain an extremely low body temperature.

During my days in the Service, I would often take five-minute cat naps, even while waiting to be questioned by police or counterintelligence agents in other countries. One night, prior to questioning, I was kept under close surveillance, and on the following day the police told me how surprised they were to see me sleep soundly before an interrogation that could decide my future.

Before going to bed with a new lover, I sometimes tell her I suffer from a serious heart condition that may kill me in my sleep after having sex. If she has been able to fall asleep at all, she wakes up to find my body cold. When she cannot detect my breathing, she believes I am dead.

Some first-night lovers have failed my test and run out, desperate to disassociate themselves from my death. Others less afraid have rifled through my personal belongings. One woman, terrified by my corpse, called her boy friend for advice, without even realizing that she was admitting she'd been sleeping with another man.

My sensitivity to the slightest change in my environment, and my craving for unusual psychological pressure have made me aware how little other people are aware of their surroundings, how little they know of themselves and how little they notice me.

Once, I attended a party given by a wealthy businessman who had rented paintings from a small, private museum to impress his guests. When the guests arrived, they were greeted with an array of works by major artists, which was passed off by the businessman as his private collection. While the other guests were engaged in conversation, I strolled over to examine the paintings. Pretending to admire a medium-sized portrait, I casually slipped it off its hook, quietly lowered it to the floor and rested it against the wall.

I made a quick tour of the room, chatting with the other guests and complimenting the host on his impressive art collection. Then I ambled back to the portrait. Under the pretext of studying the other paintings that lined the wall, I edged it along the baseboard toward a hallway. As I reached the door, I bent down, picked up the portrait and walked casually into the bedroom where the guests had left their coats. Since the room was empty, I had all the time I needed to shove the painting under the bed and return to the party. Half an hour later, I went back to the bedroom, shut the door and took the framed portrait from its hiding place. Since I was sitting on the far edge of the bed with my back to the door, anyone entering the room would have assumed I was simply not feeling well. Before the person could cross to the bed, I would have slid the painting back under it, where it would remain hidden. No one appeared, and in minutes I had taken the portrait out of the frame, pried off the staples that secured the canvas to its stretcher, pushed the frame under the bed, rolled up the canvas and stuck it up the sleeve of my raincoat. I left the party in a group of six people, with my coat slung casually over my arm. A few days later, I shipped the painting back to my host in a package with no return address.

The party was only one of many situations which have confirmed my belief that people notice only what they want to. One of my Service cover occupations required me to speak occasionally at large banquets. After delivering my speech, I would always sit down on the dais facing the audience and pretend to pay attention to other speakers or to a discussion from the floor. There was no way I could leave the dais before the speeches were concluded. Whenever the wait became unbearable, I would reach for a half-full glass of white wine, sip it, put it down and cup my chin in my hand as if I were listening intently. With my free hand, I would pick up the glass again from the table and, in one continuous movement, down the rest of the wine, lower the glass until it was hidden from the audience and other speakers by the tablecloth and position it between my thighs. Then I would unzip my pants and fill the glass. A few moments later, I would put it back on the table. Apparently engrossed in the conversation around me, I would absent-mindedly push the full glass away from me. It would remain there until the waiters cleared it away with the other glasses.

Yet the isolation I feel and resent in public is nothing like the kind I find and cherish—out of doors when the ski season is nearly over. In early spring I often visit a resort where I can easily take a cable car to the glaciers and ski slowly down the slopes. At that time of the year, I am usually one of three or four people on the entire mountain. Surrounded by snow, rock and ice, I gaze at the peaks shining in the spring sun and listen to the sound of distant avalanches. Elsewhere, countless millions of people fight for every inch of living space; here, I and a few select others enjoy a splendid private world, a wilderness broken only by occasional cable cars, mountain top restaurants and alpine shelters.

I am protective of my solitude in the mountains. I have shared it only once, with a dog, a huge animal, so strong that he could drag me uphill. When I was tired or upset he would stay close, his eyes fixed on my face, his muscles ready to respond to my slightest command. We took walks and he would run ahead of me or lag behind, scouting for unseen enemies. If I was sick, he lost his appetite. If I locked him in another room, he paced restlessly, listening for my every sound.

But I did not want his whole being to be centered on me. I felt that I had perverted his essence, taming his original animal cunning and making him a dependent creature.

When he once failed to catch an alley cat, I called him. He slunk toward me, afraid, knowing I was angry. I began whipping him with my heaviest belt, swinging my arm high. As he whined, I silenced him by kicking his head until his eyes rolled in pain and terror. He flattened like a swollen rug, his fur soaked with sweat, saliva dripping from his mouth. I stood over him, continuing to beat him, trying to force him to get up and attack me. But he would not. He cringed in the corner, bereft of any instinct for self-preservation.

One night, as he padded up the stairs, I noticed that his flanks seemed too heavy for his back legs. The next morning, his hind quarters were swaying sideways. I felt his back, and he whimpered in pain but licked my hand, his eyes searching my face, his great head pressing against my thighs. I took him to a veterinarian, who told me an incurable disease was eating through the dog's spine.

Although walking was painful for him, he insisted on following me. He stayed even closer now, his nose nudging my calves. If I stretched out on my back in the grass, he sat erect behind me despite the pain, watching for anything that moved. If I opened my eyes, I would see his head towering over my face ready to lick my forehead. Sometimes he would stretch out next to me with one of his paws gently resting on my shoulder. Every week, his flanks grew heavier, until his legs eventually gave in under him when he tried to follow me.

In the evenings, we often sat together on my balcony, looking into the valley and the mountains beyond it. As the wind brought us a child's cry or the barking of a village dog, his ears would stand up, but his eyes were foggy and his breathing was labored. Finally, I mixed a powerful drug into his food. He ate his meal reluctantly, sensing the presence of the poison. When he had finished, I spread a blanket and lay down, pretending to sleep. He listened to my breathing and sniffed the spring wind. He lay down slowly, his paws and head heavy on my legs. The breeze brought sounds of faraway life, but soon he did not hear them.

Years later, in the Service, I trained a tough little hound. I had him run about in a belt loaded with heavy metal, from which a long thin rod protruded like an antenna. When he grew accustomed to running with the added weight, I attached food to the underside of a car, a foot or two forward from the back bumper, and sent him to fetch it. Next, my partner would slowly drive the car by, and at my command the dog, who hadn't been fed for a day or two, would chase the car and crawl under its rear fender to get to his dinner. The rod protruding from the belt would bang against the undercarriage as he snatched the food from beneath the still-moving car.

During the next stage of training, my partner drove a car of a different type every day. With each test, he increased the speed and I placed the food closer and closer to the gas tank. The dog never failed. Even when the food was under the gas tank, he retrieved it successfully. He was ready.

On the day of our assignment, the three of us were up early. Expecting to be fed, the animal grew excited as my partner strapped the dog's belly with the belt, which now also contained packets of gelatinous explosive.

Through my binoculars, I sighted a large limousine parked in front of a town house at the end of the block. I could tell from its slight tremor that the engine was idling. The car's bulletproof glass was almost opaque, and now and then the driver stuck his head out to look around. Two guards lounged nearby.

The door of the house opened and two more guards briskly accompanied a gray-haired man down the stairs. The guards on the sidewalk became alert, looking up and down the street. Four of the men climbed inside the rear of the limousine and the fifth took his seat beside the chauffeur. The car pulled away from the curb in our direction, slowly picking up speed. I opened the door of our car, pointed at the passing limousine and gave the command. The hound, its tail between its legs, the rod rising from its back, slipped away and sped toward its dinner.

We drove away just as the explosion lifted the limousine and enveloped it in flames. A wave of hot air pounded our car, warming my face. The shattered glass from nearby windows rained onto the sidewalks and struck the cars parked along the srteet; everywhere, pedestrians ran for cover. Soon we heard police sirens.

Although I had expected to be upset by witnessing the explosion, I was surprised by my own lack of emotional response to the scene. Yet since I was a child I have done many inexplicable things. Perhaps the explanations for my behavior, if there are any, are rooted in an area of my past to which I have no access.

I learned from my father that before I was two years old my mother came into my room one morning and found me sleeping in my nanny's bed. Knowing that I could not climb out of my crib by myself, she called the woman and asked her why she had taken me to her bed. Nanny denied that she was responsible and claimed that almost every night for several weeks she had awakened to find me in bed with her. She had tried to get me back to the crib, but my crying was so pitiful that she let me stay with her till morning. My father did not believe her and decided to conduct his own investigation.

On the following night, my father crept into our room when nanny and I were sleeping, and crouched in the corner. After a few hours, he saw me stand up in my crib, sound asleep, climb out of it, go straight to the nanny's bed and cuddle up at her feet. My father apologized to the woman and decided to seek medical help. Several doctors examined me, but none could discover the cause of my sleepwalking. The most sensible of them advised my father to drape wet towels over the sides of my crib, so that when I climbed up against them their chilly dampness would send me back to the warmth of my blankets. I never walked in my sleep again.

I have only one memory of another nanny, a Swiss

girl who began working for my parents when I was three. One evening after she had been with us about a year, I stole a pair of scissors from her work box. Later, when she sat me on her lap and hugged me close, I plunged the scissors into her right breast. Her face became contorted, and she screamed, watching her white blouse turn red. When my mother rushed into the room, my fist was covered with blood, making her think it was I who had been wounded.

A few months later, I dropped a large earthenware flowerpot from the window of our fifth-floor apartment onto a five-year-old boy who had broken one of my favorite toys. It missed him, but a shard from the pot flew up into his face and badly lacerated an eye. Everyone supposed the pot had dropped by accident.

When I was twelve, the new government uprooted hundreds of thousands of families, my own included, and resettled them in recently annexed territories along the new border. None of the resettled families was allowed to take anything except minimal personal belongings; they had to leave behind homes full of furniture and objects collected over the years, and move across the country into households furnished with objects that others had been forced to abandon. Their insecurity was increased by the fact that the government at any time might make them surrender even these lodgings.

Since both my parents worked, I was alone every day until shortly after lunch, when my tutor arrived. One morning, the telephone rang and a long-distance operator in the Capital announced that a government official wished to speak to my father. I explained he was at work and offered to accept the call. The official came on the line and, assuming I was not a child, ordered me to write down what he was about to tell me.

In two days, he said, my father was to appear at the

offices of the department in charge of the new territories. After signing a disclaimer of ownership of his former property, he would be issued a certificate authorizing him to reside permanently in our present apartment. The official informed me of the heavy penalty for noncompliance with the orders but added that the government would reimburse my father for traveling expenses. He gave me a list of train times, the department's address, the name of the official my father was to see and the time of his appointment. When the man finished, he had me read back the instructions to make certain I had made no mistakes. He warned that only a serious accident could justify my father's failure to appear.

I gave my father the message after he returned from work. I expected him to be unhappy. The government was forcing him to abandon all hope of going back to the place where he had lived all his life. But he was delighted we would not have to resettle again. He no longer seemed to mind living among unfamiliar paintings, ugly, heavy furniture, and some stranger's bric-a-brac, using silverware with strange monograms. Only a few months earlier, he had labeled the leader of the new government a Party puppet, accusing him of condoning the deaths of countless people, including my aunts and uncles. Now, he spoke impassively of the dead as victims of impersonal Party bureaucracy. My mother remarked that the most important thing was once again having a home where she and my father could raise me as a civilized human being.

My father followed the instructions I had carefully written down. It was a trip of a few hundred miles with several changes of trains, and he was gone for two days. When he returned, he brought the government certificate, a bouquet of flowers for my mother and a box of chocolates for me.

After my parents left for work the next day, I opened the telephone directory, selected a number at random and dialed it. A woman answered. Imitating the high-pitched voice of a long-distance operator, I announced a call from the Capital. Then I lowered my voice to sound as much as possible like the official who had phoned my father. I told the woman I wished to talk to the current legal tenant of her apartment. She replied that her husband was at work and could not be reached by phone, but that she would take the message for him.

I then warned her it was imperative to write down the following instructions correctly. Her husband was required to appear in the Capital in two days' time, where, in exchange for formally relinquishing all rights to his previous property, he would receive government authorization to reside permanently in the apartment he now occupied. As I dictated, I invented an address of the department, as well as the name of the official he was to see and the time of the appointment. I read off the train times I had copied down for my father and added that the government would reimburse her husband's travel expenses upon presentation of the receipts.

I had her read the message back to me to guarantee accuracy. Assuring me that her husband would keep the appointment, she hung up. The next day I called her again, pretending to be one of her husband's business acquaintances who had been unable to reach him at his office. She replied that he had left early that morning for an appointment in the Capital and would be back at work the next day.

From then on, I waited impatiently for my parents to leave every morning. As soon as they were gone, I rushed to the telephone directory and chose people in the resettled districts. If, like my father, they had abjectly surrendered their rights, they deserved to be punished.

Alternating between bureaucratic impersonality and restrained friendliness, I recited the directions, always stressing that official proof of identity was required for the issuance certificate. The dictation process was tedious, but I remained patient. Each time, I invented a new address of the department, and when circumstances required it I improvised other details.

Some of my older victims were almost illiterate, many speaking in crude, peasant dialects. Others were hard of hearing, some unused to speaking on a telephone and many so terrified of yet another governmental intervention in their lives that they could hardly speak at all. Occasionally, I was given personal information: an apprehensive wife feared her crippled husband might not survive the trip; an aged aunt assured me her nephew would obey the summons, although on the day of the appointment his fiancée was coming a great distance for a two-day visit. A young woman speculated that, since she was about to give birth, her husband would be reluctant to leave her; a teen-aged son told me he would go on his father's behalf since the man had been traumatized into immobility by internment in a labor camp; a widowed mother spoke of her tubercular baby daughter's long-awaited appointment in the town's only clinic.

I listened to their pleas without interrupting, then gently replied that full compliance was mandatory. To disobey, I said, introducing a note of shrillness into my voice, would be to aid political saboteurs and foreigners who conspired to regain the land they had lost. Thus, no excuses were valid, and no postponements were allowed.

I kept a complete record of all my calls, noting what I had said and how the news had been received. Every day, I tried at least half a dozen new numbers and made continual checks on the ones I had called the preceding day. Of all the people with whom I had made contact, only five were still home when I checked back the following day.

If, in my calls, I came across a household that had already received a resident certification, I penalized myself by making several additional calls. No one whose number came up was allowed to escape his fate, and if the phone wasn't answered the first time, I persisted in calling the number until finally someone responded.

I called one such number twice daily for at least three weeks before a man answered. He identified himself as the sole member of the household. After I had given him the usual details, he pleaded in a tremulous, heavily accented voice for a postponement. He was a Jew, he said, and was just recovering from a massive heart attack.

I was tempted to relent, because a year before my father had been stricken with a heart attack. Casually, I asked if he enjoyed living in the new territories. After all, I said, it was possible for him to emigrate to Palestine, and I was curious to know why he had chosen to remain in a country where millions of his people had been slaughtered. He faltered and then told me that destiny had decreed that Jews were to live in the homes of others, even if they were enemies. I hesitated no longer. I told him that destiny belonged to men, not men to destiny, and the law I represented made no exceptions for heart-attack convalescents. A man who was strong enough to live alone among his enemies was strong enough to keep a government appointment in his nation's Capital. He reacted at once. All he wanted from life, he said, was peace and security, which the certificate would bring him. He read the instructions back to me and promised to follow them to the letter. I called his number the next day and for several days following that. No one answered.

A month after I began my calls, a knock on the door interrupted my family's breakfast. A harsh voice announced that the police were outside. My father's hands shook so badly that he was unable to knot the sash of his robe, and my mother turned white. She and my father hurried to the front door. When she opened it, six plainclothesmen pushed by her and said my father was under arrest. They hauled him downstairs to an unmarked car and drove off. Later that morning, my tutor's wife called to say her husband, too, had been arrested.

The following day, a policeman came to our door with orders for my mother and me to accompany him to police headquarters without delay.

As soon as we arrived at the station house, an inspector ushered us into a room and announced that treasonous calls had been made from our telephone. He demanded statements about my father's activities from both my mother and me. My mother was so distraught that she could hardly speak, but did manage to say that no one had access to our telephone except the three of us. She could not understand the charges.

The inspector said scores of innocent people were being victimized by a vicious saboteur who was using our telephone as his weapon. The inspector described the crime and told us that, a few weeks before my father's arrest, a call had been made to a citizen who already had a residence certificate. The man had reported the incident to the police, who then checked with the Capital and learned that numerous persons were being sent to nonexistent residence certification bureaus. Public notices were placed in the papers urging anyone receiving a potentially fraudulent call to get in touch with the police. Some of the victims had replied, and the police were able to trace subsequent calls to our phone.

The inspector flipped on a tape recorder and I heard myself speaking as the official. Until that moment, I hadn't realized how perfect my imitations were. The voice on the tape sounded like a middle-aged man's. My mother listened intently and shook her head, unable to recognize the voice.

I stood up and announced that I was the impostor. The inspector laughed. I insisted that I could prove it. If he would turn off the recorder, I told him, I would recite word for word the rest of the recorded message. He stopped laughing and turned off the machine.

I continued the monologue, modulating my voice as I had done so many times. The inspector called a second man into the room and ordered me to repeat the speech, which by now they were recording. When I finished, they conferred for a moment. The inspector told me that, in spite of my youth, I was under arrest. My mother was free to go. She reached for me, but they forced her away. That evening, I was transferred to a darkened room with padded walls. It contained a long table with four chairs along one wall, a single bench against another.

After I had been alone in the room for several hours, four men entered and sat down at the table. Buckets of water and several spotlights were brought into the room. One of the men ordered me over to the bench. I was blinded by the lights and could not tell which of the four men kept insisting that my father and my tutor were the real saboteurs. He claimed they had written the text of my message, trained me to imitate the official's voice and selected the numbers I had called. Now, he ranted, those traitors were letting me take the blame for them and possibly for other conspirators.

I leaned forward, squinting in the direction of his voice. My parents and tutor did not know about my calls, I shouted. I had made them while alone in the apartment. The man roared the accusation at me again. I repeated the denial. A second voice announced that unless I told the truth I would rot in prison. Since I was young, he said, I could look forward to many years of solitary confinement. I screamed out my denial. One of my interrogators rose and positioned himself between me and the spotlights. His dark bulk bent over me and he yelled into my face that I must confess. Gripping the edge of the bench, I leaned backward to avoid smelling his breath.

He grabbed me by the hair, dragged me off the bench and threw me against the table. The other three interrogators stood up and moved toward me. As I struggled to get away, one of them slammed me in the mouth and I spat blood and two teeth onto the table. Another man threw a bucket of cold water into my face and all four began to shout at once.

It occurred to me that the police were not aware of my father's heart condition. They could easily kill him by beating him or even by keeping him in confinement. I thought about my tutor, a gentle, quiet man who spoke Latin as if it were the local dialect. I myself had already been too lucky; I had survived the war. Moreover, my life involved no one but myself, unlike my father and my tutor who had to support families.

I began to mimic the speech patterns of one of my interrogators. Though the missing teeth interfered with my speech, I imitated his voice perfectly, including his vocabulary and his mannerisms. The other inspectors burst into laughter. Then, catching themselves, they grew silent. The man I had mocked made a grab for me, but I jumped up and ran around the room, never stopping my impersonation. I paused once or twice to ask mockingly if they thought my father and my tutor had coached me for this performance.

The four interrogators stormed out of the room and I was locked up once more. The next day, the man I had imitated tried to bribe me with some fruit and an imported chocolate bar. He watched me eat, then asked me why I had tortured scores of innocent strangers who were already sad victims of the war. Ignoring his question, I asked him what would happen to my father and my tutor. Both of them would remain in prison, he said, until I had satisfactorily answered his questions. I told him that if I gave him the information he wanted they would never be released. If they were to be hurt or held in prison, I suggested he kill me, because if he didn't I would someday punish his wife and children so terribly that he would regret he had ever met me. I reminded him how adept I was at affecting the lives of people I did not even know. He kicked the leg of my chair and stormed out of the cell.

Soon after, I was released from the prison and driven home in a military jeep. My father lay in bed, his swollen face covered with cuts and bruises. My mother sat next to him, applying compresses to his shoulder and abdomen. When she saw me, she began to cry.

My father gestured for me to come to him. I kissed his unshaven cheek. He held me at arm's length and said that he did not want to know what reason I had to hurt so many families. My mother hugged me and told me that even though my tutor had been released from prison, he refused to teach me anymore.

My winter vacations were spent in a small mountain village in the north of the country. When I arrived the first year, in November, I expected to find deep snow. Instead the Ruh, the wet wind from the warm lakes, swept through the region, keeping the snow and the skiers away. Yet, nature was ready for the winter. Autumn had boiled to death all the grass and weeds. The black willow branches, stripped of their foliage, curved to the ground. The potato plants decayed and the fields became bogs. The dull glow of morning hovered over the spreading gray hills, and the raindrops, the children of the Ruh, shook themselves loose from the sky, scuttling fast. The Ruh punished them as they fled, forcing them aslant and hurling them against the ground.

At daybreak, the villagers wrapped themselves in warm clothes and made their way from their homes to the market. They were all anxiously awaiting the Thule, a dry wind from the tundras.

A solitary pond fed by underground springs slowly diffused into swamps. Thickets of reeds, slender rushes and clusters of low dwarf willows grew in clumps on its banks. Every day, I joined the village boys and girls when they went to examine the lowering water level of the pond.

As the first breath of the Thule blew across the hills, dozens of us rushed to the pond to begin the game of Thule. Each child brought a canvas bag or a box containing a live animal—a rat, a dog, a cat, a duck, a goose or a muskrat—that he had captured or bought during the last days of gentle Ruh.

Attaching stones or iron bars to each animal's underbelly to slow it down in the water, we released the creatures, throwing them into the pond. Blinded by the sudden light after days of darkness, the animals hit the water, sank, then emerged breathless, instinctively swimming or thrashing their way to shore. As they struggled to keep afloat, their owners frightened them away from the banks, screaming and shouting and swinging long twig brooms with iron hooks hidden inside them. If an animal escaped or drowned, its owner was disqualified and had to pay a penalty to those whose animals were still panicking and colliding in the chilled water.

The Thule grew colder by the minute, and we pulled our woolen cloaks tighter about ourselves. Suddenly, the air seemed to contract. The pond thickened, then crackled ominously. In an instant, it turned into a platter of thin ice, its glaze broken only by the trapped animals.

We watched them struggling to crawl out of the water, but they could not grip the glassy sheet. The Thule blew around them. It slowed the blood in their veins, thinned the air in their lungs and made them sluggish. Stunned, they stared at the sky, at each other and at us, standing along the distant shore. One after another, they died, their heads cocked to one side as though listening, their eyes frozen open.

When the first snow swirled down, it stuck to the animals. Throughout the winter, they sat in the frozen pond like frosted glass sculptures from the church fair. On our way to the slopes, we often stopped to stare but never touched them. The animals belonged to the Thule, which had transformed them into creatures from another world.

When I returned the following winter, the village had completed a new ski jump, one of the largest in the country. Increasing numbers of visitors lengthened the lines at the lifts. Ski-jumping had become popular among the young villagers, and local skiers were beginning to compete against the best jumpers in the country.

One of them, the potter's son, was unquestionably the top village jumper. Speeding down the run, hunched over his skis, he would reach the takeoff and arch forward into the air, arms flat against his sides, his nose almost touching the tips of his skis as he hurtled through space.

We all stood breathless, expecting him to fall, but, stretching out his arms and bending his knees to soften the impact, he always touched the ground easily and skied to a graceful halt. In silent amazement, we'd surround him before he could remove his skis or shake the snow from his parka. This attention made him uncomfortable and he would immediately walk back to the top of the hill to begin a new jump.

He was short, with one shoulder a bit lower than the other. His head was too big, his yellow teeth were crooked and his eyes were set in a perpetual squint under a low forehead. I recalled my mother saying that a low forehead was a sign of mental inferiority. Only two inches separated my hairline from my eyebrows, but the jumper's scalp and brows almost grew together. He could never complete a sentence without stuttering, and I speculated that it was because he was slow-witted.

Some of his jumps had exceeded the national record and the villagers predicted that, once he won the Olympic Gold Medal, foreign skiers would begin flocking to the village. Several of the wealthier townspeople had already been in contact with city architects about designing new restaurants, and the more adventurous ones even considered opening a gas station.

My parents had been unable to find me a new tutor and while looking for one, they felt I was better off in the mountains than in the city. They allowed me to remain in the village until the end of January. After the holidays, though, all the other tourist children went home and the village boys and girls went back to school. As I found myself more and more alone, my fascination with the jumper intensified. I would have given anything to be able to jump as he did. But whenever I gathered enough speed to dare a hop from a mound of snow, I was tossed about like a baby bird clumsily trying to fly for the first time. While some invisible physical force launched the potter's son into the air, an opposite force drove me directly back down to earth with a humiliating thump.

I was desperate to learn all I could about my idol. I mingled among the villagers when they gathered to drink at night, pretending I was looking for someone. All they talked about was the jumper, endlessly pondering his future achievements but rarely discussing the man himself. I did learn that because of his terrible stutter he had never gone to school. He could neither read nor write, and even the priest who was forced to listen to his confessions had given up all attempts to correct the stammer.

All this made the skier seem even more extraordinary. Here was a man who had achieved fame without ever having gone to school. Even his one skill, jumping, he had developed without training, relying only on what his instinct commanded.

During the Christmas competition, which he had lost only by inches to the national champion, the potter's son became a nationwide celebrity. Radio, television and camera crews, as well as reporters, photographers and autograph hunters, came to the village in search of him. Always shy, the jumper grew even more withdrawn as the reporters pressed microphones into his face and cameras zeroed in on his every move.

Around New Year's day, a tall, dark-haired Austrian appeared in the village. From listening to the gossip in the square, I learned he was a famous ski-jumping coach, hired by several of the richest families in the village to train the potter's son for the Olympic qualifying competition.

Every morning, I followed the coach and the potter's son to the jump and watched them. Often, I was the only spectator at the practice sessions because the village children were in school, and soon both the Austrian and the jumper began to greet me with smiles.

As the jumper went through his paces, the Austrian took dozens of photographs of his run, his leap, his flight and his landing. The potter's son did not seem to pay much attention to his coach's advice and I wondered if he even understood what instructions the Austrian screamed at him through a megaphone.

About a week after the Austrian arrived, a friend of his appeared in the village. She was as tall as he but much younger. Her hair was red and she wore tight-fitting sweaters and a long fur coat, which always hung open over skirts that showed her knees. None of the villagers spoke to her. But because she had been brought to town by the coach, they all tried their best to restrain their scorn. One of them claimed that the "Red Whore" had been imported from the big city as a special reward for the jumper, who apparently had never had a woman.

I devoted all my time to spying on the woman, the Austrian and the potter's son. Many evenings, I watched the three of them drinking on the balcony of the house where the Austrian and the woman were living. When the jumper got too drunk to sit up straight, the couple would drag him into the house.

One afternoon, pretending to watch the jumper practice, I dared to move closer to the woman, who now accompanied the two men to their jump sessions.

While the jumper was climbing the distant run, the Austrian said to her that the "Flying Gnome" had to be gotten out of the village to practice jumping from higher and better-constructed ski-jumps. She shook her head, replying that the Gnome had persistently refused to leave the village. With a laugh, he answered that, after all, she had been brought to change the jumper's mind, and asked if she didn't think the Flying Gnome was in love with her. The woman said he would follow her to the ends of the earth. They both laughed uproariously, and at that moment the jumper fell. The Austrian immediately ran to him.

The woman turned toward me. She asked me my name and why I was at the jump. I blushed and replied that one day I was going to be as great a man as the potter's son was a jumper.

She sat down next to me and put her arm around my shoulder. Her eyes were pale green. I stared at her white teeth as she spoke and felt her breath on my face. She whispered that the potter's son jumped only to demonstrate his love for her. The more he loved her, she said, the farther he jumped. I protested that the potter's son had jumped well long before she had come to the village. She brought her face and body so close to me that her fur coat brushed my chin and I could feel her breasts press against me. She agreed that he had jumped well, but before her time, she said, the potter's son had been a stuttering, dumb peasant who knew nothing about life. Since he had fallen in love with her, she continued, he had become a man. If I, too, wanted to become a man, she said, I must first learn how to love.

She got up and walked over to the Austrian, who was shouting angrily at the jumper. The Flying Gnome stood silently, his head bowed.

In February, my parents found a tutor in the city

and I went home. I studied the sports pages every day to find out whether the Flying Gnome would again confront the national champion. Finally, a date was announced and the papers began carrying large photographs of both the champion and the Gnome. I continually nagged my parents to let me attend the competition, and at last they agreed.

I spent twelve hours on the train and arrived, a few hours before the jumps were to begin, in the fashionable ski resort that was sponsoring the meet. When the guards were not looking, I slipped through the rows of spectators and found a spot next to the takeoff point. I scanned the jumpers with binoculars until I saw the Flying Gnome, dressed in a blue ski suit with a tight red cap pulled down to his eyebrows. The Austrian was gesturing emphatically to him but the jumper kept his head turned away.

When I checked the area reserved for rich spectators and the jumpers' families, I saw the Red Whore. Her hair was even redder than I remembered and her make-up thicker. She was accompanied by another woman and by a man with a large movie camera. As I spotted her, she was changing seats with the other woman and leaning against the man's shoulder, her face as close to his as it had once been to mine.

I turned back to the competition in time to see the national champion establish a new record. Then I watched the Red Whore through the binoculars. She removed her coat and stood up in the loge, thrusting her chest forward, applauding and cheering wildly. She was the most noticeable of all the women, and many men in the stands were ogling her. When the crowd quieted down, the challenger for the national championship was announced over the loudspeakers.

I turned my binoculars to the Flying Gnome. He lurched forward, and I saw the blue tips of his skis sticking out of the snow. Hunched at the top of the run, he looked even smaller than he was. When he started down, he accelerated so fast that I had trouble keeping the glasses trained on him. But almost as soon as his skis left the run and he was propelled into the air, I sensed something was wrong. His body appeared to have given up, to refuse to complete the jump at all. His hands would not line up with his thighs, and his skis seemed out of control. The crowd gasped.

When he reached the peak of the ascent, his trunk turned sideways, his head bent beneath his skis, his hands flapped frantically in the air. Instead of witnessing the miraculous jump we had all expected, we saw a puppet severed from its strings. In an instant, he crashed down on the run. As his skis fell off, he bounced against the packed snow and we heard a loud crack. His body rolled down the incline and came to a stop, leaving red and brown splotches in his trail.

The screaming crowd broke through the barriers, and I shoved through the throng past the guards and the police. By the time I reached the jumper, he was being carried to the ambulance. His eyes were open and unblinking. Someone shouted that he was dead.

I looked everywhere for the Red Whore and finally found her leaving the grounds with the other woman. I grabbed her coat sleeve and she turned to look at me. I screamed at her that she had said her love would make him jump farther and farther until he became the national champion. I wanted to know why he had failed.

She whispered something to her companion and the woman left us. The Red Whore walked to a bench and sat down. I stood weeping in front of her. She embraced me, pressing me against her chest, and kissed my cheeks. If I would stop crying, she said, she would tell me why the potter's son had killed himself.

She then took my hand and guided it under her skirt, along her thighs, under the garters and the soft underwear. When I hesitated, she insisted, leading my hand where she wanted it to go. As my fingers went inside her, her expression softened. She asked if I could feel how hot she was. She said the jumper had never liked her heat and had never wanted to be where my hand now was. The jumper had grown up surrounded by rock and ice, she said, and he could live only when his bones and his body were frozen like stored meat. He saw rot in everything hot and wet and would touch her warmth only when he was drunk. And there she had been, hot and wet, inviting his touch all the time. She said he felt soiled by her love.

The air felt cold against my warm hand as the Red Whore withdrew it from under her skirt. Before my fingers could dry, she gently pressed them to my mouth and I licked them. For an instant, I felt the moisture on my tongue before it dried in the cold. Then she took my hand and kissed it, her tongue pink against her bright red lipstick. The Red Whore embraced me, got up and moved off with the crowd.

Years later, in the Service, I was waiting in a restaurant on the massif of Switzerland's Plaine Morte for a telephone call from my contact. I noticed an old man on the terrace who seemed familiar, although I couldn't quite place him. He was bald and the bright sun gleamed on his scalp. He supported his sharp chin on one hand, and his elbow rested rigidly on the arm of the deck chair, a blanket covering his legs and other hand. When he turned to the waitress, I recognized him as the Flying Gnome's jumping coach.

Apologizing for the intrusion, I asked whether he

remembered a ski jumper from a small mountain village who had been killed in a national championship many years before. I prompted him by reminding him that he had called the jumper the "Flying Gnome." As he removed his sunglasses to see me better, the Austrian exclaimed that, indeed, he did remember such a monster. He reached up to pat my shoulder, repeating the nickname with obvious delight, without asking how I came to know it. The conversation seemed to have stopped, and again I prompted his wandering mind by suggesting that the jumper had been in love with a woman with dyed red hair who had arrived in the village not long after he himself had come there.

The Austrian leaned closer to me, his expression altered as if he were about to tell a dirty joke. On the day of the Gnome's death, he related, he had accompanied him to the top of the ski-jump tower. About five minutes before his jump, the Gnome wanted to go to the men's room. The Austrian insisted that the jumper was experiencing an attack of nerves rather than a real physical need and reminded him that he had been to the toilet twice in the past hour. The jumper persisted. Reluctantly, the Austrian said, he had escorted the Gnome to the men's room, but, when they got there, both toilets were occupied. The Flying Gnome had begun screaming that he could not wait any longer, and the Austrian was about to check if the ladies' room was free, when it became apparent that it was too late. The jumper propped himself against a wall and pointed at his freshly pressed blue ski pants, now covered with brown stains. Just as the Austrian was about to ask for a postponement of the jump, it was announced that the Flying Gnome was next.

The Austrian said that he had almost dragged the jumper to the starting position. Some of the judges, press people, photographers and waiting contestants noticed the splotches on the jumper's pants and the stench emanating from him. Many people walked away; others laughed. The Flying Gnome, the Austrian recalled, turned to him and stuttered that he would rather die than have the people below laugh at him because he had soiled himself like a child. He stepped into the trail and began his flight, leaving a faint odor behind him. Seconds later, he was dead.

I asked what had happened to the red-haired woman. The Austrian's hand emerged from under the blanket in a gesture of nonchalance. She was nobody, he said, just a hooker who had been paid to keep that ape of a man happy. Instead, he chuckled, that stupid woman had fallen in love with the Gnome.

When I was in high school, I discovered that, by squeezing my member, I could force it back into my body. I practiced keeping it retracted, and later discovered that I could keep it hidden with a plastic-edged metal clamp, which made it look as if I were recovering from an amputation.

A few days after my discovery, I invited a girl I was interested in to my family home. After the preliminary kissing and fondling, I turned off the lights, undressed her and continued to caress her until she asked me to undress as well. I pretended to hesitate but at last removed my shirt, slowly unbuckled my belt and finally took off my pants.

The girl was not aggressive enough to reach for me, so I guided her fingers to the clamp. She pulled away in horror. Calmly, I explained that when I was a child, during the war, a grenade had exploded near me and metal shards had torn into my organ. A surgeon had fitted a clamp to protect the chronic wound from irritation. I told her that I was barred for life from what was considered normal intercourse, and could find fulfillment only through unusual associations. I assured the girl I would respect her right to reject me as a cripple. Ashamed of her initial withdrawal, she attempted to convince me that the absence of one part of my body did not distress her. In fact, she remarked, my deficiency was really an advantage because it freed her from the danger of pregnancy, and for once she could let herself go without fear of the consequences.

In turn, I urged her to demand anything that excited her: I was an invalid, I said, who searched for sources of release others might consider abnormal, and nothing was perverted or repellent to me. She said she was willing to try, and almost immediately began to take the initiative.

I had to avoid erection during love-making because the clamp could be sprung by the growing pressure within my organ. As long as the clamp remained in place, I felt a bit of pain, but the sense of harnessed power made orgasm crude by comparison.

Later, when the girl was too aroused to be aware of what I was doing, I surreptitiously removed the clamp and shot into her without warning. When she felt me climax inside her, she screamed. First she grew angry, although I tried to convince her that withholding part of myself was not a game but an attempt to revive sexual sensitivity. I explained that, in avoiding what we had experienced so often with so many others, she and I had made the act of sex fresh and pure.

She finally admitted that being aggressive with me had released her in a pleasurable way, and had let her feel more sensual than ever before. Her manipulation of me was more exciting than her passive surrender to her previous lovers; she said that any anger or anxiety she had suffered because of my deception was a small price to pay for her new-found freedom, her new sexual identity.

I have needed to change my identity so often in recent years, I've come to look upon disguise as more than a means of personal liberation: it's a necessity. My life depends on my being able to instantly create a new persona and slip out of the past. As for the others I come in contact with, my disguise is never simply a deception or a hoax. It is an attempt to expand the range of another's perception. Confronted with my camouflage, it is the witness who deceives himself, allowing his eyes to give my new character credibility and authenticity. I do not fool him; he either accepts or rejects my altered truth.

As I once wandered through Florence, an elegant tailoring establishment caught my eye. A metal plaque next to the door announced that the shop had been founded in the mid-nineteenth century and specialized in formal wear and military uniforms. A small window above the plaque displayed photographs of some of the shop's more prominent clients, including military leaders, chiefs of state and top-ranking diplomats.

I entered the shop and asked to speak to the manager. A Florentine with a long monk's face, delicate hands and silky white hair came out to see me.

"I would like to order two military uniforms for myself," I told him. "One for daytime; one for evening."

The manager called over two of his assistants and explained that they would take the notes and measurements necessary to fill my order. "In which army do you serve, sir?" inquired the manager.

"In a one-man army," I replied.

The manager smiled nervously. "Ah, every man's dream, is it not?" he said. "Are you then, sir, in the reserves?"

"No, but I need two military uniforms that are not copies of actual ones, either current or historical . . ."

The manager stared at me uneasily before he broke into a smile. "You must be an actor!" he exclaimed. "And these uniforms are for a play or a film? Or a television spectacular?" He looked to me for confirmation, while the two assistants, pencils poised, studied me with keen interest.

"No, I am not an actor. A one-man theater, more likely," I replied, but this time got no smile in return. "The uniforms must not link me to any particular country or military branch, but they must create the impression that I am a high-ranking military official."

He seemed suspicious of my motives. "Before we proceed further, sir," he said rather coldly, "may I inquire how you would like to pay for this order?"

"In Swiss francs, if you don't mind. And in advance."

He was relieved. "We have made uniforms here for over a century," he announced, "but I doubt, sir, that we have ever had a request like yours. You see, a uniform is a uniquely designed garment worn by persons to provide a distinctive yet easily recognizable appearance. A uniform is as definite as a date on a calendar, while what you seem to want is . . ." As he searched for a description, I interrupted.

"What I want is what you have already described, easily recognizable, distinctive. Just make it undefinable. It's difficult, but I trust the artist in you."

The manager nodded, and, after a pause, ordered the attendants to bring over albums containing sketches and photographs of all important uniforms designed in the last quarter-century.

He sat down next to me and prepared to take notes, as both assistants hovered nearby.

"Exactly what mood do you want your uniforms to convey?" He stressed the word "mood."

"Power, but restrained power. Importance, but subdued importance. I will aways wear my uniform with a shirt and tie, but never with medals or ribbons."

He jotted down what I had said, then waited for me to go on. I began turning the pages of the album marked *High Command: Twentieth Century*.

"To compensate for my narrow chest, I need wide lapels, as in this British uniform." I pointed to the sketch, and both assistants scribbled down the number. "But I want the lapels spread a bit wider to reveal more of the tie, as in this Italian uniform." I indicated a second drawing, which the assistants noted instantly.

The manager picked up another album and opened it. "Pockets as in this Swedish uniform?" he suggested.

"Fine. But to make my neck appear shorter, I would like the back collar kept high so not too much shirt will show above it."

He perused a third album. "Perhaps the collar from the Brazilian Air Force?" We both studied it carefully, but I wasn't satisfied. We finally settled on a collar from a NATO uniform and on sleeves from a Chinese one.

"Epaulets?" he inquired.

"How about these Warsaw Pact General Staff epaulets?" I suggested. "They're large and will make my shoulders appear broader." He agreed.

The cap posed problems. I explained I wanted a tall one to balance out my long nose and to extend my forehead.

"There is nothing wrong with your face, sir," he objected politely.

"It never matches what I wear," I retorted. "Since I can't change my face, I can at least design a uniform to go with it."

"Yes, of course. The German caps of the early forties would best suit your face," he volunteered.

"Too familiar. And too many associations by now, don't you agree?"

He nodded. "Yes. A bit much."

We finally decided to crossbreed the German cap with the Soviet Cavalry and the American Air Force designs.

I chose the best khaki twill in stock for the daytime uniform and dark blue flannel for evening. My uniforms were twice as expensive as the standard ones, but I paid without complaining. The delighted manager escorted me to the door, and, after telling me that the first of my five fittings would take place the next day, he said, "Of course, it's not my business, sir, but may I ask why you need these uniforms?"

"To please a woman," I said. "I excite her only when I'm in a uniform."

"She must be quite a whimsical woman, sir," he murmured.

When I returned to the shop for the first fitting, I was ushered into a large room and told to stand in front of a three-way mirror. Looking around the room, I saw tailors and assistants fitting men, some of whom stood like mannequins, often in uniforms I recognized, some in various stages of undress.

I glanced at a military man who was just leaving the room. From his epaulets, I gathered he was a colonel, but I did not know what country or branch of the military he served. When I turned toward the mirror, our eyes met.

Even though the jacket was still sleeveless and I wasn't wearing trousers, he must have decided my rank was higher than his and he saluted first. Only after I saluted back did it occur to me that my salute, like my uniform, should be a military hybrid. After some experimenting, I adopted a greeting that consisted of raising my left hand rather casually to the visor of my cap, as though my right arm had been wounded. It was a salute that I felt reflected the spirit of my uniform and of the man who wore it.

I had a chance to use the salute frequently during later fittings: any time a military man caught sight of my uniform, he promptly saluted. One was a heavily decorated general who was having his uniforms let out because of the weight he had gained. He took a look at my costume and saluted me with the warm smile of an old soldier passing the torch to a younger man. I was saluted deferentially by a young captain, who, my fitter told me, was the son of an aristocratic Spanish family. The captain paid me the respect that the new guard shows toward the veteran.

At last, the finished uniforms were delivered to my hotel. On the left breast of each jacket, where military ribbons would go, I pinned two thin cardboard strips and carefully hung both jackets out on the balcony. After they had bleached for a few hours in the Florentine spring sun, I removed the strips. The areas they had protected were now slightly darker than the rest of the cloth, and I further darkened them with a dye.

I bought fake insignia in a theatrical prop store, selecting jet fighters braced by two Cupids for my caps and turtles for my epaulets.

I donned my khaki uniform and prepared to leave Florence. When I returned my room key to the concierge, he was so hynotized by my uniform that he didn't recognize me. I gave him my name and he sprang to attention as if both of us were in the military, then apologized. "I didn't realize that you were in the Air Corps!" he exclaimed, accepting the key from me with reverence.

"I'm not," I replied solicitously. "But at one time or another, all of us wear uniforms." I punched his arm lightly and pointed to his own impressive outfit. But he refused to accept the comparison and insisted on carrying my luggage out to the car.

The hotel parking attendant saw me in my uniform and brought my car without being asked, ignoring five or six other guests who had been waiting ahead of me.

I drove across Europe wearing my uniforms. Often a traffic policeman, noticing the insignia on my cap, would promptly halt all other vehicles, wave my car through the red light and salute me as I passed. In return, I raised my hand in my own unique salute. One day, I decided to visit the ruins of a medieval fortress in a remote hill town. I simply brought my car to the local police station, parked it directly in front of the door and went inside. At the sight of my uniform, three policemen jumped up, saluted me and struggled to button their jackets.

The men remained standing at attention, although I attempted to put them at ease by explaining that I was just a tourist anxious to spend some time inside the fortress. I asked if they would mind keeping an eye on my car while I was gone. The police chief hastened to assure me he'd assign one of his men to guard it.

In restaurants with long waiting lines, I would simply walk up to the headwaiter. One glance at my uniform would cause him to order the waiters to move in an additional table or speed up a clearing. In a matter of minutes, I would be seated and served, the people in line staring at me wordlessly.

If an airlines flight I wanted was filled, I would approach the ticket counter and ask for a seat. Almost invariably, I would get a place. Once a clerk took a look at my insignia and began to apologize profusely, stammering that the only place he could assign me was a spare service seat at the back of the plane. I assured him that it was perfectly acceptable. He issued the ticket at once and called for an airline car to drive me from the terminal to the plane.

As I climbed the boarding ramp, the pilot came out to welcome me on board. He saluted and apologized that my seat was at "the wrong end" of his aircraft. The stewardess, obviously impressed by my presence, escorted me to my seat and throughout the flight paid special attention to me.

The seats on both sides of the aisle in front of me were occupied by a Ruthenian family, who talked loudly among themselves. I soon gathered they were emigrants on their way to a new country, and that the family consisted of a married couple, their six- or seven-year-old son and his two grandmothers.

The boy was sitting directly in front of me next to the window. Since mine was the last seat in the plane, it did not recline, and I was forced to stretch out my legs under his seat. The moment I tried to nap after takeoff, the boy began jumping up and down, and every bounce made the seat bang into my shins.

I leaned toward the window and called to him in a whisper. The child turned and saw me peering through the narrow space between his seat and the window. "What's your name?" I whispered in Ruthenian.

"Tomek," he answered.

"Can you see me, Tomek?" He nodded. "Can you hear me?" He nodded again. "Now, Tomek, listen carefully," I said. "Do you see that huge engine on the wing outside?" Tomek looked through the window, then turned back to me and nodded. "Good. Do you know what would happen if I fed you to that engine?" I asked solemnly. The boy's eyes grew wide.

"What would happen?" he whimpered.

"The engines would chop you up and churn you out like a long, thin sausage that would fall to earth and there be gobbled up by dogs." Tomek looked at me in terror. I leaned closer. "If you jump on your seat and wake me one more time, I will feed you to that engine."

The boy flushed and turned away. "Mama, Mama!" he screamed, shaking her until she woke up. He pointed in my direction. "This man says he will throw me into the engine and turn me into a sausage."

I pretended to be asleep, with my cap resting on my knees. The woman looked at the cap, then at me, and whispered loudly, "Stop this nonsense, Tomek. We are not in our town anymore. This officer cannot speak our language. Stop making things up. Be quiet and try to sleep." She turned away from him.

Tomek swiveled around again and watched me. For a few minutes, I pretended to be asleep, then I opened my eyes and leaned forward. "Stop making things up, Tomek," I said, "because if you don't, I'll turn you into a long, thin sausage and no one will know it except the dogs that eat you."

Tomek's face went white. "Mama, Mama," he screamed again. "This man says he will throw me into the engine. I don't want to become a long, thin sausage. I don't want to be eaten by dogs."

As his mother woke up, I shut my eyes again. "Stop that, Tomek," she shouted. Then, afraid she might wake me, she continued in an angry whisper. "No one talked to you. Stop making things up. One more lie and I'll spank you."

I waited a moment before I opened my eyes again. Tomek was staring at me, clutching the arm of his seat. I moved closer and whispered, "Your mother doesn't believe you, Tomek. No one will. Perhaps because they don't want to see me. Am I speaking to you?" The boy, his lips trembling, shook his head in denial. "Am I here, Tomek?" Again he moved his head from side to side. "But, could I still turn you into a sausage?" He nodded that I could. "Good," I said. "I am going to sleep now. Don't disturb me."

I closed my eyes and fell asleep. During the rest of the trip, whenever I woke up, I saw Tomek peering at me from around the seat. I smiled at him, but he did not smile back.

I saw him with his family at the airport. He was carrying a big Mickey Mouse doll he had been given by the immigration service hostess who greeted his family.

I approached him at passport control and, smiling, said to him in English, "What a nice Mickey Mouse you've got. I hope you have a good time here." The hostess translated what I had said and his parents and grandmothers acknowledged me with a smile, but Tomek's face remained stony and he looked through me as if I were invisible.

"Say 'thank you' to the nice officer," said his mother, putting her arm around him. Tomek looked at her wild-eyed. "What officer?" he screamed in a fury. "I can't see an officer here." His mother looked pointedly at his father, who promptly reprimanded his son for misbehaving. As they bent over Tomek and the Mickey Mouse doll, I raised my arm in a stiff salute. I walked off, accompanied by Tomek's unyielding gaze.

I have always been fascinated by the strange psychic strength that allows acrobats and stunt men to defy death easily. I find it equally fascinating that, while their professional lives demand continual risks, in their private existences they take no chances.

I once stayed at a gambling resort famous for its variety shows, which included many stunt acts. I would usually dine watching a floor show at a lavish hotel, and afterward would stroll downtown to the third-rate nightclubs, snack bars and coffee houses. As I walked through the district one evening, I noticed that one club was featuring a father-and-daughter act. The brightly colored poster showed a photograph of a man tossing a gigantic horseshoe at a young woman standing opposite him. The camera had captured the horseshoe in flight six feet above the stage, midway between the couple. The slender, shapely woman posed with arms outstretched as she faced the oncoming horseshoe.

I went into the club to watch the performance. There were fifty or sixty people in the audience, mostly men. The bartender told me that many customers who had seen the act twice in one night returned the next, drawn back not by the stunt but by the woman.

The horseshoe-thrower walked onto the stage alone. He was in his fifties, short but powerfully built. His large head seemed to weigh so much that it forced his chin down into his massive neck, spreading the layers of fat out onto his shoulders. His hair had receded beyond his jug-shaped ears, and, when he glanced around, his eyes seemed to function independently of one another.

The horseshoe he hefted was cast-iron, omega-shaped, two or three times the size of an ordinary horseshoe. Raising it above his head with both hands, he held it still for a moment, then dropped it onto the stage floor with a crash. The audience applauded and the man smiled, displaying uneven teeth.

At that moment, the woman appeared and walked toward him. She embraced him as if they were lovers.

This was the woman portrayed in the poster, but the photograph had made her look hard by comparison with what she was. Her hair, piled high on her head, was the color of ripe wheat, and her large wide eyes gave her face an innocent look. Her neck was long, her shoulders delicate, her breasts small and perfectly formed. A short silk skirt clung to her firm thighs and buttocks, and her legs were shapely as a sixteen-year-old's. She strutted across the stage on high-heeled shoes, with just a hint of a stripper's sway.

The horseshoe-thrower stepped down from the stage with the horseshoe and approached the audience. In an amiable voice that rang through the room, he asked for someone to test the weight of the horseshoe. I stood up, took it in my hand, and almost dropped it. The man took it back and raised it high over his head. He announced that he was going to throw this horseshoe at his daughter's neck, but that it would land on her shoulders without even disturbing a single lock of her hair.

He returned to the stage, where he and the girl positioned themselves about twenty feet apart at opposite ends of the proscenium, he on the right, she on the left. The spotlight encased her as she took her time fastening heavy, protective pads to her shoulders. Then the spotlight moved to the man. Apparently weighed down by the horseshoe, he bent forward, and then, as casually as a child playing with a plastic hoop, he raised the horseshoe and shook it, testing its feel in his hand. Across the stage, the girl turned toward him, completely at ease, her head held high, her hands on her hips. She nodded that she was ready.

As additional spotlights lit the stage, a drum roll began, and the man lifted the horseshoe with his right hand, kissing the metal tenderly. He set his feet and swiveled his body to the left, bringing the horseshoe down below his waist. For a moment he stood still, then suddenly spun to the right, and the horseshoe shot from his hand.

The audience gasped, and the girl was smiling serenely, her eyes fixed on the man. The horseshoe seemed to land smoothly on her shoulders, yet her whole body shuddered under its impact. The clash of cymbals mingled with thunderous applause. The girl removed the horseshoe with difficulty and carried it to the man, who met her at the center of the stage. Again, he kissed the horseshoe; as the applause continued to grow, he embraced the girl.

I paid my bill and went backstage, where I caught the pair just as they were leaving. I introduced myself and told them how stunned I was by the perfection of their act. Not only did I plan to return to the club, I said, but I would pay them the equivalent of one week's nightclub salary for a private performance. They were taken aback, but accepted my invitation to discuss the proposal over supper.

At the restaurant, the man told me he had performed the act with his wife for twenty years. After her death, he said, his daughter had begun working with him. He had been doing the stunt for so long now that he barely needed to practice, and for the money I offered he would gladly perform for me on their day off. Jokingly, he asked if I would like to take his daughter's place as the target.

While the man and I talked, the girl remained silent. I turned toward her and asked if she objected to the arrangement. She shrugged, faintly annoyed, and answered that she didn't care if one or a hundred people watched the performance.

Saying he had to make a telephone call, her father left us, and I asked the girl what I had done to offend her. After some hesitation, she replied that like all spectators, I seemed to assume that her father did the hard part of the act: after all, I had offered him the money. But no one ever realized that without her, her father would never be able to perform. He'd never find another partner. I reminded her that, apparently, her mother had also been able to work with him. The girl looked away for a moment, and then replied that it had been easier for her mother because she had been born blind.

I told her that if she would consider breaking with her father and become my steady companion I would gladly see to it that she had money and a career on the stage if she wanted it.

Her expression changed completely. Since her mother's death, she said with vehemence, she was all her father had. He could not live without her. By suggesting she leave him, I proved how little I understood people.

Her father returned to the table considerably more jovial than before he left. He announced that he was ready to celebrate our deal, and, noting his flushed cheeks, I suspected that he had taken a couple of drinks during his absence.

I ordered a bottle of champagne, and as he drank he recalled the places where he had performed and the people who had come to see his act. His daughter scarcely touched the champagne, but each time her father downed a glass, her face betrayed deep concern. Toward me she remained cool and aloof. As the evening passed, I became intensely aware of how much she disliked me. She tolerated me only for her father's sake.

As we drank, her father told me that he had run away from home as a small boy and had never learned to read or write. All he had learned, he said, was to throw the horseshoe. Later his wife took care of him and their baby. Now his daughter ran the house, worked with booking agents, signed contracts and paid the bills. Without her to control his drinking, he said, he would be reduced to nothing.

Before we parted I gave the man some money as an advance for their private performance. He took the bills, exclaiming how happy he was with our arrangement, and told me where and when to meet them.

At the appointed time, I drove to their rented trailer on the outskirts of town. It was obvious the man had been drinking and his euphoria increased when I presented him with a case of whiskey. Hearing our voices, the girl stepped out of the trailer, hardly acknowledging me. She was visibly upset when her father opened one of the new bottles and drank directly from it, but said nothing.

When she went inside to make coffee, the man explained that it did not matter to him where or at what he threw the horseshoe. He could do it on a stage, he said, in a pit, in an open field. He disappeared into the trailer and came back with his great iron prop. He handed me the liquor bottle and told me to place it where I wished. I walked the length of the trailer, set the bottle down and came back to where he stood. He waited for a moment, as if gauging the distance between himself and the bottle, boasting that he could perform the stunt blindfolded. When I expressed doubt, he asked me for a handkerchief and, in a highly theatrical manner, told me to check it for holes. I took out my handkerchief, examined it and tied it securely over his eyes.

Blindfolded, he readied himself just as he had done on the nightclub stage. He spun and hurled the horseshoe as if it were light as a lasso. It flew high up, then made a perfect landing around the bottle. The man tore off the blindfold.

Shaking my head in astonishment, I went over and retrieved the horseshoe. The man laughed, took the horseshoe from me, pitched it high in the air and caught it as if it were a Frisbee.

His daughter brought coffee. While she and I sipped it from our cups, her father picked up the bottle and began drinking from it. A troubled look crossed the girl's face, but again she said nothing.

Now the man told the girl he wanted her to stand even farther away than the bottle had been. I protested that he had performed enough that day and that I would be glad to come back another time, but he insisted that no matter how drunk his body became, his hand would always guide the horseshoe where he wanted it to go.

He bet a month's wages that he could drink a whole bottle of whiskey and still throw the horseshoe without harming his daughter. I pleaded with him to postpone the performance. She was not afraid to be his target, he said, but he could see, he shouted, that I was afraid of losing the bet. He would never hurt his daughter. But if I wanted to talk her out of it, I could try, he said angrily.

When I saw him uncorking a second bottle of whiskey, I took the girl aside and said that the only reason I had arranged a private performance was to see her and persuade her to leave. Didn't she realize how terribly she was being exploited? Each time she walked onto a third-rate nightclub stage, I said, she was sacrificing herself to an old drunk who cared more about booze than he did about her safety.

It did not take much imagination, I continued, to tell what would happen if the horseshoe hit her. The ten-pound weight would pulverize every bone in her head. Or it would crush her eyes and nose, it would ram her chin and teeth into her throat. It could break her neck and, for the few moments she would live, her head would dangle like a yo-yo on a soft rope. As I spoke, she stopped attaching her shoulder padding; her face was flushed, her eyes full of rage. In a calm voice she answered that she preferred to be maimed for life by her father than be touched by me even once.

Walking defiantly away from the trailer, she went to the spot where the bottle stood and walked far beyond it. Just as her father finished draining the second bottle, she shouted that she was ready.

The man picked up the horseshoe. I felt my heart pounding, but gave him the signal to throw. He bent, as if weighed down by the horseshoe, then in a second, he straightened out and the horseshoe shot into the air. As I looked on, the weight seemed to slow down and hover in midair before landing with a thud squarely on the girl's shoulder pads.

She removed the horseshoe and went straight to her father, laying the horseshoe at his feet. She kissed his cheek, his neck and his hands, and he patted her gently on the back, as if restrained by my presence. When she had finished caressing him, I handed him the money. I was about to leave when the girl asked to talk to me. We walked away from her father.

"Why did you bring him the whiskey?" she asked.

"I wanted him to drink it."

"So you could see me crippled or killed?"

"Or so I could imagine it happening after I've gone."

"Why?"

I did not answer.

"Because you know you can never have me?" she asked.

"Perhaps."

She gazed at me as if she were acknowledging my presence for the first time. "Tell me," she asked, "are you a gambler?"

"This is a gambler's town."

"All right. Now, I will bet you. I'll bet you anything that you would never, never have the guts to be his target when he is as drunk as he is now."

"I'm not eager to die," I said.

"But you paid money to see me die. You're a killer. I'll tell you what: if you stand as the target right now, I'll put myself up as the stake."

"Yourself?"

"Yes. You can have me. Providing you're intact enough to collect your winnings."

"I accept."

She was surprised. "If I told him that you had come here to take me away, you wouldn't leave here alive," she said.

"Tell him whatever you want," I told her, "I'm ready for him."

The man lay on the grass staring at the sky, a half-empty glass beside his head.

"We've made another bet," she said to him. "This time he'll be the target." She pointed to me.

"What?" the man grunted.

"He will stand where I did," she announced.

"Have you ever been a target before?" he asked, getting up with difficulty.

"Many times," I said.

"Is that so?" he mused.

The girl fetched the shoulder pads and escorted me to the place where she had stood before. "You sweat a lot. Better take off your jacket," she remarked, laughing.

"I sweat when I'm frightened," I replied, removing

159

the jacket. As she fastened the leather pads on my shoulders, her hand brushed my chin and she pulled back quickly.

"It does not take much imagination," she mocked, "to know that if the horseshoe hits you it will pulverize every bone in your head, remember?"

The pads felt securely fastened. "I'll leave you now," she said. "But you must stand absolutely still. If you move while the shoe is in the air . . ."

"I know. A big yo-yo on a soft rope."

She nodded and left me alone. I remembered an execution I had witnessed during the war. The soldiers had escorted a young deserter into the barnyard and strapped him to a stake. Then they turned, marched away, turned back again and formed a line. The commanding officer took his position and raised his sabre. I heard the salvo and I saw the top of the prisoner's shaved skull sliced off above his thick eyebrows. Blood, chunks of brain and bone foamed out of what remained of his head. His body tottered, went limp like a deflated rubber toy and slid down the stake to the ground.

"Are you ready?" the girl shouted.

"I am," I shouted back. I closed my eyes. It was too late to run away, and I might never know if the man had intended to kill me, miss me or land the horseshoe on my shoulder pads. Because of a whim, my future lay in the hands of an old drunk. In the silence like the one in an air raid shelter before a bomb hits, I imagined the horseshoe gliding toward me, ready to strike me at any moment.

Suddenly, two iron hands gripped my shoulders with such force that my whole body shook. Hesitantly, I reached up to touch them and felt cold metal. I opened my eyes and saw the horseshoe resting on the pads that were soaked with sweat. I tried to control my trembling and removed the horseshoe before the girl came over to assist me.

"So you've survived," she said tonelessly.

"So far, yes. I am ready to collect my winnings."

"As you wish," she nodded.

We went back to the table. The man, who could barely walk by now, wanted to toast my courage with more whiskey. I told him that, instead of drinking, I wanted to take his daughter for a ride. He settled down with a full bottle, indifferent to what either of us did.

She accompanied me to the car without saying a word. We drove directly to my motel. On the way to my room, I ordered drinks to be brought up. After the waiter had left, she turned to me casually. "How do you plan to have me?" she asked. "Straight or kinky?"

She started to undress. When she was naked, she stood before me as cool and unconcerned as the first time I'd seen her on the nightclub stage. "Any particular place?" she asked.

I pulled back the blanket, and she climbed onto the bed, grabbing a pillow and propping herself against it.

"When?" she asked.

"Now," I said.

I took hold of her shoulders. They felt too delicate to have withstood the weight of the horseshoe. "Lie down," I ordered. She stretched out. "Anything else?" she asked. In the semidarkness of the room, I moved next to her, uncertain how to touch her. As she turned her head away to avoid my lips, her hands moved lightly behind my hips and her legs spread invitingly. I took it for a sign of desire, and my body responded.

I poised myself to ease inside her, but when I tried to enter her, she was closed tight. I moved her thighs farther apart, again attempting to push myself into her. She groaned, but remained closed. I wrapped my arms around her waist and pulled her tight against me. Still she did not open herself to me. I played with her to get her aroused, sucking her nipples, burying my face in her. Finally, I tried to enter her by sheer strength. She was unyielding.

"Are you finished?" she asked, drawing up her knees and pulling away from me.

"I don't understand," I said.

"It would take surgery to open me up," she said. "I've never wanted to have the operation."

"Why not?" I asked.

"Because of men like you," she answered. She got up and began to dress.

I reached for her. "Don't," she commanded sternly. "You wanted what you won, but you'll never win what you wanted." She finished dressing and was gone.

I remember an old bicycle wheel that I used to roll in front of me when I was a boy, guiding it with a short stick. I believed the wheel was animated by a powerful spirit. I ran behind it barefoot, urging it on, the soles of my feet hard as its rim. Whenever the wheel began to totter, my stick would whip it back to life and the wheel would suddenly leap forward, as if daring me to pursue it. Sometimes, like a horse abruptly tearing the reins from a rider's hands, the wheel would escape and surge far ahead of me, slowing down and speeding up at will.

Whenever I rested and the wheel lay still, I felt impatient and guilty. Its very shape demanded movement, and soon I would leap up and send it on its way again. In the early morning, I followed it across withered fields, toward the misty blur of the forest, through the gaunt skeletons of ancient birch trees. The life of my wheel was superior to the lives of men and beasts: a dog would chase it only to surrender to its indifference; a tattered-looking crow would swoop down to investigate the mystery of its speed and then flap off into the wilderness, croaking his defeat.

On the roads, we raced past mud-covered peasants, who trudged alongside their overloaded carts and slow, bony horses. I guided the wheel with my stick, lashing at it when it slowed down, making it skim over the empty fields and ditches like a stone over water. The wind whipped my face and chilled my fingers, but I felt nothing. I was conscious only of vaulting through space.

Walking through the city now, I am inspired by that same sense of vaulting. Whom shall I draw out of the anonymous crowd of faces surrounding me? I can enter their worlds unobserved and unchecked. Each person is a wheel to follow, and at any moment my manner, my language, my being, like the stick I used as a boy, will drive the wheel where I urge it to go.

As a result of the circumstances under which I left the Service, I cannot join any professional, social or political group. Yet, to live alone, depending on no one, and to keep up no lasting associations, is like living in a cell; and I have never lost my desire to be as free as I was as a child, almost flying, drawn on by my wheel.

Now, I have devised a new kind of wheel game, which provides the human associations my current life-style prohibits. Confronted with hundreds of anonymous faces, hundreds of human wheels, I choose one and let it take me where it will. I pick a life and enter it, unobserved: none of my pseudo-family members ever know how I gain access to their lives.

As soon as I arrived in the city after leaving the Service, I applied for part-time work in the few printing shops left in the city that still specialized in hand-engraved letterheads and invitations. Most of them had been in business so long that the founders had retired, leaving the firms to inexperienced or careless younger men. The plants were severely understaffed, and I was offered jobs at all the places to which I'd applied. I finally chose to work at the most respected of these establishments.

Since the plant was months behind in filling orders, my offer to work overtime was eagerly accepted. Shortly after the shop closed each night, I was left alone. I would spend hours looking through files stuffed with letterhead samples for individual, business and government stationery. I selected the pieces I could use for each of my other identities and took them home with me. I also collected invitations to weddings, bar mitzvahs, parties and diplomatic receptions, as well as business announcements, certificates, calling cards and medical prescription blanks.

Some of the documents I needed had to be specially designed and printed. I decided that this would be easiest to do at the shop farthest behind in filling orders. I chose a place with a reputation for bad management and went to see its owner. I told him I had taken a day job but needed more cash to pay debts. I would be willing to work nights for less than the minimum wage. He hired me immediately.

I had been at the shop about two weeks when I became aware that I was being followed by a man who seemed to be working alone. At first, I considered leaving the city, but then decided to eliminate the threat instead.

One evening, I arrived at the shop with the distinct feeling that he was going to close in. I let myself into the store, locked the doors and headed for the room equipped with the powerful quartz lights that are used in photochemical treatment of large plates. As the briefest exposure to quartz light results in permanent blindness, it was imperative for the shops' employees to wear special protective goggles and keep the door tightly sealed. I put on my goggles and sat in the darkened room near the light switch.

When I heard footsteps at the door, I faked a suppressed sneeze. I knew that everything depended on whether the man had noticed the danger sign posted outside the room.

The door opened. I turned on the switch and light tore through the room like an explosion. Protected by my goggles, I could see the man held a cocked gun. Then the light must have pierced his eyes. He howled, dropped his gun and covered his face with his hands.

The man was a fool. His dependence on a mechanical weapon made him ignore, and destroy, his natural weapons, his eyes. I, on the other hand, cultivate those self-protective devices. I hook my feet around the legs of chairs to prevent their being pulled out from under me. Entering a building, I always check to see if anyone is following me. In a theater, I sit down only after everyone is already seated, and I prefer to ride an elevator alone.

I am always amazed by how many people never learn to protect themselves, especially those who have much contact with the public, for instance, salespeople. As I walk through stores, I see saleswomen with legs misshapen by decades of standing on their feet, and salesmen clutching their backs when they bend down to pick out merchandise from a lower drawer. I look at their faded faces. I study their tired eyes and the permanent squint caused by years of exposure to fluorescent lighting, as they complacently take out and put back merchandise for the ten-thousandth time. Theirs is the resignation of people who know only how to endure. They are servants who never expect any reward or help from the people they serve.

I often single out an older salesperson who seems particularly in need of an anonymous benefactor. Once I entered the luggage department of a large store and described a certain kind of suitcase to a middle-aged saleswoman. She accompanied me from shelf to shelf, showing me every item. I finally settled on one of the largest and most expensive pieces, but decided that another color would be more attractive. The woman was not certain that they carried it, but asked me to wait while she went to the stockroom to check. She returned with the suitcase, commenting on my good fortune, because it was the only piece of its kind remaining. I examined it and told her it wasn't quite what I'd pictured.

I suddenly pretended to change my mind; instead of a suitcase, I said, I would consider a large attaché case. She patiently pushed aside all the suitcases I'd been looking at and escorted me to the attaché cases. I showed initial interest in two or three, but ended by complaining that none of them had the type of lock I was looking for. Once again, she went to the stockroom and brought back several cases, each with a different type of lock. I found a flaw in all of them.

Losing interest once more, I moved toward the shaving kits. They came in an even greater variety than the luggage, but she did not seem to mind my looking over as many of them as I wanted. After inspecting at least a dozen, I could not make up my mind if I really needed one. I reflected for a moment, then said I wanted to think it over before buying anything. Disappointed and obviously tired, she must have assumed I would never come back, but still she remained courteous and friendly.

A week later, I returned to the luggage department

and went over to her. She remembered me and asked if I could wait a moment until she finished with the customers she was helping. I said I would, resisting the advances of several other salespeople. When she was ready to assist me, I asked to see, one more time, everything I'd liked. I again appeared unable to decide and pretended to be on the verge of leaving.

I started across the floor, paused and went back to her. I said I had decided to buy the suitcase she had brought from the stockroom, as well as the attaché case with two combination locks. I told her I trusted her judgment, and that, if she claimed they were the best available, I would believe her. I paid in cash, and while my luggage was being wrapped I thanked her for her gracious service and asked for her name so I could recommend her to my friends. She was beaming as I said goodbye to her.

On the following day, using letterhead stationery from one of the country's better-known industrial conglomerates, I wrote to the president of the store where the woman was employed. I complimented his organization on its unusually courteous and efficient service, and cited the saleswoman as an outstanding example of the store's high caliber. In closing, I again praised the store and the saleswoman, saying that, if some of my executives were as good an advertisement for my company as she was for his store, I would be more than happy.

Many times I've worked my way into other lives through real estate firms, insurance or employment agencies, collection services, marketing research firms, publishing houses, newspaper or magazine offices. I pretend to be suffering from a nervous disorder that has gravely impaired my speech and left my limbs unsteady. I force on the manager a crudely typed card stating I am illiterate and impoverished, and am willing to clean offices at lunch time for a third of the standard rate. With a badly shaking hand, I point out a sentence which states that I do not mind being locked in the office when the staff is out to lunch or even overnight. The manager agrees to try me out. I do an excellent cleaning job, while perusing all the correspondence, memos and miscellaneous papers in the office.

Not long ago, I was cleaning a real estate office when I came across a letter of complaint from a tenant. The woman, who lived alone, demanded assistance in protecting herself from an alcoholic neighbor. She claimed that every night he pounded on her door yelling that her poodle's barking disturbed his sleep; actually he was trying to force her out of her apartment so a friend of his could move in.

The woman was so afraid of her neighbor that, whenever she had to walk the dog or take her garbage to the incinerator, she called a woman friend in the building to stand guard while she ran across the hall or to the elevator. Every morning, she sneaked out to go to the beauty shop where she worked only after making sure that her neighbor had left his apartment. Terrified that he would attack her in the corridor, she began leaving work early to get home before he did, and went out only late at night to walk her dog. She closed by saying that her neighbor was ruining her life.

I called the woman, introducing myself as a former acquaintance of the bully next door. I told her I had run into him at a bar, and, when he was drunk, he had mentioned her by name, swearing he would put an end to her poodle's whining by killing the animal. I said I knew that her neighbor appeared to be capable of violence and urged her to keep out of his way.

The woman assured me how much she appreciated

my saving her dog's life. She said she could not afford a lawyer and complained that the landlord refused to do anything to help her.

I next telephoned the man, whose name and number I had copied down from the woman's letter. I introduced myself as a friendly citizen who had struck up a casual acquaintance in the park with a middle-aged lady walking her poodle. I cautioned him that, without any encouragement from me, the woman had mentioned him by name and described him as an incurable degenerate who picked up male and female whores every night, got drunk, took drugs and then pounded on her door, though he was too cowardly to confront her during the day. I suggested that, if this woman continued to spread rumors about him, his reputation would suffer and her lurid stories might even get back to his employers. He thanked me profusely and said he would buy me a drink any time I was in the neighborhood.

A week later, I called the woman again. As soon as she recognized my voice, she burst into tears, telling me that the morning after I called, her neighbor had angrily accosted her in the corridor and made a horrible scene. Thanks to my warning, he had not gotten the chance to harm her dog. She said she was becoming unhinged by living next door to such a monster, and, thanks to my intercession, had decided to move for the sake of her sanity. She told me I was the only man who had ever assisted her so chivalrously, and invited me to dinner.

But perhaps the most successful forays I have made into other people's lives have depended on the mail system. I often notice full mail pouches lying open and unprotected near the drab green street mailboxes or in the lobbies of office buildings. Since there is no one guarding them, and no chains secure them to the boxes, anyone can reach in and snatch a bundle of mail or even make off with the whole bag. I look upon these mail pouches as grab bags full of fascinating secrets.

Recently I befriended an older mailman whom I accompanied on his rounds. During one lunch hour, as I sat next to him, I noticed the chain attached to the master mailbox key hanging out of his pocket. Pulling gently, I extracted the key, made an impression of it in the wax block I held hidden in my hand and replaced it without his knowing. Within a week, I had my own duplicate key.

One morning, wearing a mailman's uniform rented from a theatrical supply store, I casually strolled up to a mailbox, took an empty collection bag from the large pile accumulating underneath and walked away.

Now, every few weeks, I drive around the town in my uniform until I spot a mailbox that suits my purpose. I double-park my rented sedan next to it, then check the time of the next collection. If I see there are at least two hours until the pickup, I unlock the box, gather up the mail, throw it in the pouch and drive off with it.

After parking my car in the garage, I pack the bag inside a large suitcase that I keep in the trunk and lug it upstairs to my apartment.

Anxious to see what I have won, I immediately spread the haul on the floor. I weed out fourth-class mail, packages, sweepstakes and contest entries. First-class and air-mail letters are what primarily interest me.

I slit each envelope down the side fold, slide the letter out and read it carefully.

Many of the letters are like pages torn at random from novels: they reveal a lot, but never enough. I feel cheated and disappointed. Often I endow the writers with voices, with gestures and facial expressions.

When I finish reading, I slide the letter back into its envelope and reseal it with transparent tape. A day or two later, I drop all the letters into a mailbox, assured that, in this era of automatic letter openers and outrageous mail delays, no one will notice his envelopes have been tampered with.

If I come across a particularly interesting letter, or if I want to know more about the writer or the person to whom the letter was written, I simply copy it before remailing.

Until now, in every mail collection, I find at least one letter that might enrich someone's life with an offer of a job, money, love. Intercepting such letters excites me because I feel I have found a magic passport to another's life, as well as control over that life.

From one letter I learned that a naturalized American citizen had been arrested when the airliner on which he was traveling made an unscheduled stop in his native country. He had fled twenty-five years earlier with no intention of returning. Now, the local authorities had charged him with illegally crossing the border, and had imprisoned him.

The man's naturalized citizenship was not recognized by his captors, who considered him a fugitive and an enemy of the State. They would almost certainly sentence him to a long term. The more I read the letter, the more enraged I became.

The letter gave the man's name and local address. Pretending I was a housing official making a routine check of the premises, I visited the family at their crowded three-room apartment in a middle-income housing project.

Four children, ranging in age from five to nine, followed me around as I examined windows and door frames, walls and ceilings. The children introduced me to their cat and kept showing me their toys. I also talked to their bedridden grandmother, who was obviously very ill and spoke English with difficulty.

When I asked the woman about her husband, she began to tell her story. She said that her husband and three of his business associates had been sent abroad to attend a four-day international congress of specialists in their field.

The husband's colleagues had reported that, during the airplane's stopover, the passengers had been asked to show their passports, and then proceed to the airport's transit lounge. Moments after entering the lounge, her husband was accosted by two plainclothes agents, who asked him to follow them outside. When the man refused, claiming the transit lounge was international territory, one of them knocked him out. Then the agents dragged him from the lounge in front of the stunned passengers.

His wife showed me the letter she had received from the State Department in response to her plea that the U.S. government intervene on her husband's behalf. The State Department officially informed her that the question of original citizenship was a matter solely between her husband and the foreign government that claimed him, and politely regretted that the American government could not influence the other government or assist her husband in any way. Her husband's employer had also written to her, arguing that since the man had been aware of the danger inherent in his status before he made the trip, he alone was responsible.

During the two months her husband had been in prison, she had sought aid from the Red Cross, Amnesty International and even The International League for the Rights of Man. She had written petitions to members of American P.E.N. as well as to dozens of senators and congressmen. All had tried to help, but, since her husband was still awaiting trial, no American counsel was allowed to see him. He was permitted to receive letters but was prohibited from writing them. Recently, she learned that the State Prosecutor would probably bring additional charges against her husband, even though the initial accusation was already enough to earn him years of hard labor.

The wife told me that she had been born in this country and such things made no sense to her. Even though he had grown up elsewhere, her husband had been forced to serve in the military and to pay taxes in the United States. It was absurd that he should now be claimed by a country he had not seen or wished to see for twenty-five years.

She had become the sole support of her family, working for a brokerage firm during the day and moonlighting as a cashier in a twenty-four-hour delicatessen. She cried when she told me that she had been forced to keep her oldest child at home to look after the younger children and the ailing mother-in-law. I told her not to lose hope, and promised to talk to a relative of mine who specialized in international law.

During the next few days, I hung around the consulate, the UN mission and the tourist bureau of the country that had imprisoned her husband. I began following the country's diplomats and their wives, checking the buildings where they lived and the garages that serviced their cars. I bribed several of the employees of the real estate offices that managed the properties the diplomats owned and rented, and several of them gave me useful information. I even became friendly with a nurse in the office of the doctor who treated the UN ambassador and managed to get acquainted with his wife's hairdresser.

Finally, I went to the UN mission, presenting myself as an investor who wished to discuss with the ambassador a matter relating to real estate. When I was ushered into his chambers, he greeted me cordially, and asked me to sit down. I did; then I mentioned that I had come to plead for the release of the arrested man. He immediately attempted to terminate our meeting. Getting up to leave I asked if the custom-made sports car parked outside belonged to him.

"It does," he said curtly.

"It's most impressive. It must be the only one of its kind in the city."

"Possibly."

"By the strangest coincidence, I have become familiar with the unusual terms by which Your Excellency acquired it. I also learned that when recently your government sold one of its consulate town houses here, the actual price was substantially higher than the figure recorded in the bill of sale. I believe the local realtor paid the difference to Your Excellency in cash . . ."

Ignoring my remark, the ambassador asked me to sit down. I obeyed. He asked coolly, "What is your connection with this arrested nomad?"

"My connection is his imprisonment," I answered.

The ambassador grew impatient. "Come now, we're practical men. Who sent you?"

"No one," I replied. "I came on my own."

"I don't believe you. Still and all, what do you want?" he asked.

"I would like you to suggest to your government that the man be freed and returned to his family within two weeks. I would also like you to assure me that he will be compensated for his time and treatment in prison. You can blame his abduction on a bureaucratic slip-up."

The ambassador picked up a paperweight and passed it from his right hand to his left, then put it back on the desk. "Nonsense. There was no slip-up. According to the penal code of my country . . ."

"Your country's penal code does not apply in the free transit lounge of an international airport," I interrupted. "The man was kidnapped."

"Rubbish," he interjected. "Rubbish. Your own government not only refused to grant political asylum to a foreign sailor, but returned him to his own country for trial. And you talk about 'free' transit lounges. Are you mad?"

I did not reply. He looked at me intently, then said in a firm but friendly voice, "Tell me who paid you to investigate my private life, and I promise to have that man released."

"I could tell you that it was one of our newspapers looking to discredit your government and you would believe that. I could tell you that I am employed by a personal enemy of yours at the Foreign Ministry of your country. You would believe that, too. But you will not believe me when I tell you I am alone. Why?"

The ambassador smiled, took my arm and led me politely to the door. "I don't believe you because no man acts alone," he said, "and it's precisely because I don't believe you that I'll give my word that your man will be home in two weeks. You know, I could have you charged with extortion," he added lightly, his hand resting on the gleaming doorknob. He opened the door for me.

I called the abducted man's home two weeks later. When his wife answered, I told her I was the housing official calling to inquire if my relative had been of any help in solving her problems. She told me ecstatically that her husband had returned home, and had been with his family for almost a week. She was more grateful for my help than she could ever show. She said that, just as her husband was being brought to trial, the charges against him were abruptly dropped and his arrest proclaimed a bureaucratic mistake. He was even paid damages for his time in jail and provided with free transportation back to the States. He was resting now, she told me, but she would be glad to wake him if I wanted to speak with him. I told her not to disturb him, joking that I wake up only those who do not deserve their rest.

Whether I am looking for a new acquaintance or merely trying to get to know an old one better, I like to familiarize myself with his or her professional life. In one instance, my search for a new adventure took me to the offices of a large publishing house. When I began my explorations, I didn't know anyone who worked there, but the books and authors the company published intrigued me. For the first few days, I got out of the elevator on a floor without a receptionist, then took the interdepartmental stairs to an editorial floor.

Behaving as if I were a new employee trying to learn his way around, I would take off my jacket and hang it either behind the door of an unused office or in a hall closet among umbrellas, sweaters, a shabby raincoat and a few old jackets that must have been forgotten long before. I would roll up my shirt sleeves and loosen my tie, pick up a sheaf of papers, talk with the secretaries and sit in empty cubicles, where I leafed through papers and stationery in desk drawers. Or I simply stood in a passageway as if waiting for someone, occasionally taking a catalogue or a book off a shelf and appearing to browse through it. I would enter a reference room, take a seat at a table and peruse various dictionaries and directories, chatting with the editorial assistants who frequented the room.

After I had become familiar to the staff, I would leave a floor at lunch time through the main entrance, making sure to attract the attention of the receptionist. I always joked about my arriving at the office earlier than she did and complimented her on a new dress or hairdo. Soon, we even began to gossip about other employees. I usually returned for an afternoon tour, again chatting with the receptionist as I passed through the entrance area. Then, I headed for the stairs and proceeded to other floors. I would leave the office only after most of the editorial staff had gone home. On my way out, I used to stop on the ground floor to say a few words to the night guard. I never failed to mention to him that, once again, I had worked longer hours than anyone else in the building.

After a few days of reconnoitering, I knew the location of every office in which high-level decisions were made, as well as the names and functions of those in charge. I also came to know in whose files the most interesting information was kept and if anyone had ever stopped me to ask what I was doing there, I could have provided him with a detailed explanation.

Now that I had laid the groundwork, I began to leave the office early in the afternoon, still making sure to say goodbye to the receptionist. I would return just before the end of the day, carrying an attaché case, and wait in a vacant office until most of the staff had gone home. Once the halls were empty, I opened the case and took out a pair of overalls like the ones worn by the cleaning crew. They fitted over my suit, zipped up the front and could be slipped on in seconds. When I had changed, I pushed the attaché case under a desk and began to move freely through the building. Because a number of editors were accustomed to working late, I could turn on office lights without attracting attention.

I made a daily check of the materials that the editors left on top of their desks, noting the pertinent points of unsigned letters, project proposals, manuscripts and correspondence files. In order to follow up some of them, I occasionally had to pick the lock of a drawer, file or cabinet. Only a few were locked. In addition to the business correspondence of the editors, I came across their personal mail, bank statements and address books, and photographs of families and friends.

One night, after turning on the lights in an office I had recently been investigating, I saw a man asleep on the sofa. It was too late to turn off the switch. The light had already awakened him. Jumping up from the sofa, he began screaming for me to go away. I decided to challenge him and explained that I had come to clean the floors and was paid to do my work just as he was to do his. He told me brusquely to get out of his office; I refused to budge, insisting that the floor had to be done that night and that he would have to move to another office until I was finished.

Growing taut with anger, he swore he would report me to the building management first thing in the morning unless I left immediately. I stood my ground. His eyes darted back and forth across his desk, searching for an instrument with which he could force me away. Suddenly, in desperation, he picked up a paper coffee cup and dashed the contents in my face. For a moment, I stood absolutely still; then, as I began to wipe the coffee off my face, I asked, "You're Richard Lasker, aren't you? Didn't you write *Great Naval Battles?*"

He looked at me, unsure how to respond. "Well, I collected the essays. Yes. How did you know?"

I pointed to the copy on his desk. "Last time I cleaned your room, I saw your picture on the back of this book."

"So what?" he asked.

"So you would know if a ship's gun can fire when it's turned on the ship itself."

"It can't. It would be blocked by the firing cut-out cam."

"The what?" I said. "Cut-out cam," he repeated. Then he went on, "What is this? A test? Get the hell out of my office." He began to move toward me belligerently.

"My friend," I said, motioning him to stop where he was, "you may have proved yourself wrong. You may have broken the cut-out cam and turned the gun on yourself." I flashed him a smile and turned off the lights on my way out.

I returned to his office the next night to search for information about him. Trying to think where to begin, I recalled that Lasker's latest best-selling author was Anthony Duncan. Duncan was an espionage writer who had become world-famous several weeks earlier when he had been arrested and held incommunicado after legally entering East Germany.

According to news reports, Jessica Whitehead, Duncan's constant companion, had accompanied him to the train station in Copenhagen and taken his photograph as he boarded the train for Peenemunde, East Germany, where he was going to do research on his next novel. Originally, Jessica had planned to accompany him, but, at the last minute, Duncan hinted there might be trouble with the East German police and insisted that she stay in Copenhagen. He had promised to call her in three days, but when a week passed with no word from him, she became worried and contacted government authorities.

Since Lasker was the editor of all Duncan's novels, he was quoted frequently in the press, voicing his concern for Duncan's welfare because he was both his business associate and a personal friend. He promoted the theory that the East Germans had detained Duncan because of the novelist's extraordinary ability to find top-level security leaks, of which he made liberal use in his fiction. Yet East Germany staunchly denied that Duncan had crossed the border and all U.S. attempts at locating him had failed.

I pulled out Duncan's file, sat down and began to work. I leafed through all the major news articles written about Duncan's disappearance, many illustrated by Jessica Whitehead's last photo of him. Duncan was around forty and handsome in a blond, beefy way. Smiling broadly, he posed on the steps of the railroad car wearing a tweed jacket and an open trenchcoat, dark glasses in one hand, typewriter case in the other.

As I read on, I learned that of Duncan's four novels only his first had become a big best seller in both hardcover and paperback. It had also been made into an enormously successful film. His second novel had been a best seller, but not nearly as successful as the first. The third sold rather poorly. Now Duncan's disappearance was generating new interest in both the man and his fiction. In the weeks after I began my investigation, I saw Jessica Whitehead and Lasker on television many times. Duncan's latest book jumped to the top of the best-seller lists, and hefty paperback rights were negotiated for the new best seller as well as the previous failure. Film and television rights to the new book had been bought outright by a major studio, which also took a six-figure option on the still uncompleted Peenemunde novel.

I returned to Lasker's office many times, always

careful to check it before entering. On three or four occasions, I observed Lasker sitting at his desk in the middle of the night.

Once, as I was rifling through a desk drawer, I saw a photocopied statement of long-distance calls billed to Lasker's extensions. As I scanned it, I noted that, in the week following Duncan's disappearance, the editor had placed several calls to Copenhagen. I traced the calls and found out that they were made to Jessica Whitehead and to the U.S. Embassy. The calls lasted from ten to twenty-five minutes apiece. I also noticed three collect calls from Denmark, all after Jessica Whitehead's return to New York. Each call had been placed on a different day and had lasted only three to five minutes. I copied down the number of the telephone statement, put the bills back where I had found them and went home.

Early the next morning, I called the international operator. Pretending that I worked for the publishing company and had been assigned to verify a few overseas charges that someone was questioning, I asked her if she could identify the number from which the collect calls had been made and the times at which they were received. She said it would take a few hours and I told her I would call her back. When I phoned her, she reported that the calls had been made from an inn in a Danish town near Cape Skagen and had been received after midnight, New York time. I had never heard of the Danish town and went to check it in an atlas. It was an obscure fishing village on the northernmost coast. I then placed a call to the inn. When a man answered, I introduced myself as the editor of an American travel magazine.

He told me in broken English that he was the owner of the inn and suggested I speak to his daughter, whose English was good. She understood perfectly when I told her that my magazine was doing a feature story on cold-water fishing in Scandinavia. A colleague had highly recommended both the town and the inn, and I was considering sending a reporter and photographer there. She was delighted.

I also mentioned that a friend of my colleague had been planning to visit the town about now and asked if any English or American guests were registered in her inn. She told me there was a Mr. Arthur Duffy, an engineer from Dublin. I said that was not the name I was after, but thanked her anyway and told her she would be hearing from me soon.

I called the inn again when it was midnight there. The phone rang six or seven times; the man answered. Imitating Lasker's voice, I asked for Mr. Arthur Duffy of Dublin. The man muttered that I would have to wait because Duffy was asleep.

Finally, another voice, thick with sleep, came on the line with a guarded "Hello."

"Tony," I began, stopped abruptly, then began again. "Hello, Duffy!"

He paused for a second and then exclaimed, "Dick! For Christ's sake, what are you doing?" His voice had lost its sleepiness and had lowered to a nervous whisper. "Jesus Christ!" he muttered. Then, in a milder voice, he apologized, "I'm sorry, Dick. I wasn't expecting you to call. Well, never mind. What's up?"

"Our firing cut-out cam is broken," I said.

"What the . . . ? Dick, are you tanked? Is this your idea of a joke? What do you mean, 'the cut-out cam is broken'?"

"I'm sorry, Duffy," I said in my own voice. "This isn't Dick."

There was a dead silence on the other end of the line. Then, in a voice drained of all expression, he asked, "Who are you?"

"Let's say I'm a protagonist from someone else's novel."

"A what? Look, I don't know you. There's been some kind of mix-up on the line. Call the operator and get it straightened out. I'm going back to bed."

I paused for a second before saying, "Duncan, I have an urgent message for you from Lasker. Now be quiet and pay attention. Under no circumstances must you call, write or cable Dick or anyone else. Get on the earliest available train and go directly to one of the villages near Krusaa on the German border. Once you arrive, register as Arthur Duffy in any of the following inns and wait for our message."

"Just a second," he said. "Let me get a pencil. Okay, fire away!"

I dictated a list of border towns and their hotels, and he repeated them back to me.

"That's it," I said. "Stay well, Tony, and let us do the worrying."

"Us?"

"Dick and me."

"Anyone else?"

"Not if you do as advised. All right?"

"All right. One more thing . . ." he continued haltingly.

"Yes?"

"How is Dick?"

"Oh, he's fine."

"And the others?"

"Fine. Jessica looked great on television. You should have seen her."

"Did the reprint contract go through?"

"Yes. Without a hitch."

"What about the movie sales?"

"Concluded yesterday. You're a rich man, Tony," I said and hung up.

Next day, I called the inn again and asked for Arthur Duffy. I was told he had departed without leaving a forwarding address.

I called Lasker's secretary and asked for an appointment. I said I was sent by Mr. Lasker's friend and gave her the name of a writer residing in Rome whose file I had come across in Lasker's office. She asked me to hold and then put Lasker on the line. His manner was genial and relaxed and he asked me to come and see him after lunch, around four in the afternoon.

I was escorted into his office. He rose to greet me, closed the office door behind him and made sure I was comfortably seated before sitting down himself. I watched him stare at me from across the desk.

"You're wondering where we've met before," I said.

"Well, yes, I am," he admitted.

"We met right here," I said. He was puzzled but not convinced. "One night I came to clean your floors. We talked about *Great Naval Battles*, remember?" I smiled.

"What . . . ?" He sat forward.

"That night you were waiting in your office for a phone call from a certain Arthur Duffy."

"I don't know anyone named Arthur Duffy."

"You're Anthony Duncan's editor, aren't you?"

"What has Anthony Duncan got to do with Arthur Duffy?" He betrayed a hint of anxiety.

"Arthur Duffy is an Anthony Duncan invention," I announced, "as you ought to know from your recent conversations with him."

"Recent conversations? Duncan has been incommunicado for weeks."

"I talked to him the day before yesterday," I said. "He wasn't in East Germany at all. He was in Asaa, a Danish fishing village near Cape Skagen. If you are not interested, I'll be glad to take my story elsewhere."

I started to rise but he motioned me to stay seated. "All right," he said wearily. "What do you want to know?"

"Is the girl friend in on this?"

"No. Jessica doesn't know anything about it. Tony was adamant that she be kept out of it. If he hadn't been paranoid about his new book, he never would have devised this crazy scheme."

"How is he going to explain his disappearance?"

Lasker fidgeted in his chair. "He'll claim that on the train to Germany he changed his mind and took off for the north of Denmark to do some other research. A lot of his book is set in Denmark; that's why he and Jessica were living in Copenhagen."

"And the next chapter?"

"He'll say he tried to reach Jessica in Copenhagen after the first week but no one answered the phone so he figured she'd gotten bored and gone off to see some friends of theirs in Paris."

"His phoney name?"

"Simple. He wanted to be left completely alone to work."

"Why did you go along with this?" I asked him.

He hesitated. "At first, I thought his disappearance was genuine. Then, one morning, I found a telephone message on my desk that somebody had scribbled late the night before. All it said was that Arthur Duffy called from Europe and would call back that night at twelve-thirty. I'd never heard of Arthur Duffy but I had a feeling this had to do with Tony, so I waited for the call. You appeared about fifteen minutes before it was due and almost scared me to death. When the call actually came, I damned near had a heart attack. I told him to get his ass back here on the double but he refused."

"When do you think he'll resurface?"

Lasker's eyes shot to the wall calendar. "He's supposed to get in touch with me within the week."

"What if he doesn't?"

"He will," he said with a weary smile. "And anyway, I know where to reach him."

"No, you don't. Not anymore," I told him. "Now I'm in charge of the plot. It's my novel."

He began to grow agitated, raising his hand to his forehead as though testing for fever. "What do you mean? Has something happened to Tony?"

"Don't concern yourself with fact. Stick to fiction. Remember, your cut-out cam is broken."

All of a sudden, he seemed to give up. "What do you want me to do?"

"As soon as I leave, telephone Jessica and tell her you've heard from Duncan and that he's fine. Next, call a press conference and tell the truth."

He thought it over. "No," he said at last. "I can't make that decision for him. I edit his books, not his life."

I rose, preparing to go. "Duncan might never surface again. Remember the cut-out cam!" I said. Lasker got up, went over to the window and stared at the skyline. I opened the door and left the office.

The next day at noon, I turned on the TV and saw Jessica Whitehead and Richard Lasker being interviewed by reporters. They both beamed as they announced that Duncan had called Lasker from a village in Denmark and was shocked to hear the disappearance story. He was still in the village finishing up his work but would be flying back to New York in a week or two.

Around eleven-thirty that night, as I was preparing to leave for Lasker's office, a special bulletin flashed on the news. Anthony Duncan had been found dead on the Danish side of the Danish-German border.

The writer's body had been discovered behind the wheel of a rented car and the local coroner had established that death was due to carbon monoxide poisoning. The car had been parked at the edge of some woods a quarter of a mile off a highway near the township of Krusaa, and the Danish police theorized that Duncan had pulled off the road to sleep but had kept the engine running for warmth. A leak had infused the sealed car with lethal fumes. Although Duncan was alone in the vehicle when his body was discovered, the ashtray was filled with lipstick-smeared cigarette butts, from which the police concluded that Duncan had been traveling with an unidentified woman.

Often I invite the unpredictable simply by being in the right place at the right time. When I am restless at night, I take a taxi to a deserted section of the city. Once the taxi drives off, I wander through the dark, unfamiliar streets alone, armed only with a small leather case. Inside is a tape recorder designed to look exactly like the walkie-talkies used by police and other enforcement agencies. I can activate prerecorded messages inconspicuously by pressing one of the bolts on the bag's handle.

As I walked a short path between the piers one night, I noticed a limousine with its lights off, parked close to the wall of an abandoned warehouse. I moved closer to it, expecting to hear the sound of an engine, but the car seemed empty.

I was just about to take out a flashlight and examine the license plate when the interior lit up. Both of the car's left-hand doors opened simultaneously and I faced two men, one in the driver's seat, the other directly behind him. They remained in the car, pointing their guns at me. Two other men peered at me from inside the car. I pressed a button under the bag's handle and a long antenna sprang out. "Hey, you, come here," commanded the man behind the driver. The click of his gun signaled that it was ready to fire. The light from inside the car shone on his dark hair and on the short barrel of the gun. I hoped he would notice the antenna before he pressed the trigger. As I moved toward him, very slowly, my steps echoing in the silence, I kept my finger on the bolt of the bag's handle.

The man beside the driver handed him a flashlight, which he shone on me. At that moment, I realized I had not checked the recorder's batteries or the tape before going out. If my gimmick failed, he would kill me.

The man motioned to me with his gun. "Hey, man, come over here. What's that you're carrying? Drop it!"

I pressed the bolt. The device in my bag beeped twice, and a loud message blasted into the night as if it were being transmitted from somewhere nearby. "Three-zero-four, three-zero-four. We have your position. Moving from both sides. Over."

The gunman at the wheel slammed the front door and instantly turned the ignition. The man behind him sat back in his seat with his gun still pointing at me. Only as the car screeched forward did the gunman slam the other door shut. In a second, the car was gone. My eyes, which had been blinded by the glare of the flashlight, began to readjust to the darkness. I lowered the antenna and rewound the tape, feeling as satisfied as if I had physically beaten each of my assailants.

When I was eighteen, I took my final exams early and moved to the ski resort in mid-December. Having accepted the fact that I would never be good enough for slalom or downhill racing, I decided to perfect a ski stunt in which I could exhibit an equal amount of skill and courage. At the height of the season, the lines of skiers waiting to go up in the cable cars were so long that they extended around the corner of the cable car station to an area at the base of the main run. So as they waited, the crowds that lined up around the terminal could watch other skiers speeding down the last leg of the run. The best skiers, aware of their captive audience, would take the steep last section at full speed, then make an abrupt, well-executed stop.

There was a flight of twelve steep steps on the side wall of the station. Around the corner from the top stair, and at a level slightly higher, there was a balcony about the size of a station wagon attached to the front of the terminal, almost two floors above the ground. Because it lacked a railing and was encrusted with ice and snow, this balcony was never used in winter.

My stunt would consist of skiing straight down the slope, approaching the station at great speed, jumping over the entire staircase and stopping dead center on the balcony. As I began the run toward the steps, the people waiting below would think I had lost control and was about to fall down onto them. I could imagine the crowd scattering with fear, but I would land on the balcony, side-slip, stop in an upright position and calm them with a nod.

To do the stunt without crashing into the staircase or sliding off the balcony would require painstaking practice, for if I failed, I could be crippled or killed. I designed a very strict regimen. I stopped skiing early in the afternoon, ate dinner long before dusk and was in bed by six.

After midnight, when the slopes were deserted and the other skiers were either carousing or asleep, I would get up, dress, pack up my ski gear and call a taxi. The drivers would always explain that the lift was closed, and I would answer that night-skiing was my passion and that I enjoyed climbing up the slope in the dark. Once at the station, I would walk only the few hundred yards to the last leg of the run. The cab drivers never waited for me and I would have to walk back to the lodge after practice.

I taped one flashlight to the balcony, another to the stairs and a third to my chest. During the first week, I practiced skiing downhill and jumping parallel to the staircase until I could gauge the thrust needed to lift my body over the steep steps to the balcony. The second week, I took off the skis and practiced leaping from the top step onto the balcony itself to develop the speed and balance necessary for turning and stopping.

After weeks of intensive practice, I could successfully jump onto the balcony, but I still had to take care that my lateral momentum created enough friction to stop me from crashing into the wall or flipping off the balcony. To prevent injury, I rigged a net from the balcony's outer edge to the roof overhanging it. If I misjudged, I ended up with my skis entangled in the net, irritated by my failure but unharmed.

Even when I jumped as many as twenty times a night, the risks did not seem to decrease. The physical strain began to show. My friends complained that they hadn't seen me at the nightclubs for a month and commented on how thin I had become. Some of them suspected a secret vice was sapping my strength. One claimed I had lost my mind because, driving home from a midnight poker game, he had seen me walking alone in full skiing gear with skis and poles slung over my shoulder. I denied both vice and night wandering but offered no other explanation.

Despite my practice, the net was still saving me at

least twice a night. My body was bruised from the punishment it had taken, and I had twisted my ankle when my skis caught between two steps. Still I persevered until, at the end of the second month, I was satisfied with my performance.

My debut would be made on Sunday, when hundreds of skiers were lined up below the balcony to wait for the cable car. Both exhilarated and apprehensive, I took the car up early Sunday morning and at the highest station ordered a breakfast I couldn't eat. My hands shook, my mouth was dry and I could not stop my nervous cough. For a moment, I felt that the adulation I anticipated would not compensate for the danger, but that moment passed. If the largest possible crowd was to witness my performance, I had to begin immediately. I put on my skis with shaking hands and started carefully down the slope.

In forty minutes, I sighted the cable car terminal below me. Slightly out of breath, I paused before the final stretch and checked my skis and bindings. My breathing grew more regular and my heartbeat steadier. Letting go, I took off straight at the staircase. It looked steeper and shorter in the daylight, and, as I sped toward it, I could envision it spattered with my blood.

People crowding the run screamed when, with one motion, I brought my skis together, leaped, cleared the stairs and reached the balcony with a loud thud. Even before I touched down, I had known that my angle was correct and my body ready for the landing. I came to a perfect halt an inch or so from the edge of the balcony.

I unfastened my skis, entered the station through the balcony door, walked down the inside steps and out to the cable car line. As I emerged, the crowd applauded. I took my place in line and accepted the admiration modestly. I made five jumps the first day.

After my debut, when I walked down the main street, I noticed people pointing me out to their friends and waving to me as I passed. Several of them came over to ask my opinion on the best skiing equipment and training programs.

I lived from jump to jump. At the cable car station, I talked with skiers who had seen the stunt before and now treated me as an old friend, wishing me well on the next attempt. Their awe elated me but did not dissipate the terror I felt at the top of the run. After a few weeks, I became aware of the animosity of the local ski instructors. By now all of them had seen or heard of my jumps, but they knew I was merely an average skier who excelled only at a single ingenious stunt. Whenever they could, they embarrassed me in front of tourists by challenging me to compete on the slopes, not on the balcony.

Late one afternoon, I was sitting with a few friends in the summit restaurant. Several local skiers came toward me. One of them, a tall, strong garage mechanic, made certain that everyone heard him bet me a week's salary that he could beat me on the resort's toughest run.

I agreed that he could win because I was just not as good a skier as he was. In response, he charged I was a coward whose successful balcony jumps were sheer luck. His friends added their taunts to his, calling me a big city show-off interested only in tricks. I admitted that I enjoyed showing off but denied being a coward, implying that jumping the staircase was far more dangerous than the resort's toughest run.

Among the other diners, I noticed a girl probably in her early twenties, quietly watching me take on the locals. She sat alone, in a stiff, formal pose, unsmiling and silent. When I saw her staring, I announced that

I was willing to bet the equivalent of the mechanic's weekly salary that none of the local skiers could successfully perform my stunt, adding that I would jump as many times as challenged.

The mechanic accepted at once, followed by four of his companions. We went to a corner table to arrange the terms of the competition. I took a seat against the wall to keep my eye on the girl. A local ski instructor had offered to serve as referee. It was decided that the challengers and I would jump one after the other, and that I would pay each of them as he succeeded. We agreed that, regardless of the weather, we would jump the next day, after the last cable car had descended and the area was clear of other skiers. As their judge, the locals proposed the owner of a hardware shop, who was well known as the inventor of a new ski binding. While the girl watched, I solemnly nodded and shook my challengers' hands. I proposed my own judge: the girl.

When my challengers turned to stare at her, I walked over to explain what I was asking her to do. She introduced herself, mechanically reciting her name and address in the resort as if anticipating I would ask. After the challengers left, I thanked her and invited her to dine with me, but she said she had made other arrangements, and walked away.

That night, I sat in my room, staring at a tiny icicle hanging from the window frame. I had now made over two hundred jumps, but success had not increased my confidence. I was well aware that I could be tipped over by the smallest incident—a sneeze, a sudden hesitation, a momentary swirl of snow, the accidental release of a binding. I checked and rechecked my boots, skis, bindings, even my clothes and goggles. Then I locked the door, pulled down the shade, undressed and closed my eyes.

I thought about the girl who was my judge. I knew which chalet she stayed in; by cutting across the fields I could reach it in twenty minutes. I dressed and walked out. The frosty air speeded my movement and, as I walked, the powdery snow went over the tops of my boots, melting down into my socks.

The downstairs window was lit in the chalet. I pulled on a skiing mask that left my eyes and mouth uncovered, then I looked in and saw the girl. She sat alone at the large table reading an illustrated magazine. Four breakfast places were already set on the table. I felt an impulse to knock on the window, to startle her with my mask. The girl would ask what I wanted and I would admit I was frightened of my jump. I would also tell her that I had proposed the bet to the local skiers merely because I wanted to attract her attention.

I tapped the window gently. The girl raised her head and, uncertain, glanced in my direction. I ducked down. When I looked in again, she was absorbed in her reading. I thought of knocking at the window once more but I did not. Suddenly the drama of my jump seemed more immediate than the possibility of a relationship with the girl. I walked away.

Back in my room, I decided to forget about the contest; having accepted the challenge, it was out of my control. I went to sleep. I awoke later than I had planned, though still in time for the competition. The taxi driver recognized me as the night-skier, but seemed indifferent when I told him I was no longer skiing alone in the dark.

My opponents and our two judges had already gathered at the station. As I shook hands with the girl, I saw that her eyes were as unresponsive as ever. The challengers and I drew matches to determine the order of our jumps. One of the skiers drew first jump and was driven up the slope in a snowmobile. At the starting point he got off, positioned his goggles and waited for the signal. When the judges raised their hands, he started down the run with a confidence that initially misled me, but as soon as he had gained speed, I realized that by unfolding his body too soon, he was aiming too high. He landed near the outer edge of the balcony and slid off as smoothly as if he had planned to.

We heard his skis splinter as he fell. When he tried to get up but failed, two of his fellow challengers ran to him and carried him to a friend's car, which immediately took off for town. In an unemotional tone, I asked the remaining challengers if they wanted to yield. They exchanged glances, and took a vote. Their decision was to continue, but it was not unanimous, and the one skier who disagreed was pale and uneasy.

I was second jumper; I put on my skis but left off my parka, so that I'd have as much freedom as possible. Instead of riding the snowmobile, I asked to be towed behind it up the run, hoping to loosen up and generate some warmth before making the leap. From the top, the staircase and the balcony looked absurdly small.

At the judges' signal, I took off, my skis vibrating on the well-packed snow. Just before I aimed at the staircase, I glanced at the girl. She was looking at the balcony, not at me, as if only the moment of impact mattered. Countering a sudden tension, I pitched myself over the staircase, my feet underneath my hips, my hands dropping down, my body automatically flexing to the side. With my chest bent over my knees, my skis touched down on the balcony, then rasped along its icy surface. In a moment, I stopped. I took the skis off and calmly returned to my place. The girl's eyes were still fixed on the balcony.

The next skier was halfway up the run in the snow-mobile before I realized that it was the mechanic who had challenged me initially. When he took off, I did not want to watch him, yet I could not shut out the sound of his skis rattling on the snow. After a moment, I heard the crash, followed by a scream. Everyone watching raced toward the stairs. From a distance I saw the mechanic fall; his head smashed against the edge of the balcony, his skis lodged between the top two steps. He was unconscious. His companions lifted him gently and put him into a car, which slowly made its way down the road.

The girl and the other judge told me they had decided to end the jumps but that I would be paid what I had won. When I asked if the girl would walk back to the town with me, she looked at me coldly and refused.

For the last few years, I have frequented a bar in the theater district. Its barman is a retired police officer, and his bar is a quiet place without much late-night business. I often drop by twice the same evening and, while I sip my drink, I chat with the barman. He seems to enjoy my stories and I leave a big tip.

Whenever I assume a new disguise, I always test it on him. On one such occasion, I came in earlier than usual, disguised as a laborer. There were five or six men sitting at the bar and a few couples at tables in the rear. The barman came over but did not recognize me. I ordered a drink. When he brought it, I insisted the glass was dirty. He glared at me but took it back, spilled the contents into the sink, made a point of washing the glass and poured a fresh drink. As he pushed it toward me, I knocked it over with my elbow. Loudly blaming him for the accident, I demanded another replacement. After he ignored my request, I made fun of the photographs of him in his police uniform and insulted his medals and insignia, which hung on the wall above the bar.

Trying to contain his rage, he suggested I leave. I replied that, until I was served the drink I had ordered, I would not go. He came out from behind the bar, and hissed that if I wouldn't leave on my own he would be glad to help me.

I challenged him to do it. Prompted by the other customers, he grabbed me by the shoulders, dragged me to the door and propelled me onto the sidewalk. I hailed a taxi and went to my apartment. Three-quarters of an hour later I was back, this time without the disguise. The barman was pleased to see me and said he needed me to cheer him up because he'd just had a bad time with a customer. He insisted I have a drink on the house, and I amused him and the other patrons with a few anecdotes as I drank. When I finished, I tipped him heavily, bade them all good night and left.

I returned to the apartment and donned a second disguise. In half an hour, I was inside the bar again. It was late, and there were only four customers left. Once more, the barman did not know me. In a deep Southern accent, I ordered an imported beer. He told me he did not carry it, and I started swearing. Soon, he was fuming and gesturing toward the door.

On my way out, I heard him explaining to a customer who had witnessed the previous incident that this was the first time in his fifteen years behind the bar that he had had trouble twice in one night from perfect strangers. He blamed it on the fact that so many weirdos were coming to the city now to get drugs.

About that same time, I began to review the photos

I have always kept of myself. There are snapshots of me with my parents, with the university ski team, with my army unit and with friends.

And there are shots of myself making love to various women. These photos were taken by cameras equipped with a delayed action mechanism. When I think about the energy expended during the past decades in picking up these women, and in taking, developing and enlarging these photographs, I am overcome by its pointlessness.

All that time and trouble, and still the record is a superficial one: I see only how I looked in the fraction of a second when the shutter was open. But there's no trace of the thoughts and emotions which surrounded that moment. When I die and my memories die with me, all that will remain will be thousands of yellowing photographs and 35 mm. negatives locked in my filing cabinets.

I spent an entire day sorting and enlarging negatives and didn't go out until late that evening. On my way out, I saw an attractive young prostitute get out of a taxi and walk in a leisurely way past a corner bar. I accosted her and told her I wanted her to come with me. Her only reaction was to name a price. I hailed a taxi and gave the driver one of my addresses. During the ride the girl said nothing except that she had clients in my neighborhood.

As soon as we got to the apartment, I offered her a drink, which she refused. I paid her, then pointed out all the spotlights and the cameras attached to tripods. I told her I had picked her up, not only because she was attractive, but also because I was sure she would photograph well. I handed her an album of center-fold-size photographs of women, both clothed and nude. As she flipped through it, she mentioned that the only pictures she had of herself were a few Polaroid shots taken by her brother.

Among the subjects in the book, she recognized another prostitute, a girl she had met once in the city jail. She asked why I would choose a hooker over a professional model. I answered that prostitutes were much more at ease in front of a man than models were.

By this time, she appeared quite relaxed, and I suggested we begin our session. I assured her that she should not feel obliged to pose naked, as I was equally interested in photographing her clothed. She said she didn't mind my taking pictures of her nude. If the photos turned out well, I said, I would bring them by her beat the next night so she could look through them. I promised her that she could keep some if she liked. She went to freshen her make-up while I arranged the spotlights and prepared the cameras.

At first, she posed self-consciously, and I kept changing the lighting and the angle, attempting to capture her when she was least aware of it. I photographed her dressed and naked. I caught her unbuttoning her blouse, removing her bra, pulling her skirt down, peeling off her stockings. At the end of the session, she was astonished when I told her how many rolls of film I had used. I asked for her phone number or address, but she refused to give them to me. On her way out, she mentioned that, unless she got arrested, I could find her on the same beat every night.

As soon as she was gone, I began developing the negatives. I selected only the most glamorous poses, each of which revealed a startlingly different aspect of her beauty. By dawn, I had printed them to resemble professional fashion photographs and cropped them to tabloid size.

I waited impatiently for evening to come. At dusk,

I carried a portfolio full of the photographs to the street corner where I had first met her. The other girls were already lined up along the block, but my model hadn't arrived. I opened the portfolio, took out one of her photographs and showed it to another girl, asking if she knew where my model was. She told me I would have to be patient because my friend usually arrived last. The prostitute was very impressed with the photograph and asked if she could see the rest of them. I told her I never showed photos without the subject's permission. She remarked that discretion was important in her line of work, too, and drifted off to talk to another man.

After waiting over two hours, I saw my model get out of a taxi. She had completely altered her hairstyle, dress style, and make-up, but was just as alluring as she had been the day before. Afraid I would lose her to another customer, I dashed across the street. At first, she did not recognize me. But when she saw the portfolio, she smiled and asked if I had brought her pictures. I said they had turned out better than I'd hoped and invited her to have a drink while she looked at them.

We sat in a corner booth in a bar, and, once we'd ordered, I began pulling photos from the portfolio. The bartender, who must have seen her cruising many times, whispered something to his customers, who stared at us. I laid the photographs on the table, on the empty seats and on the floor around us. The girl was amazed. She said she had not really expected any pictures because she was used to clients photographing her, but they'd never show up with the pictures they promised. After hesitating for a moment, she asked if she could buy all the photographs I'd taken of her, and possibly commission more.

She could not afford my prices, I said. I was paid

more for one photograph than she made in a week. I confessed that I had chosen to photograph her only because I wanted her, and suggested that she earn her pictures by making love to me. I promised that each time she brought me to a climax, I would pay her three photographs. I told her that even if she didn't accept my offer she could keep any four shots.

She quickly gathered the pictures into a neat stack and flipped through them; then she went through them a second time, placing the pictures she liked in a pile. She re-examined the photos she preferred and eventually narrowed the stack down to four.

She was eager, she said, to work for more photographs. Her only stipulation was that she visit me in the late afternoons; since she worked all night, she had to sleep during the day.

The next afternoon, she arrived wearing a fashionable suede suit, and told me excitedly that she had shown the photographs to some of the other girls. They had urged her to collect a portfolio for modeling or acting interviews. A legitimate job would offer protection when the cops tried to arrest her.

Accepting the drink I offered, she changed into the clothes she had brought for the session and I photographed her. After we made love, she chose nine more stills that I'd taken two days before.

She came to my apartment every day on her way to work, always wearing a different outfit, wig, shade of nail polish or lipstick. I was careful to compliment her looks because I could see how much it pleased her. She complained half-seriously that, not only did my spotlights tire her eyes, but the means I used to induce her orgasms exhausted her before she went to work at night. Only then did I remember that she would be spending her night embraced by one man after another.

One evening, after she had left, I was restless. I put on a disguise and walked to her beat, where I watched her from across the street. When a squad car approached, I saw her and the other girls scatter, and return after the police had driven off. Later, I watched her talking with a middle-aged man. His face remained rigid and expressionless, while his head shook constantly. His elbows and wrists flexed in regular, involuntary spasms and his right hand seemed paralyzed into a permanent, immobile claw.

I assumed the girl would reject this cripple, but she did not. The two of them got into a taxi and went off. I stood on the street, missing her, wondering what he would ask of her and how she would accommodate him.

During our next encounter, I asked her about the spastic man. At first, she admitted, the cripple had been repugnant to her. When I asked her to repeat with me exactly what she had done with him, she appeared shocked by my request.

Gradually, the more of my sexual demands she fulfilled without disgust, the more persistent became my fantasies of what she must have done with other men. More and more often, she claimed, I involved her in things none of her other clients had even hinted at, yet she was willing to meet my every demand. When I asked her why she obeyed, she replied that thinking of the photographs I would take kept her going. My pictures, she said, proved that, regardless of how debased she was, I really saw her as clean and beautiful, and my demanding her return meant that I really wanted her.

As I became more experienced in photographing her, I discovered that, at certain times, she appeared refined and delicate, while at others she looked hard and vulgar. The photographs I took of her became increasingly diverse and, as her desire for them grew, choosing only a few each day became more and more difficult for her.

To earn as many as possible, she began probing for what would bring me to orgasm, with a passion that few of my past lovers have displayed. Just as I focused on every potential of her features, she examined my needs, looking for new ways to excite me.

One day, she asked if I would meet her at her corner, instead of waiting for her at my apartment. She was late, as usual, and I was chatting with another girl when she arrived. She apologized, explaining that the owner of a bar downtown had paid her extra to stay longer. Later, she told me it had upset her to see me talking with the girl and added that, if I liked the girl I had been talking to, she would gladly arrange for the two of them to come to my apartment or, if I did not want both, the other girl could come alone. All she wanted, she said, was my word that I would not photograph the other girls. She assured me that, from now on, she would come to my place any time I wanted her. From then on, we began meeting in the evenings. She would usually arrive late. It was un-avoidable, she said, because she could not tell in ad-vance how long an encounter would last. Some clients got aroused slowly, and those who paid for special services insisted on additional time. Since I worried that she had been arrested or had left me, to find she had been delayed merely by another man's love-making was a relief.

As I was locking the door one morning, a man hold-ing a revolver stepped into the corridor from the stairwell. He motioned me out to the landing, kicking the door shut behind us. When he announced that he was my model's brother, I told him there was no rea-son for the gun. I assured him I was merely a photographer who had agreed to shoot her portfolio pictures so she could get a legitimate cover job. Aiming the gun at my stomach, he muttered that his sister supported him and his girl friend. Since she'd been seeing me, he said, his sister was bringing home less money every night.

He said he had destroyed every single photograph I had taken of his sister. If he ever found out she was trying to start a career as a model, he would sell her to a black pimp, who would mess her up so badly that no one would ever want to photograph her again. I quickly promised not to see her again and mentioned that I had to leave town on the following day. He backed down one flight of stairs with his gun trained on me, then tucked the weapon in his pocket, and raced down the rest of the stairs. That night, instead of meeting my model, I moved to another of my apartments.

Sometimes, I would return to her beat in disguise and mix with the watchers, penniless old men who, in exchange for occasional sex, maintain tabs on an unsuspecting girl for her pimp. A watcher will note every time the whore turns down a potential client, how many coffee breaks she takes, how long she stays with a customer and how often she is harassed by the police or the vice squad. He keeps in contact with the pimp from a public telephone booth.

I once witnessed an episode involving a watcher and a girl who insisted on working alone. He waited until she had gone off with a customer before summoning a pimp. The girl came back, wearing a low-cut, thigh-length dress. All at once, a band of ghetto boys, paid by the pimp, converged on her with ink bottles and sharp-edged rulers.

As the pimp looked on from his limousine, the boys splashed the girl with ink and slashed her with the rulers until her breasts, arms and thighs were red and indelible blue. While she cried and swore and fought, passersby looked on, fascinated by the spectacle. No one moved to help her.

The attack ended quickly. Before the last boy fled, he punched the girl in the pelvis and snatched her purse. The pimp stepped out of his car, went over to the girl and, whispering to her, tenderly embraced her. He must have convinced her to accept his protection because, after a few minutes, they both got into his limousine and drove off.

A few nights later, I noticed this pimp's limousine discharge another woman. She was my model.

I watched her walk, her form-fitting clothes advertising her supple body. Many potential customers looked at her but hesitated to approach. Only when she glanced at a man encouragingly would he speak to her. When I approached her, she recognized me but waved me away. Her eyes were glassy and vacant. Before I could move off, her pimp came up behind me and knocked me to the ground. I got up and left.

I began keeping track of the pimp's movements. One night, I saw him park in front of a local restaurant and go inside with some friends. I strolled past the car, and slipped a glassine bag of white talcum powder through a half-opened rear window. Next, I made an anonymous call to the police, telling them that the steel gray luxury sedan parked in front of the restaurant contained a stash of heroin and that the car's owner, a pimp, was heavily armed.

As soon as I spotted a police car approaching, I went inside the restaurant and asked for the pimp. I was escorted upstairs to a private room, where he and his friends were eating. I ran to him and whispered that I had seen a man throw a bag of white powder into his car. Before I could finish, the pimp dashed outside to the car and I followed him out to the street. As soon as he peered into the back seat and saw the bag, the police came up and announced themselves. The pimp panicked, jumped behind the wheel, started the motor and hit the gas. The car swung out sharply. The police opened fire and the car veered up over the curb, plunging straight into a wall. I checked my watch while they were dragging the body out of the wreckage; fifteen minutes had passed since I dumped the bag in the car.

During that experience with the prostitute I continued my review of old photographs. I spent days organizing the prints chronologically, although there is one period in my catalogues which seems out of place; directly after photos which show me as a young man, there is a series in which I look much older.

The reason is that I once devised a photographic process that reveals the gradual aging of the human face. When I first perfected this technique, I fitted an industrial camera with special filters and loaded it with film coated with an emulsion I myself prepared. I posed under powerful industrial lights and let each exposure focus on a different part of my face. I processed the negative in several chemical baths that highlighted those parts of the face and neck that age most rapidly. Then I made enlargements, rephotographed them, and copied them again through various filters. The finished photographs showed my face years older than it was.

While organizing my prints and negatives, I set aside several files for documentary photographs. I often carry a small automatic camera and a couple of extra rolls of film in my pocket. If I happen upon an accident, collision, fire or shoot-out, I snap as many shots as possible and later arrange them into a complete photographic reconstruction of the incident.

Recently I saw a young woman slip while crossing the street, falling directly in the path of an oncoming taxi. Just as she slipped, she screamed, and I raised my camera, getting photos of the entire incident. Her shoulder and neck smashed against the front fender, which dragged her five or six feet. I rushed over to her. While other bystanders tried to comfort her, I began taking pictures from every side. I wanted to establish on film the precise angle and position of the wheels at the moment of the collision, the distance that the woman's body was dragged and the exact nature of the cab's contact with the body. By the time the police and ambulance arrived, I had used three rolls of film. When I told the taxi driver that I had photographed the accident, he said he was anxious to have the prints for his defense. He gave me his name and address, and I promised to contact him. Next, I told the police I had photos of the collision and was eager for the woman's family to see them in case they decided to sue. I was immediately supplied with the name and address of the woman, who at that moment was being lifted into an ambulance.

In my apartment, I developed the negatives and enlarged some of the photographs. I selected shots for the cab driver that could best prove his innocence: according to his set, the woman had crossed the street in the middle of the block and tripped because of her high heels. The street surface had been wet, slippery and slightly inclined, and the traces made by the cab's sudden braking indicated it had stayed within its lane.

The woman's set of photos, which I mailed to her relatives, suggested she had been hit by a careless driver who hadn't noticed her crossing. It looked as if she had waited on her side of the dividing line for the cab to pass, and had fallen only after its fender had knocked her off balance.

I was motoring up the coast, along a scenic highway flanked by the ocean on one side and the bay on the other. A large turn-of-the-century house, towering on a cliff over the water, attracted my curiosity. I decided to explore it, and turned when I reached a private road leading to a gate.

I saw from a sign on the gate that the property was for rent and started up the drive. The road was overgrown with grasses, and the pavement was buried under a blanket of moss. Farther from the highway, the drive became even more forbidding, and I had to force the car across roots and dense underbrush. The grounds were as unkempt as the road; weeds choked the flower beds, bushes had grown into huge grotesque shapes completely obscuring the windows of the house. I parked the car, got out and walked up the steps to look at the realtor's sign affixed to the padlocked door. Standing in front of the house as the sun set, I surveyed the huge expanse of land and noticed a small guest house a little way off, set up on a knoll. Anxious to reach the highway before dark, I made my way back through the foliage and drove to the nearest town.

Early the next day, I visited the realtor. He was an older man, proud of the community in which he had lived all his life. I asked if I could lease the property for a year, explaining that I was attracted by its privacy and easy access to the beaches. I explained I was an investor whom ill health had forced into early retirement, that I had no family or relatives and that I was anxious to enjoy a year of uninterrupted rest. I offered to pay the year's rent in advance, and casually indicated that, if I leased the property, I would also rent, through his firm, a sailboat, a motorboat and a car. Intrigued by the prospect of an additional commission, the realtor hurriedly assured me he foresaw no problem in obtaining the lease.

I learned that the property was called the Park, and consisted of over two thousand acres. It was controlled by the estate of a woman who had died in her nineties, about a year earlier. She had lived alone all her life, but toward the end she had shared the place with dozens of cats, all of whom were provided for in her will. A small residential community had grown up next to the property. The Park was protected on one side by the ocean and on the other by the bay, as well as by one of the largest Indian reservations on the Eastern seaboard. The old woman had left the property to her nephew with the strict provision that it be maintained exactly as it had been. The heir was legally prohibited from selling the property or any part of it.

The real estate agent revealed that, when the nephew found himself in financial trouble, he had used the property as collateral with his bank. Now the bank was stuck with it until his death, being bound by the terms of the will. The small property owners of the adjacent community were pleased that the Park had remained intact, even though they were not allowed to enter it. Yet, they were all afraid that the bank might win its court case and sell the property to land speculators, who would turn it into a gigantic development.

Two days later, the lease was ready for my signature. The realtor told me that the bank was pleased he had found a tenant, even if only for a year. My presence would calm the neighbors, he said, and reassure them that the bank had no intention of selling.

In looking over my copy of the lease, I noticed that the realtor had provided bogus references, listing me as an associate of various firms with which he claimed to have done business. I signed the papers with the realtor's wife and son-in-law as witnesses, and paid the year's rent in cash.

I took possession of the estate at the end of the week on a hot June day, the air buzzing with insects. Parking my newly rented convertible in the driveway, I set out to inspect the property. On the ground floor of the main house were several drawing rooms plus a dining room and kitchen. The second floor consisted of numerous small bedrooms and bathrooms, furnished with a mixture of good antiques and cheap patio furniture. The heating was primitive and the wiring archaic.

The guest house was more livable. Compact and comfortable, it had a living room and den with beamed ceilings, modern kitchen and bathrooms, two bedrooms, an attic and an attached garage. Since it stood on the highest point of the property, from the attic windows I could see the entire length of the long driveway, the Indian reservation, the expanse of land sweeping out toward the bay, the high dunes on the ocean beach and, with the help of binoculars, the outlying Park grounds. I felt like a lookout in a fortress, able to observe and be ready to receive any unwanted intruders. I decided to use the guest house as my base.

The first night I slept there, I was awakened by headlights shining into my bedroom. Through the window, I could see a young couple emerge from a car parked near the main house and disappear into the woods. Later, I was awakened by the sound of a boat approaching the beach. When its engines stopped, I heard the voices of drunks singing army songs.

During the day, I inspected the Park and came across tire marks, footprints, used prophylactics, traces of recent picnic fires, discarded liquor bottles, crushed beer cans and several empty rifle cartridges.

I drove into the city and bought a camera and military field glasses, both equipped with infrared attachments, a pellet revolver, a wooden replica of a submachine gun from a theater supply company and a dictionary of the language spoken by the neighboring Indians. I also acquired several sets of powerful sound detectors specifically designed for outdoor use.

I spent the following week installing my transmitting and receiving system: I hooked up most of the rooms in the main house, as well as the attic and basement of the guest cottage. Then I placed directional microphones and loudspeakers in the trees and even wired the abandoned wells and half-buried boat wrecks scattered among the dunes. These warning devices worked on various frequencies and were controlled from a central switchboard in the attic of the guest house. They would alert me if anyone trespassed on the property or attempted to break into either house.

Late one evening, my sound monitor alerted me that a boat had pulled onto the beach: I distinguished three male voices. Soon I heard the men digging a pit, lighting a fire, roasting hot dogs and trying to improve the reception on their battery-operated TV. After a few beers, their comments on the ball game became increasingly raucous.

One of my speakers was hidden almost directly above the men, in the tall, dense grass of the dunes. Just before the ball game ended, I began bellowing Indian phrases through the speaker. The men panicked, splashed around in the water, and almost forgot to take the ice chest and television as they fled.

The Park continued to attract trespassers, by day and night. Trying to reach the beaches, some of the drivers simply lost their way on the Park's unlit road. Often, a car would stop in front of the main house and its driver would knock at the door. I never bothered anyone who wandered into the Park by accident; I was interested only in those who came to play.

I saw the realtor when I picked up the boats I'd rented from him. On several other occasions, as a neighborly gesture, he and his wife stopped by the house. During one visit, I complained about the trespassers and reported that at night I often heard Indians chanting. The realtor nodded sadly and said that the reservation Indians often got drunk and celebrated some fertility rites at their cemetery bordering on the Park. He speculated that they might be using the Park as a place in which to sober up before returning to the reservation. There was apparently no legal way to stop them.

He warned me against taking matters into my own hands. The big-city radicals always took the side of the Indians, he said, and a violent incident could give the bank reason to break up the Park. His wife agreed, assuring me that the Indians were irritating but harmless, and suggested that I should simply lock myself in, take a shot of whiskey and sleep through the howling.

The next morning, I paddled an inflatable dinghy out to my boat anchored in the bay, and spent a few hours hooking up my remote-control receiver-transmitters. As I worked, I recalled sitting on a quay in Monaco, gazing through binoculars at yachts anchored a few hundred yards off shore. I could see their crews, the stewards rushing around with trays, the passengers' tanned bodies lounging on sundecks.

It was in Monaco that a small boy saw me staring at the boats and sat next to me. He was about ten years old, barefoot and thin, wearing clothes that he had outgrown. After a while, I asked him what he would most like to do. He pointed at the biggest yachts and said he would like to torpedo them. I asked how. He turned toward me, flushed with excitement, and said all he needed were a few battery-operated toy submarines loaded with real dynamite. He would stage the attack at night, when the passengers were returning from the casino. His deadly flotilla, ready to destroy on contact, would move slowly through the calm waters, passing unseen in the shadows.

The boy spoke rapidly as he described the explosions that would wreck the yachts, illuminating the port like fireworks. He imagined musicians forsaking their instruments, waiters dropping their trays, captains deserting their crews, men abandoning their women, women their children, and children their playthings. He described how the yachts would slowly sink in the darkness, servants and princes fighting one another for places in the dinghies.

Inspired by the boy's scheme, on my last trip to the city I had bought several battery-powered miniatures of amphibious naval carriers. The toys could maintain a steady course for several hundred yards in smooth water as well as run on the sand on their rubber wheels. I loaded each toy with a waterproof packet of explosive powder, which I could detonate by remote control.

One Friday night, I was awakened by sounds of boats and people. I quickly dressed and made my way to the dunes, scanning the waterline through infrared field glasses. Two pleasure boats had beached there and two young couples were busy setting up a midnight picnic. There was no moon, and, unobserved, I launched the dinghy and rowed to my boat. Through earphones attached to the directional microphones, I continued eavesdropping on my visitors, who were growing rowdier with every drink.

After waiting an hour, I began broadcasting through one speaker my single Indian incantation. The picnickers were startled but I heard the men assuring their women that as long as there was only one Indian they could easily chase him off. Armed with driftwood, they crawled inland looking for the drunken native. I waited for a while, then I activated the second speaker hidden in the bushes, creating the impression that the Indian had moved away from the beach. Next I turned on a third speaker at the opposite end of the woods. Through various directional mikes I followed the progress of the pursuers, who still thought they were chasing only one Indian.

With the men in the woods, I launched my amphibious toys. The little boats bobbed through the water and rolled onto the sand.

I pressed a button, and the first boat exploded in a white flare with the noise of a firecracker. Seconds later, I sent moans and Indian phrases through several of the Park's most powerful speakers. Stunned by the explosions and the ghostly voices from the depths, the picnickers rushed back to the shore. I stopped the chanting but rapidly detonated the remaining toys. When one of the women screamed that she saw Indians arriving in canoes, the couples fled, abandoning their belongings, their boats churning up the shallow waters of the bay. I went back to the guest house, had a shot of whiskey, as the realtor's wife had suggested, and slept till late morning.

The summer was at its peak, and the Park was full of wild flowers. When I drove down the path, my car had to plough through lush foliage and blossoming shrubs. The meadows abruptly changed their color as gusts of wind blew back and forth across them.

One afternoon, from my attic, I saw a girl of about twelve bicycling slowly down a narrow path, with a boy of six or seven trotting behind her. I immediately switched on a speaker in one of the wells and began moaning and sobbing. The sounds were multiplied by echoes. The girl whirled around and bicycled furiously back toward the gate. The little boy ran after her, weeping.

In less than two hours, they returned with nine other children, ranging in age from about six to thirteen. Carrying slingshots, stones and bows and arrows, they crawled through the bush like seasoned guerrillas. When the band approached the main house, I activated a speaker hidden in the grass several feet from them, and started my incantations in throaty whispers gradually rising to howls. The children were ready for their prey and shot their missiles directly at the voice. I began to moan as if I had been hit, and, suddenly frightened, the children ran from the Park, shouting.

I called the theatrical supply company and asked if it could provide a life-size dummy of a dead male Indian, which I needed for a play. They told me the company accepted orders for dead Indians only by the dozen, and that a single body would be quite expensive. I called several shops in the city before finding one that had recently acquired top-quality dummies from a bankrupt Hollywood studio. I made arrangements and drove in to pick up the dead Indian.

Following my specifications, the make-up man at the supply company had dressed the Indian in only a headband and loincloth. I asked him to cover the body with bloody wounds supposedly inflicted by the sample arrows and slingshot pellets I had taken with me. Because the play was to be staged outdoors in the daytime, I explained, it was important that the corpse look real. The make-up man complimented me on my feeling for detail. He advised me that, although standards had slipped elsewhere in the business, his mannequin was made of high quality plastic that closely resembled the texture of skin.

In a few hours, my Indian was ready. His skin was mottled with gray spots, and the blood seeping from the wounds around the arrows was amazingly realistic. To prevent his wounds from chipping and smearing, I wrapped the dummy in a blanket and placed him carefully in the trunk of my car. Next to him I stashed a can of imitation blood I had bought from the make-up man.

In the Park, I removed the speaker and placed the dummy in the grass at the exact spot where the children thought they had attacked an Indian. I scattered their arrows, stones and pellets over and around the dummy, then soaked the ground with imitation blood. I dribbled clear corn syrup on the wounds, and by the time I left, a swarm of flies had arrived to feed on the syrup.

As I had expected, the children returned to the Park after school. Carrying bows, arrows and slingshots, and axes, hammers and wrenches, they crept through the woods quietly. I loaded my camera, hung my wooden submachine gun on my shoulder and fastened the microphone of a tape recorder on an outside pocket of my military jacket. Soon two of the children had spotted the flies and discovered the dead Indian. The other children gathered around.

Just then I stepped from the brush, and aiming my gun, ordered them to drop their weapons and put up their hands. I shouted that anyone who disobeyed my orders would be shot. The children were terrified. They dropped their weapons and clasped their hands behind their heads. The younger ones started to cry.

Pointing at the dead Indian, I told them I had seen them kill him when he was peacefully returning from the cemetery, where he had gone to pray. I had not moved the body or reported the crime only because I knew that sooner or later the killers would come back.

I put the gun in the crook of my arm and raised the camera to photograph the children. In unison, they shielded their faces from the camera with their hands, like criminals being led into court. I raised the gun and threatened to present the police with their corpses instead of their photographs. They dropped their hands. After I finished the group photographs, I took a full-face and profile picture of each of them and had them dictate their names and addresses directly into my tape recorder. I warned that lying would implicate them even more seriously.

I announced that they would all be charged with the murder of an unarmed, innocent Indian. Each one of them would be sentenced to many years of solitary confinement, and their disgraced parents would have to change their names and their jobs and move to another state. Their coldly premeditated crime would make headlines in the newspapers and the whole world would see their vicious faces on television. As I talked, some of the children turned pale; others trembled and cried, begging me not to denounce them. They whimpered that they would do anything for me. The older ones, with what they considered adult arguments, pointed out that, after all, Indians never went to church or to the movies or to shopping centers and didn't send their kids to school, but just drank and slept all day, living off the taxes of the whites who worked.

I hesitated for a long time, as if deep in thought, then told them I had reconsidered my decision and decided to protect them for the sake of their families.

I promised that the body would never be discovered. The children flocked about me, sobbing with relief. After they calmed down, I said I wanted to take one final photograph for my own private album.

Willingly, the children now formed a tight circle around the Indian. Great hunters displaying their kill, they smiled proudly at the camera. I promised that, in a day or so, I would leave a photograph for each child in a plastic bag under the oak tree near the main gate. To protect the cover-up, I said, I would keep the negatives in my bank vault. One after another, they swore themselves to secrecy and thanked me for what I had done.

I suggested that, in case we were being watched by the Indians, they should not leave the Park together. They scattered obediently, some through the gate, others by the dunes and beach.

I buried the dummy near the guest house, developed the film and made dozens of wallet-sized prints of each picture. As promised, I left the photographs in plastic bags near the gate, and the next morning, through my binoculars, I watched the children come one after another to collect them. Later in the day, a few of the older ones sneaked back to the Park to make certain no traces of their crime remained.

In the following days, I continued to lead a quiet life, going into the village only when necessary. But, whenever I drove my convertible through town, men and women waved to me, and I knew I was considered a member of the community, like it or not.

Soon, I discovered the children had not kept our secret. One man complimented me on my handling of the young intruders in the Park. A couple remarked how generous I, a newcomer, had been to the neighborhood kids. A local door-to-door cosmetics saleswoman gave me two complimentary sets of her men's products, as a reward for what she called a "communal service."

One weekend, I went to the local bar where men were spending the evening sitting in front of their beers, hypnotized by the flickering image on the television set suspended high over the bar. Although we had never met, the bartender shook my hand. He poured me a double and said it was on the house. All the men turned toward me, and those sitting in the back moved closer to get a better look. Others kept on toasting me and slapping me on the back. I toasted them in return, downed my drink and left. Five of them left with me. Outside, their spokesman launched into a speech of gratitude. He said that he was the father of one of the children that I had saved. Everyone realized, he told me, that it was only to protect the children that I had put the fear of God into them.

Looking to the others for approval, he announced that all five men were members of a group devoted to civic betterment. Whenever any group member needed help, the others rallied round him. My deed entitled me to become one of them. I told him I was grateful, but that I was shy and tended to avoid groups in favor of more intimate contacts. They again assured me that they would be standing by if I ever needed them. We parted like old buddies.

I spent the entire week in the main house, cleaning a bedroom, checking the wiring of my hidden microphones, repairing furniture and hanging curtains on many of the windows. I stocked the refrigerator and the liquor cabinet and bought rubber floats and beach blankets.

When the house and the beach were ready for guests, I returned to the city and moved into a section of town known for its gay bars. I visited one coeducational gay bar every night, and, after a while, picked out a striking couple whom I began to follow.

One was a pale, handsome woman in her thirties, over six feet tall, with short blond hair. She usually wore a man's suit, complete with shirt and tie. Her lover was a small, delicate black girl with large breasts, not much over twenty. She dressed in ankle-length skirts, embroidered blouses and sandals.

After I had been watching them for a week or so, I introduced myself as a retired insurance broker who had been admiring them both. At first, they snubbed me, but I persisted. Eventually, I suggested we all have dinner and then go to a very fashionable gay cabaret. The younger woman urged her companion to accept.

At the restaurant, when a couple of drinks had put them at ease, I told them that I admired them because they seemed to live without camouflage. Only recently, I said, had I admitted to myself that I'd long been drawn to women who love each other. Now, I confessed, I'd decided to pursue that fascination. I told them I lived alone on a large estate not far from the city and would be pleased to have them stay with me for as long as they chose to. They would have access to a large house, a boat and a car, and I would, of course, cover all their expenses.

The women stared at me incredulously, waiting for a catch, then flipped through a dozen color snapshots of the Park I showed them. I pressed forward, reminding them that the entire house would be theirs. I suggested they might wish to verify that the estate was really mine, and gave them the name and phone number of the realtor, as well as my own number at the Park. By the end of dinner, it seemed settled that they would visit me.

I returned to the Park. Within a week, the couple

phoned to say they would be arriving in the morning. I met them at the railroad station, pleased to see they were dressed as oddly as they had been in the city. It was a warm day and I drove back to the Park along the community road with the car's top down. With both of my passengers sitting on top of the back seat to see better, I proceeded slowly through the residential area bordering the Park. Some of the men from the bar were working around their lawns, and when they waved at me I waved back, as did my passengers. When we entered the Park, they were impressed with how large the estate was.

After inspecting all the bedrooms in the main house, they settled on a second-floor corner room, whose windows faced the guest house. When I pointed out that through my fieldglasses I could easily spy on them from my attic, Alex, the elder one, stroked Linda's hair and said they wouldn't mind. After all, she said, I had admitted from the outset that I was fascinated by women in love. She asked whether, given the chance, I would be more excited by listening or watching. I replied that I would rather hear them. Since they might at some point discuss me, I would learn things about myself, as well as about them, whereas by watching them I would be completely uninvolved.

Our daily schedule depended on the weather. On cloudless days, they sailed around the peninsula on the sailboat I had rented for them. From my attic, I watched their boat and listened to their conversations over a transmitter hidden inside it.

On cloudy mornings, Linda and Alex strolled around the Park, picking mushrooms and wildflowers and looking for foxes, which hid in the dense underbrush. Always, I listened to their talk.

Later in the day, they would often drive to the

shopping center or walk along the ocean to the far end of the peninsula. Occasionally, I went with them, aware of the curiosity we aroused. At sunset, we would sit on the porch of the main house, drinking and talking. I would photograph them from time to time, and eventually they stopped paying attention to the camera. For a change of pace, I would urge them to dress up in their most outrageous clothes, and we would go to dinner in one of the big restaurants.

The three of us were becoming a familiar sight, and one night I took them to the bar where earlier I had been toasted. Alex was wearing a form-fitting man's suit that emphasized her small waist and slim thighs, and Linda's full breasts were shown off by her semi-transparent dress. As we entered, every man instantly stopped talking and stared at us. Acknowledging the impact, Alex swept off her hat and bowed theatrically to the astonished men, who quickly looked away. I led the girls through the crowded room to a corner table. As we had our drinks, the bar was silent.

On our way out, men winked knowingly at me. I whispered that both women were recent acquaintances staying at the Park for a few days, and implied that they were drifters whose perverted life interested me just as it would any other man.

The following day, while Alex and Linda sunbathed naked, the monitor alerted me that the Park was being invaded. Through my binoculars, I sighted several men crawling across the dunes toward the beach. My receiver picked up their whispers as they cautioned each other to be quiet until the women started making love. They swore at the heat and at the insects, but refused to abandon their stake-out. When the women got up and walked to the boat, the disappointed men crawled away.

From then on, the men often sneaked into the Park

222

or hung around the beach. Alex and Linda told me that one afternoon their sailboat was almost swamped by men in two motor launches. Another time, as the women made love on the porch, I spotted two men watching them from the edge of the woods.

One night, five men came close to the main house. I listened in as they outlined a scheme to abduct the women and drag them down to the beach for what they called "fun and games." The men argued for a long time until they agreed which room the girls slept in and which staircase would offer the easiest access to it.

After the men left, I went over and knocked on the couple's bedroom door, calling to them to get up. I explained that the locals were planning to raid the house and rape them. Alex, who was adept in karate, was sure the three of us could easily deal with the intruders. But I insisted the risk was too great. Reluctantly, they agreed to leave.

Helping them pack, I suggested playing a trick on the men to get even. The two of them could help me by leaving me some of their clothing and make-up. They were glad to donate a bra, an old blouse, some bikini underpants and several other items.

I drove the women back to the city well after midnight. When I returned to the Park, I took the can of remaining imitation blood, soaked several pieces of the women's clothing in it and splashed it all over their mattress and sheets. I dragged the mess into the heaviest undergrowth, dug a grave big enough to have held both my guests, and buried the bloodied clothes, sheets and mattress, planting the underpants almost on the surface. Smoothing the raw earth, I covered it with bushes uprooted from another part of the Park. Then, I rigged up a set of directional microphones in a nearby tree.

I washed down the women's bedroom, using a disinfectant with a pronounced odor, making sure that a little "blood" had dribbled between the floorboards. I placed Linda's bra on the path to the grave.

Late that afternoon, my monitor detected the five men, cautiously approaching the main house from the dunes. One kept watch, while the others crept up the stairs to the women's bedroom. When they discovered that the women were gone, they were enraged. They strode around the room, making crude jokes about how the women could make love without a mattress. When somebody mentioned the pine smell of the disinfectant, commenting that the girls kept a very clean floor, another noticed the traces of blood. Now they all became excited and raced downstairs. Outside, they had no difficulty following the trail, and it wasn't long before they reached the grave site.

By then, the men had reconstructed the events according to my plan, but they could not decide what to do with their knowledge. One suggested the police. Another countered that once the press and television got hold of the story the Park would become a tourist attraction. A third pointed out that they had no business being there themselves, a fact that was certain to be noticed. They fell silent. After a few minutes of indecision, they decided to leave things as they were for the time being, and left.

The monitor woke me well past midnight. Through my binoculars, I could make out six or seven men heading for the grave. The glow of their high-powered lanterns dimmed as they moved deeper into the woods, but I picked up their voices as if I had been only a foot away. They began digging at once. In a few moments, they must have reached the blood-covered mattress, because I heard a horrified groan. When they did not find the women's bodies underneath, they began to argue among themselves. What was under the mattress was clearly virgin soil. I heard a cigarette lighter click, and a voice suggested that a new possibility had now to be considered. The two dykes could be anywhere on the Park's two thousand acres—next to the dead Indian, for instance. One by one, they began to imagine what would happen if the police exhumed the body of the man their children had killed. Anxiously arguing about what they should do, they decided to burn the mattress, sheets and clothes. As soon as the bonfire died down, the men buried the ashes in the grave and left.

They came back the next day, claiming they were looking for a lost dog. I welcomed them. They crisscrossed the Park several times. On my monitor I overheard their excited comments when they found a scarf buried in the dunes. They burned it on the spot, then left.

That evening, I went to the bar. The regulars nodded, but this time they were less than cordial. One of the men edged over and asked about my girl friends. I smiled sadly and said that they had sneaked off, taking some of my things. The theft wasn't worth the sheriff's time, I said. I added that, when it came to picking my next lovers, I would be two women wiser.

A man casually asked if I knew how to get in touch with my guests. I answered that they had been with each other for some time and probably had no other friends. I doubted I could find them even if I had to. As an afterthought, I added that, in the next few days, I myself planned to leave the Park and travel abroad.

On the following day, I dismantled the rest of my network of monitoring equipment and resold it to the supplier in the city. Toward the end of the week, as I lay sunbathing, I heard cars pull up. The sheriff and two of my midnight visitors got out and greeted me. I

invited them to have a drink, and asked what had
brought them.

The sheriff announced that the community was
concerned that during my absence the Park might become a squatters haven. To discourage this, and to
facilitate a police patrol, his two companions had
volunteered to enlarge the Park's narrow paths and
even clear some new ones. Naturally, he agreed, I, as a
tenant, would have to make the final decision. I said
I could not answer for the legal aspect of the matter.
But aside from what the old lady's will stipulated, I
could only welcome such changes.

We drank in silence, watching a solitary turtle
calmly crossing the grass in front of the house. Forcing
a smile, the sheriff asked if I was lonely without my
young companions. I replied that our arrangement
had not turned out to be what I had hoped for. Apparently, I sighed, I still had a lot to learn about
women. The men laughed uneasily, finished their
beers and were off.

Later in the day, my helpful neighbors returned
with two tractors. I watched the machines pass over
the main road and head for the gravesite. I heard the
engines strain and whine as plows ripped through the
dense greenery, building a network of roads and high,
hard-packed hills where low dunes had been only
shortly before.

The next morning, just as the sun was coming over
the humped, pitted sand, I noticed the sheriff's blue
car slow down as it passed. I wondered if he noticed
how naturally the new mounds joined the rolling
dunes that stretched all the way to the Indian reservation.

I left my apartment one day just as people began
pouring out of their offices for lunch. A group of
teen-agers in shabby orange robes and sandals with

broken leather straps moved through the crowd beating drums and chanting. Some of them accosted passersby, offering leaflets that people took and promptly crumpled up. Office workers sunned themselves in the plazas of high-rise buildings, eating sandwiches, smoking and ignoring the chanters. On the sidewalk, the dense, rapidly moving crowd forced the young people back to the curb, where they continued dancing and chanting.

One girl dancing near me had straggly hair and acne-marked skin. The loose armholes of her oversized robe revealed her flat breasts. With head thrown back and eyes closed, she was chanting in unison with the rest. I touched her arm to ask where she was from, and she muttered, "Chicago," without stopping her swaying.

"And the others?"

She answered without looking, "New York, the Rockies, Texas, California. We're from everywhere."

"Why do you do this?" I pursued. "All these people rushing past you—all of us, we think you're crazy!"

The girl wiped the sweat off her neck with the edge of her robe. "We don't care what you think," she told me, and went back to her chant. A Japanese tourist stepped between us to get a good photograph of the dancers against the bustling midtown backdrop. I strolled on.

Within a few blocks, I discovered a sex peepshow that guaranteed a variety of new twelve-minute porn films, each one divided into three-minute segments. I went inside.

A few businessmen were wandering around the darkened room, jingling the change in their pockets and studying the film descriptions posted outside each booth. I chose one, went in, and paid my quarter. The film had been playing for a minute or so when I heard the sounds of a struggle coming from the adjoining booth. I stepped out and peered into it. In the light flickering from the screen, I saw a tall sailor wrestling an old man to the floor. I took out my spray pen and squirted a drop at the sailor's neck. He immediately slumped down.

The old man scrambled to his feet, stuffed his shirt into his trousers and zipped his fly. He must have thought I was from the vice squad, because he seemed as frightened of me as of his assailant. "He attacked first. He broke my glasses," he shouted, pointing at the sailor, who was tossing around on the floor, mumbling and groaning and swearing.

Meanwhile, other customers scurried out of the nearby booths, and, without checking to see what had happened, they fled the theater.

The theater manager hurried over to us. "I run a clean place here and I'm calling the cops," he said nervously.

The older man pleaded, "There's no need for that. Please. It's not necessary. Nothing happened."

By then the sailor was getting up groggily. He shoved the old man aside and stepped out of the booth, shouting, "That old faggot came right into my booth. He grabbed me and said he would pay me if I let him . . . you know. When I told him no way, he sprayed me with some kind of poison gas and I passed out. Call the cops!" he shouted at the manager. "Call the goddamned cops!"

The old man was shaking with fright and blinking compulsively. "Please don't call the police. It's not necessary. I'll pay you; I'll pay all of you." I realized that without his glasses he was almost blind.

"I saw what happened," I interjected. "The sailor is lying." Now I pointed to the old man. "He threatened this gentleman and demanded money from him. It was a holdup."

The sailor lunged at me, stopping short of contact, and said menacingly, "You didn't see nothing, man."

"You're not on board ship now, sailor," I retorted. The old man edged toward me and I put my hand on his shoulder. To the manager I said, "Go ahead; call the police, but just remember you're in trouble, too. You may run a clean place, but you don't provide adequate protection for your customers." The manager said nothing and the sailor brushed off his uniform. "Would any of you have the time and the money to press charges and pay bail lawyers and court costs?" I asked, looking at all three of them.

The sailor picked up his cap, shrugged his shoulders, and left the theater, grumbling. I took the old man's arm, led him to the exit and invited him to have a drink with me.

We sat at a table in a nearby bar. The old man was short and lean, his cheeks pink with a network of tiny broken veins. When he spoke, his lips gaped like a rubber ball slashed in half. He told me that since the death of his wife, ten years before, he had lived alone. Because he was retired, he had to budget his pension and social security money carefully to cover the rent on his one-room apartment, food and other necessities. He ate less than when his wife had cooked for him, exercised every morning and rarely drank anything stronger than wine. Minor illnesses occasionally prompted him to consult doctors, but, once seated in the waiting room, he was always bothered by the fact that the appointment was as expensive as a night with a whore.

Only the week before, he said, a scrubbed young nurse had called his name as he sat in a doctor's office.

She led him into one of the examining cubicles, asked him to undress and told him the doctor would be right along. When she left, he overheard her and the other nurses down the hall chatting about cosmetics, interns, Caribbean vacations and diets.

He told me how he pretended to appear uninterested when the young nurse pushed his shoulders forward and spread his legs to prepare him for an x-ray. As she manipulated his body with her cool hands, he wanted to express the same contempt for her that she showed for him. After all, he said, collecting feces and urine didn't make her any better than a hooker, who at least provided pleasure while she earned her money.

He said that during the first months following his wife's death his most important needs were shelter and sex. As he sat watching television all day, he dreamed of the evening ahead.

He had invented a continuous fantasy of sexual sequences, in which the only element left to chance was the climax. Some women could relieve him, but others, who had initially aroused him just as much, could not. Over the years, he had compiled a list of erotic qualities to shop for in a woman, even though he often failed to find what he wanted.

When he went out at night, he dressed in his most threadbare clothes in order to get away with paying as little as possible. He carried only one identification card.

He was as aroused by his need to overcome his sense of a woman's disapproval of him as he was by her looks or love-making techniques. Whenever a prostitute could make him articulate his desires, and not make him feel guilty, he would pay her an additional amount.

Frequently, he would accost a prostitute and tell her she had gone with him once before, describing the tricks she had supposedly performed for him. If she denied knowing him but not the tricks, he would ask her how much she charged for gratifying such needs. By then, she would have sized him up as a lonely old man. Thinking he might become a steady client, she would often offer a special introductory rate.

The man was proud of the hard bargain he drove with every woman. Since a whore usually demanded more money for each successive climax, he had developed a sexual con. He turned off everything but a night light while she undressed. As she smoked or drank, he caressed her until he climaxed without her noticing it. She would have to work twice as hard, not knowing it would be his second orgasm. He would rate each of his orgasms by the rapidity as well as by the number of its spasms, and would keep a record of the most intense spurts. No woman, he bragged, had ever suspected how many orgasms he managed to get for the price of one.

One night, he picked up a whore and went to a hotel room with her. She offered him a rubber and he refused, insisting he was too eager to feel himself inside her. After he had caressed her for a while, she moved on top of him with his head under her belly. He split her open like a black melon. The flesh inside was pulpy and pink, and he licked and sucked and bit until her raw flesh smeared his face with slime. He strained to engulf all of her with his mouth, inhaling her steamy warmth. When her belly contracted and she bent forward to gaze down at him, he could see the dim, red glow of the night light reflect in her eyes.

After the woman left, he fell asleep. Minutes later he awoke in a sweat, stricken with a sensation that an infection she carried had seeped into him. He was terrified. The disease would spread like fire, swelling the roof of his mouth, the base of his tongue, the narrow passage of his throat. It would inflame his windpipe and his voice would die. Neither food nor breath would pass through his swollen mouth. His own flesh would suffocate him.

To kill the germs within him, he gargled with a powerful antiseptic until his mouth burned and ached. He bathed with antibacterial cleanser, but her scent seemed to persist as though it had permeated the deepest layer of his skin. Although he scrubbed himself raw, he was convinced the woman's odor lingered for days.

In recent years, he told me, he had begun sensing disaster everywhere. Each time he rode the subway, he was convinced that his train would stall between stations and catch fire. He visualized hysterical young men and women stampeding while old people like himself stumbled and fell under them, suffocating or choking on their dentures.

The subway also terrified him because he felt it a bearer of cancer. He believed that all living creatures grow new cells to replace the sick, decaying or dead ones. All the defective cells are steadily pressed out onto the surface of the body, where they are killed by soaps and detergents or released into the environment. He insisted that crowds discard these cells in such quantity that soon malignant clouds of cells form and hang in the air. The subway, with its many stations and miles of tunnels, is an ideal breeding place for the decay. Every time a crowded subway train moves through the tunnels, it farts billions of freshly shed cells. They accumulate like bacteria in a cesspool, adhering to the humid walls of subway tunnels, where they incubate for years. During the incubation, the cells interact spontaneously with other living tissues, such as mold and mosses, and begin to mutate. The mutants are many times stronger and more malignant than the original cells and have double strength to penetrate the body.

Even before he became aware of this ubiquitous contamination, he confessed, he had never liked the city. He had dreamed of traveling across Europe in search of the perfect place for a peaceful, solitary death. It would be a small village, he told me, on a high slope, above the moist vineyards yet below the frigid breath of the glacier. Every sunrise, he would step outside to gaze at mountain peaks. Serenity would come to him from measuring the insignificance of his own life against these peaks. Later in the day, he would walk down to the square, greeting other villagers who accepted him as one of their own. He would sit at the town café watching the tourists pass, amused by their accents.

Every week he would go alone to the local church to gaze at the medieval frescoes and sculptures of the saints. After the snows melted, he would ask a neighbor if he could borrow a horse, and, of course, would be urged to take the handsomest animal in the stable. At first, he said, he would let the horse walk so he could hear the dogs barking and the branches rustling in the orchard. Then he would urge it into a canter, soon coming upon unknown roads, crossing glittering brooks, whipping past the motionless black pines that cling to the slopes. He drew from his wallet a creased and crumbling magazine photograph of a small Swiss village, and told me he dreamed of a place like that.

These days, he went on, he had taken to visiting the porn shops, where he could browse at leisure through the magazines and books. He would buy a few inexpensive ones, go home and spend the afternoon poring over the pictures. As he prepared for the evening, he would study himself in the mirror for a long time; then his desire would propel him onto the street.

One night, he said, he stumbled into a midtown peepshow. As the projector whirred, he gazed at two women and a man locked in a circle, each face gripped by the other's thighs, each mouth tasting the other's flesh. Enlarged by the camera, tongues flicked in and out, penetrating and licking layers and mounds of tissue. Strands of transparent fluid stretched like gossamer from the tongues. Only after repeatedly viewing these close-ups did it occur to him that he had never paid attention to the shape, texture or color of his women's tongues.

He had begun frequenting porn theaters to make contact with men. At least twice an evening, his glance and nod would be acknowledged. The rapidity of the transaction aroused him. He would follow the other man into the booth and drop a quarter in the slot. In the darkness, he could not see the face of the stranger squatting in front of him. When the three minutes were up he would drop another quarter into the slot to make sure the red light would keep others outside.

Staring at the film, he felt the stranger's disembodied touch on him and was excited by the anonymity of the exchange. Like the quarter dropped into the slot, the other's mouth triggered a silent film inside him. In the darkness of the booth, he and his screen confronted each other.

His only fear in the peepshows, he confessed to me, was that he might encounter the Snapper, a well-built blond youth who prowled the porn houses. None of his victims could describe him accurately because he had never been seen in bright light. Like everyone else, the Snapper would stand in front of the booth and nod at an older man, who would promptly follow him into a booth. The young man would squat on the floor while the older one dropped a quarter in the slot and unzipped his pants. The boy would take the man's flesh into his mouth, easing it gently into his throat, then suddenly bite down. With one bite, the victim's organ was severed. The Snapper would push through the booth and run down the center aisle, his mouth full of blood and scraps of flesh. Once on the street, he would disappear into the crowd. The man left in the booth would crash against its screen and walls like a blind moth, then stagger out, mad with pain and terror, screaming, his guts erupting. The other customers would scurry from their booths like silverfish and flee into the street. With blood oozing through his pants, the victim would clutch his groin and beg the peepshow manager not to summon the police.

Listening to the old man, I recalled the war experiences of one of my associates in the Service. He had been a Nazi officer, attached to General Andrei Vlasov, the Soviet general who had defected to the Wehrmacht, and had been stationed on the Eastern front. Clad in specially designed uniforms, unbound by military discipline, the Vlasovites made punitive raids on towns sheltering Jews or partisans. They raped, looted and murdered with a zeal that revolted even their Nazi superiors. The Vlasovite deputies were notorious for the pride with which they displayed the trophies of their amorous conquests: necklaces of female nipples, which they had bitten off, strung together, and dried like the strings of mushrooms the peasants hang up in winter.

I applied for work as a copy-machine operator in a large, prestigious law firm. Producing a reference letter from the printing shop where I had been employed, I got the job. I soon became a trusted member of the office, moving easily amid the bright, eager young lawyers and efficient secretaries. Because of the nature of my job, I often handled documents that junior executives of the firm were prohibited from seeing.

If the text of a will, the draft of an industrial merger or secret corporate minutes had to be reproduced in the presence of a senior partner or his private secretary, I would scan the documents, apparently to decide on the correct setting. I was actually memorizing as much of the document as I could, and, as soon as I got home, would record the pertinent data on index cards for my files. Whenever I could safely do so, I made an extra copy. As if it had been a misprint, I immediately tore it halfway across or wadded it up and threw it into a wastebasket. Later, I would retrieve it and add it to my file.

In the course of my job, I learned of a thirty-five-year-old businessman who had recently received a large legacy when both parents died in a plane crash. His was a wealthy industrial family, and he was by far the best of my candidates. Nominally the chief executive of his family's multinational textile corporation, he frequently traveled on the pretext of inspecting the company's plants in the U.S. and abroad. Actually, he made the trips to ski. He suffered from a skin problem that made it mandatory for him to avoid swimming and heat, but skiing seemed to improve his health. He was so passionately devoted to the sport that he had subsidized a ski school and established an international ski prize in his name.

He had never married, but for several years had lived with a former stewardess whom he had provided with a substantial bank account. She had recently left him for another man. I knew I could use this man to great advantage without his even knowing I existed.

During the time I was employed by the law firm, I came across a woman named Veronika. Her skin was too pale, her hair too fine, her nose too short. She was almost flat-chested, and her hands and feet were too large for her body. But she was striking nevertheless. Her broad smile, graceful bearing and engaging accent made up for her deficiencies. Like an actress who never lets down her guard, her every movement and gesture was studied and controlled.

I learned that she was Belgian and, although only in her early twenties, had been divorced twice. Her first husband had been a Belgian count three times her age, sickly and impoverished. She had come to America with the few thousand dollars she got from the divorce and quickly became the mistress of a well-known theatrical agent.

To allay his wife's suspicions, the agent arranged for Veronika to marry his teen-aged nephew. While the marriage lasted, the agent developed the habit of lending Veronika to close associates or top clients. He did nothing to forward the movie career with which he had initially enticed her. When Veronika finally became a U.S. citizen, she divorced the nephew and broke with the agent. Finding herself alone, with little money and a bad reputation, she made her debut as the star performer of the wet set, a group of men with odd sexual inclinations.

I called her for a date. Names of mutual acquaintances were not even necessary. Sitting across from her after a dinner in her apartment, I came directly to the point. I told her I knew a lot about her. She had been clever enough to transform her plainness to beauty, I said, but as her youth faded, it would take more and more time and money to maintain the masquerade. I warned her that now was the time to provide for her future.

Because I liked her, I said, and because I had selected her for a certain role in my life, I was willing to help her, if she followed my advice. I knew of a man she could marry. He was rich and tolerable. In return, she would make herself unconditionally available to me sexually, whenever I needed her. She would have to be prepared for, and always accept, any number of additional partners that I might provide myself or procure through her. Her emotions were of no interest to me, but her availability was imperative.

I advised her that our relationship would continue as long as she had any connection with the wealthy bachelor. I cautioned her that I had direct access to this man's private life and thus would be able to keep track of her at all times without her being aware of it.

I then told her that I had already entered into similar relationships with three women. I admitted that two of them had reneged on my contract. I showed Veronika newspaper clippings that detailed their bizarre fates. One of them had married a well-to-do stockbroker. In the second year of their marriage, after they had returned from dining out one evening, she began complaining of headaches and abdominal pains and of alternate burning and numbness in her feet and hands. Their doctor was away for the weekend and his young associate came to see her. He prescribed a sedative. The numbness in her hands and feet persisted; her fingers and toes swelled and reddened, then blackened and shriveled. She was hospitalized and her condition diagnosed as acute gangrenous poisoning caused by eating a fungus-infected product. Her toes and fingers had to be amputated. No foul play was suspected.

The second woman had married a restaurateur. Several years after her marriage, a stranger came to the door carrying a dead poodle he claimed to have found outside her gates. Distraught by the death of her pet, she was stammering her thanks when the man drew an aerosol can from a bag and sprayed her with an acid that hideously scarred her face and breasts. No motive was ever established and the man was never found. The third woman was still happily married. I emphasized the fact that she had never broken her agreement with me.

I gave Veronika a dossier on her future husband and twenty-four hours to decide. If she was interested, I said, she would have to start changing her life immediately. She must disconnect her phone, cancel all her charge accounts, break the lease on her apartment, sell her car and tell her few friends she was moving without a forwarding address.

To prove that I was serious, I showed her enough cash to keep her more than comfortable for a year and assured her it would be hers as soon as she agreed to my offer. Three hours later, she called to accept.

In a few weeks, she obtained her new driver's license and a passport that had just been issued in the name I had chosen for her. I also had opened savings and checking accounts for her and applied for several credit cards in her new name. But I warned her that a careful investigator could still discover her real identity.

Veronika immediately left for Vail and hired a ski instructor. Since she had learned to ski as a child, I expected her to progress rapidly. After only a month of lessons, she had placed third in an intermediate competition.

Her call stimulated my fantasies. I imagined flying to Vail to see her. In my improvised dream-scenario, I check into a hotel across the street from hers. The next morning I discover where Veronika's lesson is to be held and in the afternoon I rent skis and boots. I arrive at the cable car station wearing my ski boots and carrying my skis but still dressed in a business suit and silk tie. I wait until Veronika and the instructor arrive in his sports car. He takes their skis from the rack and together they walk toward the cable car.

Veronika is dressed in a skin-tight white outfit with yellow side stripes. Its glossy surface gleams in the light. Her face is deeply tanned, her hair soft and shiny.

I don't wait for them but take the gondola that is just leaving. On the top of the mountain, I put on my skis and wait. Veronika and the instructor get out of the next gondola, step into their skis, and start down the slope, with the instructor slightly ahead. I follow Veronika, admiring her grace. When the instructor is far ahead, I pass her and come to an abrupt stop in her path. Barely missing me, she halts angrily.

She does not recognize me behind my goggles and assumes that the stranger in a suit and tie is a clumsy novice. Just as she turns, I call her by her former name. She stops short. I remove my glasses and she recognizes me. Before she has a chance to speak, I tell her that I very much wanted to see her ski during her last days in Vail, but that I'll leave her alone because she does not attract me on the slopes as much as she does in the city.

I turn away and ski down the mountain at full speed. She attempts to follow but I disappear from sight. Farther down the mountain, I spot the instructor waiting for Veronika. I ski across the backs of his skis and race away. He is livid and asks Veronika if she saw the clown in street clothes who almost ran into him.

When Veronika returned from Vail, I telephoned the bachelor's personal secretary, pretending to be a European supplier. She told me her boss was staying at a private chalet in the French Alps, and gave me the name of a hotel nearby, where he picked up mail and messages.

Two days later, I escorted Veronika to the airport and, as we walked through the departure lounge, I noticed that all the men in the room turned to stare at her. In a few days she called from abroad. She had already set up a date with the bachelor, after attracting his attention during a ski competition. In a couple of weeks, she telephoned to tell me she had become the bachelor's lover and was about to fly to Chile to ski with him. She advised me to keep an eye on the society pages. In a month, he married her.

Following her marriage, Veronika and I began to talk regularly on the phone. Before the year was out, the calls had become a catalogue of her complaints. She claimed that she found her duties as wife and hostess increasingly tedious; she was exhausted by the ceaseless travel to the same few places, she said. She was sick of her life and sick of her husband. I commiserated with her.

Despite her disenchantment, Veronika had hired a press agent to establish her reputation as an international celebrity, and her photographs began appearing regularly in fashion magazines and society columns. She was shown attending a ballet class in Leningrad. She was photographed beside an antique car in Rhode Island and dancing at an after-hours bar with a celebrated rock star. A well-paid society photographer caught her skiing with the Shah, or reasonably within the vicinity of his person, and there was even a photograph of her in a tailored cloth coat visiting a Harlem orphanage. She disclosed in a TV interview that she was working on an autobiographical novel.

During the second year of her marriage, she came to see me only six out of the fifteen times I summoned her. On three of these occasions, she stopped on her way to another appointment, staying only an hour or two. The third year, she visited me only twice, and both times she refused to participate in what I prepared for the two of us. After that, whenever I called using my own name or voice, her secretary would dismiss me with a transparent excuse.

I decided to confront her at her apartment building. As she came out, I approached and embraced her like an old friend. Kissing her cheek, I whispered that if she didn't go with me she would regret it. An attendant brought her car. I got in next to her and gave her the address of one of my apartments she had never visited. As she drove, I told her about a young call girl who had been with me the day before. The girl reminded me of her, I said, because they were both common hustlers.

The girl told me, I continued, that although she tried to select as clients only well-behaved men, she still had had her share of accidents and arrests. One of her customers, she said, had kept her in his apartment bound and gagged for two days, while he ate, slept and watched TV. He abused her during the commercials.

Another time, a middle-aged businessman had approached her in a hotel lobby. He invited her to join some other girls and his business associates at a party he was giving out of town. He appeared respectable, and when he offered her in advance twice what she would normally make in a night, she agreed to go. He had rented an entire motel, and within an hour his chauffeur-driven limousine had reached it. There, the men gave her and the other hired girls plenty of food and drinks, then asked them to put on a show in which they made love to each other and to their employers. By midnight, additional men had arrived.

The night was turning out to be more than the girls had bargained for, and they demanded to be taken back to town. Instead, the men raped and beat them. When she was too exhausted to respond, they forced whiskey down her throat and ice cubes and pep pills up her rectum. Then she was gang-raped again.

At dawn, the men took money and costume jewelry from the girls. Then they dragged them into cars and dumped them in the woods. After crawling for two hours, the girls reached the highway, where they were picked up by the state patrol for vagrancy and prostitution and kept in jail overnight. The girl told me that she had lost several pounds. Still, she wasn't complaining, she said. Every profession had its risks and hers was no exception.

When I finished the story, Veronika made no comment. She turned on the radio and kept on driving.

We parked her car a few blocks from my building. I took her arm to guide her toward the elevator, but she pulled away.

Inside my apartment, I drew the curtains and turned on the lights. Even before she could put down her purse, I shoved her into a heavy armchair, bound her to it with electrical cords and taped her mouth shut. She strained against the chair, and her terrified eyes followed my every move as I filled a disposable syringe with colorless fluid.

I squatted beside her, removed one of her shoes and rolled down her pantyhose. Holding her leg fast between my knees, I found a vein near her ankle, dabbed the skin with alcohol and carefully pierced the vein with the needle. I slowly squeezed the fluid into the vein, then removed the needle and disinfected the area again. After pulling her pantyhose back up and replacing her shoe on her foot, I sat down across from her and waited. Not knowing what to expect increased her dread, and she trembled and cried.

Had it never occurred to her, I asked, that the man who was now her husband had paid me to find a girl of a certain type he could marry and that she was that girl? Was she stupid enough to believe that I would let her forget her personal debt to me or that she could abort our relationship when it pleased her to do so?

I planned to leave her bound in my apartment, I said; I would be back in less than an hour, I told her, but if, for some reason, I did not show up, and accidents do happen, I hoped her last thoughts would be of me.

Turning off the lights and drawing the soundproof curtains behind me, I left the apartment. I locked all three locks and walked out from the building through a side entrance. I hailed a cab and told the driver to take me to a run-down section of the city. He was surprised I wanted to go there and asked again for the address. When we arrived, I told him to follow me in his cab as I walked along the derelict-littered streets. I finally settled on three men, two blacks and a white, who swayed as they staggered, as if their knees were about to buckle. Their bodies were covered with lesions and carbuncles. They all appeared to be middle-aged.

I took each of them aside, flashed some bills and said I was willing to pay twice that amount for two hours of his time. All he had to do was come to my place, where my girlfriend was ready for a bad boy she had dreamed about but had never had. Short of killing or crippling her, he could do anything he wanted to her, and I would be taking pictures of whatever he did. The photos, I said, were just for her and me, to excite us when we were alone. The men looked at me in disbelief, and when I asked how often they had been paid to screw a lovely young girl they giggled like pubescent boys. I handed each of them a cash down-payment, and they got in the taxi with me. In the rear-view mirror, I caught the driver's disapproving glance.

Soon, the four of us stood in front of my apartment door. Slowly unlocking one lock after another, I remarked that from the inside the door could be opened only by someone who knew the combinations. This, I added jokingly, should keep them from attempting anything foolish with me. I let the three of them enter first. Shutting the door behind us, I secured the locks. During the brief moment that we were in darkness, I smelled the men's unwashed clothes and sensed their nervousness. Then I drew the curtains apart and turned on the lights.

The derelicts saw Veronika sitting as I had left her, blinking at us in the sudden glare. They stared at her slyly with downcast eyes, like dogs who've been regularly whipped. I came closer, patted her head and looked into her face. When I removed the tape from her mouth, she told me she was thirsty and a little dizzy. I mockingly introduced her to our guests, and they smiled sheepishly, unsure of themselves. After I invited them to help themselves to a drink, they rushed to the bar. A pungent odor of brandy spread through the room.

I gave Veronika a stiff shot of vodka, making sure that she drank it all. She demanded that I untie her, and I told her that our guests would do that. While I set up the spotlights and loaded the cameras, the men, still gulping liquor, watched me, waiting for instructions. I told them to take off all their clothes, and, when they started for the bathroom door, I suggested they strip in front of the girl.

The derelicts began undressing clumsily, embarrassed that Veronika and I were not joining them. They hesitated before they took off their trousers, but finally stood nude before us, their naked flesh more fetid than it had been when clothed in rancid rags.

I began snapping pictures of them posed around Veronika. Then I suggested they begin. I reminded them that she didn't mind being roughed up. Veronika grew pale. She watched our every move. They hesitated a moment, then set about untying the cords. The white man approached Veronika first. As she stared at him he grew excited. With a twist of his mouth that resembled a grin, he grabbed her hair, yanked back her head and forced his mouth on hers. He drew her up out of the chair and raised her skirt. In one quick move, he thrust his hand up into her. She arched her back, writhing; her whole body tensed, pinned by the man's mouth at one end and by his fist at the other.

Now the other two men moved in. They threw her down on the carpet. All three of them swarmed all over her, licking and squeezing. I climbed on the desk and took pictures from above. The spotlights shone on her hair, on the embroidery of her dress, on the derelicts' gaunt bodies. The men's arms moved over her like skeletons' limbs, peeling off her clothes until she was naked and spread-eagled on her back, her arms flailing at the three scrofulous heads that eagerly bent over her.

Looking at her naked body, the men momentarily stopped as if shocked. But they quickly regained their courage. Their hands ran tentatively over the length of her body, stroking Veronika's flanks with their fingers. They played with her as though she were a small girl, passing her gently from one to the other. They rocked her in their arms, caressing, sniffing and kissing her, pressing their mottled chests against her belly and buttocks. As the alcohol built their courage, they began nibbling at her nipples. They sucked and chewed on her flesh, their bloody gums studded with a few broken teeth. Like leeches, they seemed to be drawing nourishment from her. When one of the bums bit her, short spasms shook his emaciated frame.

Two of the men turned Veronika sideways, and, steadying each other with their hands, squeezed into her simultaneously from the front and rear. Her harsh moans rose to a howl of pain. Quickly, the third man twisted her toward him, straddled her narrow chest, and pinned her arms and breasts under his buttocks. Her face framed by his spindly thighs, his scrawny hands on her chin and forehead, he plied her jaws open and filled her with his flesh. The screams subsided into a gagged silence. I moved in for close-ups.

The men were spent. They looked to me for further instructions. I suggested the bathroom treatment. They grinned, grabbed her by her hands and legs and dragged her, like a marionette, into the bathroom.

I heard their snickering mingled with Veronika's pleas, their wheezing and her retching, then silence, then again shrieks.

Then it was over. The men, exhausted and giddy, dressed quickly, as though anxious to leave before I changed my mind and punished them. Each one seemed relieved when I gave him his wages. I turned off the spotlights, picked up Veronika's clothes and handbag and went into the bathroom. She was lying in the tub, shivering and moaning, her eyes open but unfocused, her face, belly and thighs smeared with dirt. When I leaned over her, she uttered a short cry, then struggled to get up on her unsteady legs. She stretched and turned on the shower. I left her alone, locking the door after me.

I escorted the men down the service elevator and

put them into a cab, which would deposit them where I had found them. After I returned to the apartment, I was surprised to see how quickly Veronika had pulled herself together. She had stopped shaking and her make-up was artfully applied. I told her I had arranged the session to give her a hint of what diversions I planned for her if she decided to cut me off. I suggested that she have herself checked for disease, making certain that her doctor was discreet. Now she was free to leave, I said, but she would hear from me soon. As I opened the door for her, she looked at me and said she would never forget her blind dates.

I called her house the following week. She was out. I called several times. She was never there. It was obvious she wanted nothing further to do with me.

I began trailing her. Although she took great precautions against being followed, such as changing taxis two or three times and walking several blocks out of her way, I traced her repeatedly to the apartment of a sculptor, a young man who had recently arrived from Europe. In the trade, he was considered an untalented fraud. He would present his smaller sculptures to various society and show-business people who were known collectors, then use their letters of acknowledgment to claim that his trash had become part of their permanent collections. As he could hardly be earning a living from the few sales he made, I assumed Veronika was supporting him.

I decided to visit the sculptor while Veronika and her husband were abroad. I noticed a maintenance crew working on various floors of the building the sculptor lived in, and one day, just after they all left for lunch, I put on a pair of overalls, picked up a spatula and a bucket of cement, and arrived in his studio claiming to be sent by the management to fix the cracks in the floor of the terrace. The sculptor led me out through a large studio full of partly chiseled blocks of stone. On a table near the window stood a framed photograph of Veronika. When I finished patching up the terrace, he offered me a beer, and, as I drank it, I wandered over toward the photograph, commenting on how pretty the lady in it was.

I began talking about women. I said that the day before, when I had been doing some work in the apartment of a beautiful woman, a model, I had overheard her tell someone on the phone that the man she had been seeing had left her. I couldn't understand, I said, why some men desert gorgeous women so easily. I told him I wished I were dashing enough to console the model, who certainly seemed to want and need a man. The sculptor casually asked where she lived. I gave him an address, finished my beer and left.

I quickly called the girl with whom I had made an arrangement. I described the sculptor and asked her to encourage his advances. She reported the following day that he had come by on a flimsy pretext. I told her to get him away from his apartment for a whole night. When I phoned the next afternoon, I got her answering service: she had left a message for me that she would be gone overnight, which meant she had been successful and the sculptor would not be spending the night in his apartment.

I entered his apartment around one in the morning and went through his file cabinets, his desk, his closets. In one drawer, I found his personal diary. Reading it, I discovered that Veronika had met the man when she was a student in Europe. He had been her first lover, and their affair had continued over the years. It was through her husband's political contacts that Veronika had arranged for the artist's emigration. In a separate folder were Veronika's letters and postcards, all written in Flemish, which I read with only slight difficulty. They were recent and had been sent from abroad. I flipped through them until I came across a letter dated a few months earlier. In it she described how easy it was to convince the world that her husband had given her the power to run his estate, and unlimited access to his family's wealth. No one suspected, she wrote, that in reality neither she nor he had control of the estate yet.

She mentioned with pride that she had commissioned a well-known city reporter, who had already published articles about her, to write an illustrated book about her and her husband's life, their houses and their guests. In addition, she bragged, several publishers would gladly bid huge sums for the rights to her still unwritten novel. It was obvious to them, she claimed, that the book would succeed because of her power and fame. She hinted that she expected her novel to create a scandal, since one of its characters would be clearly modeled on a potential presidential candidate with whom she was intimately involved, and the book would have many passages that dealt with his unusual sexual appetites. She went on to describe the fringe benefits of fame: hairdressers who dropped other appointments to accommodate her whims and charged her only nominal fees in exchange for the privilege of listing her among their clients, couturiers who gave her absurd discounts because they considered her a walking advertisement. But, she wrote her lover, she was lonely. She did not bother to hide her contempt for her husband. The entire middle section of the letter was devoted to a recurring dream in which her husband died in a ski accident, leaving her free and rich.

When, almost as an afterthought, she mentioned that her husband had drawn up a new will naming her the chief beneficiary, I realized that what she was describing in minute detail was no dream, but a murder plot, or at least an incitement to murder. It occurred to me that if her husband was murdered there would be an investigation of her earlier life, in which I had played a part. I folded the letter, put it in my jacket pocket and left the apartment.

A few weeks later, I read of plans for a political dinner to raise money for the incumbent vice president's presidential campaign. The tickets were several hundred dollars apiece, and Veronika's husband was listed on the organizing committee.

At the candidate's headquarters, I introduced myself to the chairwoman as a man of independent means who was an enthusiastic supporter of the vice president. I was planning to make a substantial contribution and was looking forward to the dinner. I added that in recent years I was often abroad, and was somewhat out of touch. As an afterthought, I mentioned to her the name of Veronika's husband and asked if, since I planned to attend the dinner alone, she would be kind enough to seat me at his table. I was anxious to meet him, I continued, since he was a pillar of the community and, like myself, a known admirer of the candidate. The woman immediately telephoned the office of Veronika's husband and asked if there was room at his table for a personal friend of hers who was also a generous supporter of the candidate. She was told he would be delighted to have me at his table and would arrange for an extra place.

The night of the dinner, affluent guests in tuxedos and evening gowns flocked to the hotel to honor the vice president. Security men were everywhere, and my name and ticket number were matched against the guest list twice before I was permitted to enter the ballroom. Once inside, I was led to my table by an usher.

Veronika and her husband had not yet arrived. I introduced myself to the people already at the table and sat in one of the three unoccupied chairs. Spotlights followed governmental dignitaries as they pushed through the crowd to their tables. Then I saw Veronika, her hair cascading onto her bare shoulders. I hardly noticed the husband walking at her side.

Just as they reached our table, the vice president entered. The guests stood up and applauded wildly. Veronika and her husband remained standing with their backs to the table, applauding with the rest. I tapped Veronika's husband on the shoulder and introduced myself as the man who had been mentioned to him by the chairwoman, and whom he had so graciously invited to his table. After greeting me very cordially, he called to Veronika. She turned toward me, smiling, her hand outstretched, but when she saw who I was, she blanched. I thanked her for including me at their table and she forced a smile.

During the speeches, I leaned over and whispered that I wanted her to visit me the next day. She sipped her wine and did not respond. I mentioned that I had recently come into possession of a letter in which she outlined the plans for her husband's murder. If he died mysteriously, I would supply the police with the letter, as well as with additional information about her past. She would certainly be convicted of murder.

Playing with her wine glass, she whispered that she could afford the best lawyers. Circumstantial evidence might prove her guilt, but she would never be convicted. Moreover, she would exploit the trial, monopolizing the media and exciting the world's imagination. The case would be priceless publicity for her budding literary career. She had worked hard on her image, she continued, and a trial would only magnify her status. Vindicated and triumphant, she would be free to do anything she pleased. As the waiters served dessert and coffee, there was a short break in the speeches. Everyone at the table began talking.

When attention was again focused on the podium, Veronika informed me that her intention was not to kill but to divorce her husband, as he was about to come into the balance of his trust. She reminded me that she did not intend to repeat the precedents of her previous divorces. This time she would have top legal counsel. She had no doubt that her settlement would run into millions. She remarked that she was already romantically linked by the columnists to a powerful senator with an excellent chance for the presidential nomination of the opposite party.

Later in the evening, I watched Veronika and her husband exchanging pleasantries with the vice president and some senators and wealthy backers. As the cameras flashed, Veronika pretended to be oblivious of them, yet I knew that she was constantly posing. She and her husband returned to the table and I wished them good night. Her husband hoped that they would see me again soon. I thanked him but said I was about to leave town. Long-range plans were unrealistic for me, because of my poor health. Veronika smiled distantly.

A few days later, I read that a major aerospace company was opening its doors to the public to commemorate its fiftieth anniversary. The celebration was to include an exhibition of the company's collection of old planes as well as a presentation of the newest military jets. To brief myself, I called the public relations department and asked for recent issues of the company's monthly, an elaborate magazine printed in color on glossy paper.

One issue featured an illustrated article on the company's test pilots, describing their backgrounds and families and briefly interviewing each man. The pilots were in their late thirties or forties and many had served in the recent war. I focused on one, a man in his mid-forties. In his interview, he mentioned how pleased he was that the company had extended its retirement age for pilots. He also spoke of the fatigue and increasing tension men of his age had to cope with during each test flight.

I telephoned him and introduced myself as a well-to-do businessman, also in the aerospace industry. After complimenting him on the interview, I told him I would like to discuss future business opportunities with him. He agreed to meet me for lunch at a restaurant near the company's testing grounds.

I arrived at the restaurant early and watched him pull up in a compact car. He was a short, lithe man. We introduced ourselves.

I was surprised, I said, to see one of the better known pilots in the aerospace industry driving such a modest car. He laughed and explained that, unlike airline pilots, test fliers were not unionized. Since his profession, like car racing, had been glamorized by the media, the aerospace companies had been attracting more than enough applicants. Consequently, his salary was much lower than that of a commercial airline pilot. As it was, he admitted, his wife also had to work to support their four teen-aged children. I expressed interest in the company's forthcoming aircraft exhibition and revealed that my proposition involved the show.

When I asked if he would be demonstrating any of the new planes, he guardedly replied that he might be. I told him that a young lady friend and I were anxious to see one of the Snipe jet fighters and that if he were to show it to us I would gladly reward him

for his efforts. He laughed and told me I didn't need
him as a guide. Now that the Arabs were buying them
by the dozens, several Snipes would be displayed for
public inspection. Kids love pilots and planes, he said,
and there would be pilots in full flight gear everywhere to answer any questions.

"Still, I have a small favor to ask," I added. "At the
show, while you're in the pilot's seat and my girl is
standing in front of the Snipe, I want you to turn on
the radar."

"To do what?" he asked.

"Turn on the radar," I repeated.

"I can't do that. If the radar functions while the
plane is on the ground, there's a serious radiation
hazard. Do you know what radar radiation would do
to her?"

"I do."

"It would kill her."

"That will not be your business. You will simply
forget the plane is on the ground. Afterward, you
won't remember you ever saw me and the girl."

"Listen to me," he said solemnly, "radar is so powerful that it can detonate an explosive."

"My girlfriend is not an explosive."

"But she'll absorb a fatal dose of radiation. She'll
die a slow and horrible death. That's a hell of a way
to kill a person."

"If you refuse me," I said, "I'll have someone wrap
a heavy towel around her head to muffle her screams,
and club her repeatedly with an iron bar until her
blood soaks through the towel, and her skull, jaw and
spine are smashed. Is that more merciful?" I paused.
"I'll pay you well," I added.

He bent over the table, his drink in one hand while
the fingertips of the other traced swirls and slashes on
the frosty glass.

"For the last few years," I continued, "you've been involved in testing fighter jets. Any defects you find are instantly corrected. Even if there is nothing wrong with the product, it is constantly being improved upon. Thousands of skilled people and elaborate computers are at your disposal. Money doesn't matter, either. You know better than I that, although a plane is built to last only half the life span of an average light bulb, it costs about thirty million dollars. You've been spoiled by a world of relentless perfecting; I have not."

"I'm not testing aircraft to kill," he responded. His fingers stopped playing with the glass.

"You're not?" I broke in. "In your interview, you mentioned flying Snipes in Southeast Asia on low-level bombing missions deep into enemy territory. Your plane was hit twice; both times you ejected and were rescued by navy helicopters."

For a moment, we sipped our drinks in silence. Then I continued, "The radar of those planes you flew can track simultaneously over two dozen separate targets, such as foot soldiers, sampans, roads, railways, bridges, airports, buildings. The computer assigns priority to these targets. This is the priority system you call the 'logic tree,' isn't it?"

"Yes, but . . ."

"Let me finish. To disregard the computer's logic tree is called 'overriding,' isn't it?"

"Yes."

"In combat, you always obeyed that logic tree, never overrode it, never assigned your own priorities."

"No, sir, I never did!"

"The computer selected the targets, released the bombs and fired the rockets, but it was you who were cited for bravery. A lot of people died because of that logic tree."

"A lot of pilots died, too," he broke in.

"Quite so. Every issue of your company's magazine carries the obituaries of employees who have died. I noticed that some of the pilots recently killed in job-related accidents were much younger than you. That fly buzzing across the windowpane may outlive you. So might my girl friend."

"But what reason have I got to expose a perfect stranger to radiation?"

"You found reasons to machine-gun, bomb and napalm thousands of perfect strangers. All I want you to do is switch on the radar. Instead of a village, its screen will show a single, human-shaped target. After a moment too brief for proper identification of the object, you will simply switch the radar off. Your mission will be over and for it I'll pay you as much cash as you were paid for all your combat missions put together. How's that for a logic tree? Can you override that?"

The pilot pulled a paper napkin out of the dispenser and, taking a ball-point pen from his pocket, did some quick computations. After a moment, he pushed the napkin toward me. "Would you really pay as much as that?"

I looked at the figure. "I would," I said. "Furthermore, there is no risk involved. This girl travels constantly in private jets, all of which are radar-equipped and any of which could have been the source of the radiation. By the time she gets ill, even Sherlock Holmes wouldn't be able to trace her ailment to you."

He continued to sip his drink in silence. Then he dug into his pants pockets for his car keys and got up. "On opening day, I'll wait for you near my Snipe," he said. "The plane is usually displayed on side runway number six. Orange and black paint job, you can't miss it." He leaned close to me. "I don't care what you pay me," he said. "I'll activate the system in the plane and I'll show you where the switch is which actually starts the radar, but I won't trip that switch. That woman is your target, not mine."

He turned and walked out of the restaurant. I watched him get into his car and drive off.

I called Veronika and told her I had only barely survived a recent attack. My doctors admitted the prognosis wasn't good, and I had decided to settle in a small mountain village. Since I was about to step out of her life, I wanted to say goodbye, and wondered if she would accompany me to an air show near the seashore. If she refused such a small favor, I said, before my departure I would give the information about her past, as well as all the photographs I'd ever taken of her, including the ones of her with the three bums, to certain friends of mine who would find the most effective means of blackmailing her. If, however, she agreed to see me for one last time, I promised to destroy them all. Veronika agreed.

I telephoned the test pilot and confirmed that I would be bringing my girl friend to the show early in the morning. He told me to be at the gates as soon as they opened, to skip the first exhibits and go directly to his plane.

Veronika picked me up in her car. I mentioned to her that I was particularly interested in a special supersonic jet and that they might let us look at it more closely before the crowds came. The highway was empty and it took less than an hour to reach the exhibition field. It was a cool, clear day, and, as we walked, the wind blew through Veronika's hair and wrapped her beige silk dress about her.

The test pilot was standing near his aircraft. When we approached him, he introduced himself as if we had never met. I asked him several basic questions about the plane and he answered them succinctly. I also asked if I could see the cockpit.

He went behind me up the narrow, thin steps, and stood on the top step, while I sat in the pilot's seat. Leaning into the cockpit, he pointed at the instrument panel and console, and, in a detached voice, described the functions of various switches. When he got to the radar control switch, his hand hovered over it. I nodded. Taking out of my pocket several packs of well-worn bills, I separated the packets and spread them on my thighs. He fanned through each packet quickly, stuffed them inside the zippered compartments in his flight suit, and activated the radar system.

With camera in hand, I leaned out of the cockpit and shouted down to Veronika to stand directly in front of the aircraft's nose so that I could take pictures of her. I mockingly told her there was no danger of being caught in the propeller. When she was in position, she waited impatiently, pacing in a small circle around the spot where I wanted her to pose.

After snapping several pictures, I called down and asked her to lift her hair above her head with both hands. She complied and the camera clicked. Then I told her I had to change the lens. She nodded. I sat back, and tripped the switch. Instantly, the hazard light began flashing. The silvery radar display indicator brightened and the luminescent dots at the center of its screen began to coalesce into a blurred shape, like rapidly multiplying cells.

I glanced at Veronika through the jet's open canopy. Posed against the peaceful green field veined with white runways, she had no idea that invisible missiles were assaulting her body and brain.

I turned to the pilot. His face was flushed. He

stared at the screen's dim glow as though it reflected something horrible. I switched the radar off, and the screen darkened, then went black.

We descended from the cockpit and I said goodbye to the pilot. He did not answer, but stared at Veronika, who came over to thank him. She and I left and, hand in hand, walked across the field, passing the other planes, which were already surrounded by the first wave of visitors.

On the way back to town, Veronika asked about my health and departure date. My health had deteriorated, I said. I was leaving soon. I could bear the thought of never seeing her again only because I knew a part of me would always be with her. Nothing would please me more, I said, than to know that there would be days and nights when, unable to sleep, she would recall our arrangement and how it had ended.

Whenever I am in a large city, I often go for walks around three or four o'clock in the morning. I feel like a solitary visitor in a vast, private museum. At that hour, one can easily imagine that mankind is nearly extinct. The only signs of life are occasional: a solitary bum slouching along the sidewalk, a speeding taxi, a couple crossing a distant street. All this makes me feel that I am one of the few survivors left to contemplate the urban remains—deserted glass and steel structures, as yet untouched by time. Sometimes I am still up at dawn, the gradual increase of noise and motion reminding me that I am not alone.

I know that behind the countless walls in the thousands of buildings that fan out around me, flaccid bodies, winding in their blankets and dreams, begin to open their eyes, stretch their aching limbs, detach their bodies from brief embraces, and begin the daily ritual: soon they will grope toward narrow doors and shuffle out onto dirty streets.

One morning, just as the sun was beginning to give the city color, I stopped in front of a building I had never noticed before. It was in a part of town I enjoyed most. I decided to take an apartment in it. Later that morning I asked to see layouts of the various suites. I noticed that one plan perfectly matched my specifications. Its windows had the correct exposure and it was near the service elevator. When I asked the superintendent to see it, he suggested one on the next floor down, explaining that the one I wanted was occupied by an old bachelor who had lived there for years, paid the rent religiously and went out only twice a week. The super joked that only death could move that old crab from its hole.

I tipped the super generously and promised him more if he would let me know when the old man vacated the place. As I was leaving, the super urged me to consider the apartment below, repeating that it would be a waste of time to count on the tenant's moving.

I found out the bachelor's name from his mailbox and had him put on a number of mailing lists to receive illustrated brochures from retirement villages and information from Florida real-estate agencies catering to senior citizens. In addition, every week I sent him pamphlets proclaiming the advantages of spending one's old age in the Sunshine State. In case he might be attracted by a drier climate, I mailed brochures of retirement colonies from southern California and sent him the latest issue of *Arizona Highways*, as a complimentary inducement to subscribe. Twice a week, he received a manila envelope from me, stuffed with newspaper clippings that were vivid evidence of the rising rate of crime against elderly persons living in the city. Other items dealt with the criminally negligent medical treatment offered to the aging, the skyrocketing cost of city life and, above all, the lethal effects of pollution.

Several weeks later, the super called to tell me the old man had decided to move to Florida because he couldn't stand the loneliness and city hazards: his most valuable possession, a color TV, had blown out right in the middle of "The Match Game." The set had remained in the repair shop nearly a month, and, when the repairman brought it back, he had charged an exorbitant sum for having it fixed. Two days later, the set went dead again. The bachelor suspected that the repairman had cheated him by removing perfectly good parts and substituting old ones, but he could not prove it. When he called the repairman to look at the TV, the man claimed that it needed an expensive new part and demanded a large deposit. The bachelor considered suing the repairman, but a lawyer told him that the small-claims court had a backlog of one year on its docket. Fed up with the city, the bachelor had decided to move to the Golden Years Community in Florida.

I moved into the apartment even before it was cleaned and painted. When I opened the front closet, a torrent of leaflets and clippings, many of them from me, poured out. As I looked through the material in the course of throwing it away, I began to wonder about the nature of a community consisting entirely of the elderly. The young and middle-aged came into contact with these people only in the briefest, most fleeting way. Such an environment must be radically different from the ones in which its members had spent most of their lives.

As soon as the new apartment was in order, I took a plane to the Sunshine State and headed for the Golden Years.

I saw before me a town whose sole purpose was to provide a place where people could sit in the sun, their lives slowly evaporating like moisture in the desert. Everything was of the same pale color, as if faded by the light.

"I'm surprised to see so many convertibles here," I told the attendant at the car-rental agency. "I thought that people didn't buy them anymore and Detroit had almost stopped making them."

"You're forgetting where you are. This is the senior citizens' capital of America. There are probably more people in their eighties and nineties in this one community than in any other town in the U.S. of A.," he announced proudly.

"What does that have to do with convertibles?"

He leaned against the car that had just been brought over and patted its canvas top. "Everything. It's a lot easier for the old folks to get in and out of a car when the top's down. Bending is a real chore for them, you know. I buy convertibles on special order, and in this community there's always a demand."

As I drove toward the main lodge, I went by vast golf courses, and parked my car among a dozen other convertibles.

At the registration desk, I noticed a stack of large-type newspapers on the counter.

The young clerk came over to me and asked, "Are you visiting your parents?"

"No, they died a long time ago."

"Another member of your family?"

"In a way," I said, strolling toward the dining room.

The middle-aged hostess introduced herself as Hannah and patted my shoulder affectionately. "Will you be eating with your folks?" she asked. I told her I was staying by myself and that I planned to lunch in my room but would like to join one of the larger tables for dinner.

"Dinner is served from five to six-thirty. Come down whenever you want and I'll seat you with Harry and his cronies." She paused. "Harry is right up there in his eighties, like all the rest of them, but what a character! You might have to buy your way into the group with a bottle of wine."

When I went downstairs at six-fifteen, the dining room was blindingly bright and very noisy. Dinner was just ending and all the tables were crowded. Hannah spotted me and led me over to a group of aged men and women. She introduced me to Harry, who greeted me exuberantly while his tablemates nodded. Only when I sat down, did Harry recall that we hadn't yet shaken hands, and eagerly extended a veiny claw, speckled with enormous brown splotches.

"Where is your wife?" asked a man in a wheelchair on my right.

"My wife died many years ago," I answered.

"This is Tom," announced Harry. "Tom never married."

Tom asked why I hadn't remarried. When he spoke, one side of his mouth moved ahead of the other. Before I could answer, Harry announced, "We'll marry you off here." Then he continued, "How about marrying this nice gentleman, Miriam?" From across the table, Miriam turned her head and aimed her hearing aid toward him, and Harry repeated what he had asked. She nodded but said nothing. Harry pointed at me again. "He looks sickly," he said, "but if he can get up so easily, I bet he can still get it up. Can't you?" His eyes focused on me through thick lenses. One pupil was larger than the other and he never stopped blinking. "You are so thin," he said. "You should eat more. Or maybe you're being eaten? A cancer? How are your bowels? Is your mouth red and blistered? Stick out your tongue." He coaxed me as if I were a child.

"Harry's been married four times," interrupted Miriam. "Once before he came to Golden Years and three times since. He has children from his first wife," she continued. "They're all married. Even their children's children are married and have children."

"I have no children," barked Harry.

"Yes, you have, Harry. You have a boy and two girls. You're even a great-great-grandfather, aren't you, Harry?" she went on, raising her voice.

"I have no children," muttered Harry roughly. "They may think they have a father, but I know I have no children."

"Harry's been married four times," repeated Miriam, ignoring what he had said. "Harry's wives all died. They left him their money, didn't they, Harry?"

"I married three times, not four," Harry snorted angrily. "And when they died, they only left to me what I had coming. I never accepted anything I didn't earn."

"Harry's wives died without even being sick," said Miriam, smiling serenely. "Harry did something to them. They weren't killed by his love alone." She tittered, pounding the table with her fists.

Tom laughed with her and rolled his chair closer. He was wheezing with excitement. "Tell us what you did to your wives," he demanded, but Harry pretended he hadn't heard. "Harry didn't do anything to his wives. You know why? Because he couldn't! He couldn't do a damned thing!" Tom sought my approval, then continued with a crafty smirk. "Harry married his wives to lift their skirts. Then he took a long, hard look, and that's all they got. It was his long, hard looks that killed 'em." The table went wild with laughter. Harry gnawed his lip, struggling to remain calm. Tom renewed the assault. "After his last wife died, Harry paid the colored girl who mops the floors here to let him shave her between the legs with his electric shaver. Didn't you, Harry? Now, whenever she pulls on her panties, her crotch tickles her and reminds her of Harry." Everyone laughed uproariously.

Harry's jaws began to jerk in spasms. "You are making this up," he screeched. "You are making this all up. If you don't stop lying, I will not give you any more money. Not one more dollar." Tom suddenly stopped laughing and stared blankly at Harry.

"You have to pay him, Harry," Miriam reminded him patiently. "You made a contract with him. Through a lawyer."

Tom looked as if he would cry. "You have to give me the money, Harry. Every month. Otherwise, I couldn't afford to stay with you. Then you would be all alone, Harry." He was gripping the arms of his wheelchair with such desperation that his knuckles turned white.

Harry clutched my arm. His grasp was weak and his face twitched. "I'm rich," he said. "I always was rich, but Tom never had anything because he had no guts."

"I worked very hard," Tom shouted back. "I was rich. The richest. Once I even owned a mansion. A genuine palace."

"So why can't you pay your own bills? Why? Why?"

"Depression, Harry. The depression. And now you pay me to play bridge with you and eat lobster with you and look at the colored girl's twat with you and listen to you babble. But you know you'll get it back when I'm gone. Your lawyer made damn sure that you'd inherit the little I have. Every penny. You'll benefit from the passing of your only friend." He began to sob.

Harry impulsively grabbed a piece of bread, stuffed it in his mouth, then spat it out and began wringing his hands. "Don't believe him. Don't believe him. He's lying through his teeth. Tom's the one who hopes to make the profit if I go first . . . but I won't." He paused, wheezing with impotent rage.

"How do you know you won't be the first to go?" sneered Tom. "Who told you, Harry? Did the colored girl tell you?" He turned to me, trembling, his sunken chest rising rapidly, his breath whistling and gurgling in his throat. "I'm younger than Harry. I am at least two years younger. At our age, every day counts. Harry, you know, goes to the bathroom all the time. He can't hold his water for more than five minutes, and when he passes it, it's green and gravelly. That's why Harry wears a plastic bladder!" Abruptly, he broke into a happy grin, as if he had ridiculed not just Harry but the whole human race.

Harry struggled to his feet and reached for Tom's throat, but the effort was too much for him and he fell back onto his chair, coughing and spitting out saliva and bits of half-chewed bread. Everyone at the table frowned in disgust. Harry tired quickly; the cough grew hollow, then stopped. "You know what's going to happen to you, Tom?" he gasped. "Any day now, your nerves are going to wither away. You'll wake up one morning and your mouth won't open." He chuckled and smirked malevolently. Tom glanced up, puzzled. He opened his mouth to prove to himself that he could still do it, then looked at me, begging for help.

Everyone else at the table waited expectantly. "You won't be able to open your mouth except when you see someone yawning in front of you," said Harry, emphasizing each word. "You'll eat only when you yawn," Harry went on. "Then they'll have to stuff the food down you. Only then. No yawn, no food," Harry repeated triumphantly.

With sudden dignity, Tom looked at Harry with a firm, unflinching expression. Harry instantly detected the change and attacked again.

"You know what this means, don't you, Tom? It means that I will also have to pay for your yawner. What if I can't find one? What if I find a badly trained yawner who yawns only once a day? A yawner who manages only one quick yawn every twenty-four hours?" Harry was moving in for the death blow. "How much lobster could you swallow in one quick yawn, Tom? How much?"

Miriam was upset by now, but it took her so long to stand up that Harry spotted her before she could get away. "Miriam," Harry chided, "must you go to the bathroom?"

Everyone's attention focused on Miriam. She looked down at the floor, pretending to ignore the others, but scooted her chair back close to the table and began to buff her nails with the edge of her pink cardigan.

Harry raised his voice. "Miriam! For God's sake, don't do it here! Leave the table if you must!" Miriam frowned and then smiled sweetly, as though she had everything under control. "You know I can't just after I've eaten. I always keep it inside for a while so you can watch me when I do it in my bathroom, Harry." Everyone at the table pretended to retch.

I asked Hannah to bring us a bottle of wine. When it arrived, I poured it into all the wine glasses. Harry's friends rolled their eyes upward as if in prayer. Then they grabbed their wine and gulped it in a race to the second glass. I ordered another bottle, which was drained instantly.

No one spoke. They stared at each other with beady eyes. Whenever one of them fidgeted, everyone else glared at him. Tom began to push his chair away from the table. The others noticed his maneuver, but Tom, intent on the operation, didn't realize he was being watched.

"Tom is leaving us. He can't hold it in anymore!" Harry announced joyfully, and his voiced stopped the other man as he began to turn around. Tom's chair moved a few inches before he gave up and dejectedly turned back to the table.

Suddenly, everyone turned toward the dining-room door. A tall figure, supported by a nurse, was making its way haltingly through the now silent room. All eyes followed its progress from table to table. The figure was wrapped in soft white cloth; like a giant bandage, the cloth covered it from head to toe, disguising the contours of its head and body.

I grabbed Harry's wrist and asked who it was. When he turned to me, I saw he had gone chalky. "It's Ono," he whispered.

"Ono?"

" 'Ono' means 'It,' " Harry said, "because it isn't a man or a woman anymore."

"Why?"

"Ono is older than anyone else here. Cancer has eaten its whole body. It's a monster. They should kill it."

"Why is Ono here?"

"It pays for its keep. Like everyone else. It's fed by tubes, but once in a while Ono likes to walk across the dining room, just to frighten everybody. They shouldn't allow it to do that. They should put Ono to sleep."

I studied the figure. With the nurse steering it between the tables, Ono plodded on. It reached the far door and hesitated at the threshold. For a moment, I imagined that Ono would turn and face us, unwrap the bandages and reveal itself to us all. From one of the tables came a single hysterical shriek. Prodded on by that sound and by the nurse's shoves, Ono crossed the threshold and was gone. The waitresses resumed clearing the tables and the room exploded with voices.

I returned to the city. One evening I was photographing a girl in one of my apartments, when I ran out of film. I called the drugstore and asked them to send me half a dozen rolls, but they told me the delivery boy had already left for the night. I decided to run down for the film myself. On my way out, I told the girl that I would be back in ten minutes, and didn't bother with the three combination locks. I got into the elevator and, as it glided down to the street level, I noticed that the light panel indicating floor numbers was not working.

When the car paused, I figured it had reached the lobby, but the doors did not open, and immediately the elevator began to rise again. I assumed the doors would open at the top, but when the elevator hesitated again, presumably at the top, it began to descend silently again. I pressed the "Stop" button, but the elevator did not respond. I pressed "Alarm," but no alarm rang. I touched all the floor buttons simultaneously with my forearm but the car continued noiselessly. I pounded the stainless-steel door with my fists, but the sound seemed to die.

The elevator persisted in its constant shuttle, rebounding off the top floor only to begin its journey down again. Using the sole of my shoe as a lever, I attempted to force the doors apart, but they remained tightly shut. I then tried to pry open the instrument panel with a pocket knife, but the blade was too flimsy and snapped off at the base. Next, I used the edge of a metal money clip, but I managed only to twist the clip out of shape. The protective devices I always carry could defend me against hostile passengers, but in an empty elevator they were useless.

I began to wonder if I had been trapped so that someone could enter my apartment. My first thought was that the girl was part of the plot. Then I imagined what her captors would do to her if she wasn't.

The temperature inside the elevator rose until it was easily over ninety degrees. While I sweated from heat, I was also beginning to shiver from panic. I guessed that whoever had imprisoned me had not just wanted to break into my apartment, but had planned on my body breaking down so I'd die from apparently natural causes.

My wristwatch was the only contact I had with reality. Although I could gauge exactly how long it took the elevator to get from top to bottom, when the car hit the ground level it rebounded instantly, and I did not have time to attract the attention of people who might be waiting for the elevator. Then, I realized that, at that time of night, the lobby would be deserted anyway and that my attackers would certainly have taken precautions to get any potential help out of the way.

I looked at my watch: I had been in the elevator for almost forty-five minutes. Perspiration was streaming down my body, and the persistent loss of fluids made me feel dizzy. Although I had both tranquilizers and stimulants with me, I decided not to take any, since I could not predict how I might react to them in my dehydrated state. In order to conserve my energy and body fluids, I undressed and sat naked on the linoleum-tiled floor.

From time to time, I shouted, kicked and banged on the door, but no one came. I was exhausted. Overcome by helplessness, I collapsed against the steel wall.

Three hours passed. I vomited. Then my stomach began to contract and I eliminated on the elevator's floor. I was breathing with difficulty.

Although I have always thought of myself as moving horizontally through space, invading other people's spheres, my life has always been arranged vertically: all my apartments have been at least midway up in tall buildings, making elevators absolutely essential. Now, one of these necessary devices had suddenly become a windowless cell. The forces that propelled it up and down seemed as arbitrary and autonomous as those that spin the earth on its axis. Here, in the solitude of my capsule, I sensed a curious time warp. Encased in a steel and rubber sarcophagus, I was completely cut off from my past: a royal mummy, safely cradled and sealed for the long voyage ahead.

I fell asleep with exhaustion and woke to voices. The overhead light had gone out while I slept, but the car still glided up and down. I looked at my watch: I had been imprisoned for eight hours. When I listened more closely to the voices, I realized that men were working in the corridors of several floors. I began to shout for help and at last someone shouted back. Several minutes later, the elevator abruptly stopped, then inched jerkily to the nearest floor, opened its doors and released me.

The building superintendent told me that, the day before, a sign had been posted in every hall, announcing that the elevator was out of order. Someone had removed my floor's warning. "Probably a child," he said, "probably a prank." He asked if I had pressed both the up and down buttons to get the elevator to arrive faster. I admitted that I had. He speculated that, by pushing both buttons, I must have caused a further breakdown, which had cut out all floor stops.

When I returned to my apartment, the girl wasn't there. She had left a note explaining that she had become bored and eventually gone home. The apartment was in order and there was no trace of intruders.

I gave myself a large injection of vitamins, took a bath, ate a light breakfast and fell asleep.

I look out my window. Far below, the ice-skating rink stands out like a bright corona against the dark mass of the city and the park. The skaters move smoothly in their circle of light, gliding in uninterrupted movement to slow, silent music. From the rink's apron other figures spill onto the ice, find an opening and blend in with the flow.

Now the rink appears to revolve around the skaters as they stand like frozen sculptures growing out of the ice. I close my eyes. I remember a great old army tank, hit decades ago by an enemy shell, sunken in a shallow lagoon. The iron flaps of the tank's turret are rusted open, steadily washed over by the waves; its corroded gun defiantly trains on trenches and machine-gun nests, long buried in the sands of a deserted beach.

Tihon began coming straight to the point: "Legally you are well-nigh invulnerable—that is what people will say first of all—with sarcasm. Some will be puzzled. Who will understand the true reasons for the confession?"

FYODOR DOSTOYEVSKY, *The Possessed*

ABOUT THE AUTHOR

JERZY KOSINSKI won the National Book Award in Fiction for *Steps*, and France's Best Foreign Book Award for *The Painted Bird*. He is the recipient of the National Institute of Arts and Letters' Award in Literature and has also written *Being There, The Devil Tree* and other works. His books have been translated into most major languages. Mr. Kosinski has been Professor of English Prose at Wesleyan, Princeton and Yale universities. Since 1973, he has served as President of the American Center of P.E.N.